choice
and challenge

choice
and challenge

contemporary readings in marriage

Edited by:

CARL E. WILLIAMS
and
JOHN F. CROSBY

Indiana University

WM. C. BROWN COMPANY PUBLISHERS
Dubuque, Iowa

contents

Preface

The purpose of the following pages is to bring together in a single volume some of the best articles which have appeared in the popular press in recent years. These articles are all related to the central theme of marriage and marital life styles. Criteria for selection included the following: Is the article a legitimate and valid contribution to the field of marital relationships and life styles? Is the article written in lay language? Does the article speak its message directly or does it engage in double-talk or in a jungle of statistics? Is the article thought provoking, challenging, and/or controversial? Does the article compromise itself by failing to emphatically state its own value position? Will students be challenged to ask self-directed questions concerning their own goals and values?

Articles were selected with one basic intention in mind: For use by students taking a basic functional course in marriage and/or persons wishing to know more about the thinking of practitioners and facilitators of marital counseling and marital enrichment groups. Indeed, we feel this collection of writings could be beneficial to any person, married or unmarried, estranged or divorced, happy or hurting.

We hold no brief for these selections; we will not argue that they are the only good ones or necessarily the best. Increasingly the popular press will carry thought provoking articles written by highly qualified people. In no way do we expect agreement between student and writer. We are concerned with ideas, values, critical reaction, and, most important of all, the forging of the student's own goals, values, and expectations regarding his or her own life style.

We would like to thank each of the contributors and to acknowledge our appreciation to the students who have encouraged us to make these articles available in a single volume.

Our appreciation to Bob Nash and Sandy Hirstein who have been extremely helpful in bringing this book to fruition. Furthermore, our thanks to Vicki Williams who did the index and to all those others who have been supportive.

Carl E. Williams
John F. Crosby

Contributors

Gina Allen is a free lance writer whose articles have appeared in *Woman's Home Companion, Ladies Home Journal, Woman's Day, Family Circle,* and *Redbook.* She has written numerous books for children, short stories, and articles for publication in this country and abroad. Her other books include *Rustics for Keeps, Odyssey, Gold,* and the award-winning novel, *The Forbidden Man.*

Mark Arnold is a reporter for *The National Observer.* His articles in the *Observer* have covered such topics as school busing, welfare, military morale in an unpopular war, education against mass drug addiction, mass transit, government eavesdropping, and prison unrest.

George R. Bach is director of the Institute for Group Psychotherapy in Beverly Hills, California. In addition to *Pairing,* Dr. Bach is co-author, with Peter Wyden, of *The Intimate Enemy* and wrote the textbook *Intensive Group Psychotherapy.* He is also author of numerous articles appearing in professional journals.

Sam Blum is a free lance writer who has written articles appearing in *Esquire, Harpers, New York Times Magazine,* and *Redbook.*

Vivian Cadden is a free lance writer. She has written articles for *Redbook, McCalls, Reader's Digest,* and the *New York Times Magazine,* and formerly served as Senior Editor of *McCalls.*

Matt Clark is Medicine Editor of *Newsweek.* He is author of the following cover stories appearing in *Newsweek:* "Diet: Heart of the Matter " "Birth Control: The Pill and the Church," "The Heart: Miracle at Capetown," "Abortion and the Law," "Probing the Brain" and "Heart Attack: Curbing the Killer."

John F. Crosby is assistant professor of Marriage and Family Relations at Indiana University. He has done research on the effects of family life education on the attitudes and values of adolescents and has written an article appearing in *The Family Coordinator* reporting this research. Mr. Crosby is the author of *Illusion and Disillusion: The Self in Love and Marriage.* He is a marriage and family therapist.

Ronald Deutsch is a free lance writer and has written the following books: *Is Europe Necessary?, The Nuts Among the Berries, The Grass Lovers,* and *The Key to Feminine Response in Marriage.* He has also written over 200 nonfiction and humorous pieces that have appeared in such magazines as *Saturday Evening Post, Reader's Digest, Better Homes and Gardens, Redbook, This Week,* and *Ladies Home Journal.*

Richard Farson is a consulting psychologist and co-founder and chairman of the Board of the Western Behavioral Sciences Institute in La Jolla, California. His articles have appeared in *New Perspectives on Encounter Groups, Networks, Urban Affairs Quarterly, New Woman, Experiences in Being, Environment, Planning and Design, Look, Forbes, Journal of the Industrial Design Society of America, Glamour, Psychology Today, Harvard Business Review, Journal of Psychology, Adult Leadership,* and *Counseling.* He is editor of the book *Science and Human Affairs* and coauthor of *The Future of the Family.* His most recent book is *Birthright.*

Ivan B. Gendzel is a member of the clinical faculty, Department of Psychiatry, Stanford University School of Medicine. He has written the following articles: "End of Marriage: How Do I Find Intimacy," "Marriage and the Age of Maturity: Meaningful or Fearful?," "Marathon Group Therapy: Rationale and Techniques," and "Marathon Group Therapy and Nonverbal Methods."

Morton Hunt is a free lance writer who has written over two hundred articles on a wide range of subjects—mostly in the behavioral sciences, particularly psychology and sociology. His articles have appeared in *New Yorker, Ladies Home Journal, Seventeen, Redbook, Reader's Digest, New York Times Magazine, McCalls, Family Circle, Look, Saturday Evening Post, Holiday, Harpers,* and *Cosmopolitan.* His books include *The Affair, The World of the Formerly Married, Her Infinite Variety,* and *The Natural History of Love.*

Sidney M. Jourard is Professor of Psychology at the University of Florida. He has published articles in the *Journal of Abnormal Social Psychology, Journal of Consulting Psychology, Journal of Humanistic Psychology, Journal of Existential Psychiatry,* and *Review of Existential Psychology and Psychiatry.* His books include *Personal Adjustment: An Approach Through the Study of Healthy Personality, The Transparent Self,* and *Disclosing Man to Himself.*

Aron Krich is a psychologist who practiced psychotherapy and marriage counseling in New York City. He has edited two volumes of the publication *The Sexual Revolution* and has written numerous articles in professional journals.

Alice Lake is a free lance writer who has written articles for *Good Housekeeping, McCalls, Ladies Home Journal, Reader's Digest, Saturday Evening Post, Seventeen,* and *Redbook.*

Clement Martin is a medical doctor and coauthor of the book *Intimacy: Sensitivity, Sex and the Art of Love.*

Fredelle Maynard is a free lance writer whose articles are concerned with problems associated with education and human relations. Her articles have appeared in *Good Housekeeping, Reader's Digest, Saturday Evening Post, Seventeen, New Republic,* and *Parents Magazine.*

Margaret Mead is Curator Emeritus of Ethnology at the American Museum of Natural History. She holds over twenty honorary degrees, has held numerous positions and lectureships since 1925, and is renowned for her expeditionary work among South Seas peoples in Samoa and Bali. Among her numerous publications are: *Male and Female, New Lives and Old, And Keep Your Powder Dry, Growing Up in New Guinea, Coming of Age in Samoa, Culture and Committment: A Study of the Generation Gap, Rap on Race* (with James Baldwin).

Herbert A. Otto is chairman of the National Center for the Exploration of Human Potential, La Jolla, California. He has published numerous articles in such journals as *Journal of Marriage and the Family, The Psychiatric Quarterly, Social Casework,* and the *International Journal of Social Psychology.* He is editor of *Explorations in Human Potential,* and *Human Potentialities: The Challenge and the Promise* and co-editor with John Mann of *Ways of Growth.* His own publications include *Guide to Developing Your Potential, Group Methods Designed to Actualize Human Potential, More Joy in Your Marriage, The Family Cluster,* and with his wife Roberta has coauthored the book *Total Sex.*

Alix Shulman is a free lance writer who has written children's literature, and whose articles have appeared in *Women's Liberation: A Blueprint for the Future, Women in Sexist Society: Studies in Power and Powerlessness, Redbook, Atlantic* and *Life.* Her books include *Memoirs of an Ex-Prom Queen, To the Barricade: The Anarchist Life of Emma Goldman, The Most Dangerous Woman in the World (Emma Goldman, 1869-1940)* and is editor of *Red Emma Speaks: Selected Writings and Speeches of Emma Goldman.*

Philip Slater is Professor of Sociology at Brandeis University. His articles have appeared in the *American Sociological Review, American Journal of Sociology, Merrill-Palmer Quarterly,* and *Sociometry.* His books include *The Temporary Society, The Glory of Hera: Greek Mythology and the Greek Family, Microcosm: Structural, Psychological and Religious Evolution in Groups,* and *The Pursuit of Loneliness.*

Clark Vincent is Director, Behavioral Sciences Center, The Bowman Gray School of Medicine, Wake Forest University. His articles have appeared in such journals as *Sexual Behavior, Physician's Management, International Journal of Gynecology and Obstetrics, The Family Coordinator, Medical Aspects of Human Sexuality,* and *Journal of Marriage and the Family.* He is editor of the book *Human Sexuality in Medical Education and Practice* and author of the classic study of *Unmarried Mothers* and *Sexual and Marital Health.*

Ardis Whitman is a free lance writer who has written articles concerned with human relations that have appeared in numerous magazines including *McCalls, Reader's Digest, Redbook,* and *Seventeen.*

Carl E. Williams is Assistant Professor of Marriage and Family Life Education, Indiana University. He is author of the *Independent Study Course, Family Development,* and is a marriage and family therapist.

Barbara Wyden is Women's Editor of *The New York Times Sunday Magazine* and is coauthor with Dr. Phyllis Harrison-Ross of *The Black Child,* a manual for parents and teachers.

Introduction

There is little question that alternate life styles such as multilateral marriage, cluster families, permissive monogamy, mate-swapping, and homosexual marriage are here to stay. Further, it is becoming increasingly clear that alternate life styles and marital-familial patterns need to be openly recognized as both legally and socially desirable for those who, for whatever reason, choose them. Nevertheless, we feel that the emerging patterns and styles do not sufficiently come to grips with the marital predicament of the vast majority of our society who are committed to a traditionally monogamous pattern even though that pattern is destructive and productive of malaise, ennui, and disillusionment.

The overall encompassing issue appears to us to be: How can "traditional" or "patriarchal" monogamy be changed so that a dyadic union may remain monogamous, yet based on equalitarian premises and dedicated to the mutual growth of the partners and their offspring? In short, we are calling into question the roles and the role-binds that are implicit within traditional monogamy: We are further calling into question the traditional nuclear family as to its viability in producing healthy, growing human beings.

The future may belong to an "equalitarian monogamy," a "permissive monogamy," an "open marriage," or "liberated marriage." Actually, none of this is new. Alternate life styles such as communal arrangements and group marriage are quite historic. During the middle decades of this century the term "companionate marriage" was used to denote a changing function and expectation of married dyads. Even if not new, the issue is now more crucial than ever before. Traditional monogamy is not doing the job. However, we are somewhat at a loss to replace the traditional style until we have sufficient evidence concerning its pitfalls, weaknesses, and failures.

The selections which we have included deal with the most basic issues relating to monogamous failure and disillusionment. The selections deal with expectations, romantic mystique, readiness for life together, risk taking, self-awareness, identity, autonomy, female liberation, conflict resolution, the acceptance or rejection of our feelings, power balance, and relationships with offspring. The editors believe that in order for marital health to be a reality there must evolve a type of dyadic union which is committed to the individual growth of the partners and which is so designed that the maximum opportunity for self-fulfillment is guaranteed. Our answer to Herb Otto's article, "Has Monogamy failed?" is a qualified yes! *Traditional* monogamy is no longer a viable alternative for countless millions of people. It has failed to keep up with the humanizing goals of sexual equality and individual growth.

We remind the student that variations on a theme are not only possible, but may prove to be the most fertile ground for the recreation and reshaping of all our institutions. Today there is the possibility of choice. We can first choose our life style. If that life style is a dyadic monogamous union, we may further choose to define and shape that dyadic union into a living arrangement which avoids pitfalls of traditional monogamy yet preserves the benefits and joys of dyadic living. This reshaping, the redefining, and reinventing, may be a growth producing process in its own right.

We hope that most of the selections, if not all, will elicit the feeling-reaction of the student, even to the extent of raising one's anxiety level. This would indicate that something within oneself is either threatened or in some way bothered by what they read. We hope that critical thinking and serious questions will be focused upon monogamy, the nuclear family, romance, societal expectations, intimacy, and children. While we do not believe that marriage is doomed as a way of life, we do raise the question as to whether monogamy can survive, and under what conditions. Issues dealing with life and vitality within the marriage are not always comfortable subjects, due primarily to the ethic stating that people should bear up and stay together, even if love is dead and misery is the order of the day. The charade helps us pretend that all is well and all is normal, when underneath we are alienated most crucially from ourselves.

Marriage ONE
Styles

The selections in this section raise questions and present issues related to marriage in the traditional, patriarchal monogamous sense. The most basic issue is marriage structure. Is the nuclear family with father-mother-children able to fill the most basic primary needs of its members? Structure (or form) in marriage and family is at least partially determined by the functions that the marriage and family are expected to fulfill. Are the functions of marriage changing? If so, what are the reasons people seek primary relationships? If we were to take a cross-cultural viewpoint we would discover that marriage and family structure have shown great variation, ranging from matrilineal societies to polyandry, polygamy, and multiple variations of extended family forms. History does not confirm any absolutes other than man's basic drive to form cross-sex liaisons. If the functions which marriage has traditionally fulfilled are no longer necessary, what, we must ask, is the function of marriage? What might the marriage of the future be like? Can there be different marital categories? What roles will husbands and wives assign to themselves and to each other, assuming that there is a freedom to choose roles?

The first selection, "The Future of Marriage" by Morton Hunt, serves as an overview of the marital scene today. Hunt sees the changes taking place in marriage as a sign of health and vitality, a necessary adaptation to modern life. He sees marriage as evolving from a rigid patriarchal monogamy into a dynamic and flexible institution. The only truly revolutionary development is group marriage, and on this score Hunt reflects a mood of pessimism due to the innumerable difficulties inherent in such a relationship.

The second selection, "Has Monogamy Failed?" by Herb Otto, gives us a further glimpse into communal and group arrangements, the cluster, and his own concept of the "new marriage." Otto sees marriage as a framework for the development of personal potential. Otto feels that monogamy has not failed but that it is an evolving institution which, hopefully, will become an asset in the development and unfolding of human potential. His article quickly lays to rest any utopian or panacea type answer to the problem of marital stagnation and rigidity. Indeed, if monogamy is to be vital, dynamic, and alive, it requires a mutual commitment of the partners to a total "growth model," wherein the couple as a pair plan and execute the stages and steps so necessary for mutual human growth.

The third selection, "Marriage in Two Steps" by Margaret Mead, is a classic statement of one method of defining trial marriage. Mead's article is included here because it reflects neither a radical new type of marital structure nor a drastic change in marital function. Mead believes that a significant degree of marital failure is due to the way in which people enter the union without preparation and with inadequate conceptual expectations based on romanticized and idealized visions of marital life. She further believes that marriage in two steps would significantly decrease the divorce rate and, more importantly, the incidence of unhappy, misery infested, pathological unions which turn fairly normal individuals into neurotic marriage partners.

The final selection, "A Challenge to Every Marriage" by Alix Shulman, is included here as an example of a yet more concrete form of marital relationship wherein the partners spell out their roles and role expectations. The reader may react to Alix Shulman's precise contract, yet the Shulmans have discovered that this is the best way to get at the unspoken, traditional, and binding expectations of the closed contract of patriarchal monogamy. The Shulmans are a couple who have done what theorists and therapists have been talking about. The Shulman article also serves as an example of the kind of renegotiation which must take place if the male sex is to truly unlearn the male superiority role and learn an equalitarian role which provides for the possibility of both male and female growing into self-actualizing persons rather than the male growing at the expense of the female's stagnation or social immobility.

Under the pressure of subcultures and social movements, matrimony is changing from the old patriarchal pattern to a new form of partnership.

THE FUTURE OF MARRIAGE

by Morton Hunt

Over a century ago, the Swiss historian and ethnologist J. J. Bachofen postulated that early man lived in small packs, ignorant of marriage and indulging in beastlike sexual promiscuity. He could hardly have suggested anything more revolting, or more fascinating, to the puritanical and prurient sensibility of his time, and whole theories of the family and of society were based on his notion by various anthropologists, as well as by German socialist Friedrich Engels and Russian revolutionist Pëtr Kropotkin. As the Victorian fog dissipated, however, it turned out that among the hundreds of primitive peoples still on earth—many of whom lived much like early man—not a single one was without some form of marriage and some limitations on the sexual freedom of the married. Marriage, it appeared, was a genuine human universal, like speech and social organization.

Nonetheless, Bachofen's myth died hard, because it appealed to a longing, deep in all of us, for total freedom to do whatever we want. And recently, it has sprung up from its own ashes in the form of a startling new motion. Even if there never was a time when marriage didn't exist, there soon will be. Lately, the air has been filled with such prophecies of the decline and impending fall of marriage. Some of the prophets are grieved at this prospect—among them, men of the cloth, such as the Pope and Dr. Peale, who keep warning us that hedonism and easy divorce are eroding the very foundations of family life. Others, who rejoice at the thought, include an assortment of feminists, hippies and anarchists, plus much-married theater people such as Joan Fontaine, who, having been married more times than the Pope and Dr. Peale put together, has authoritatively told the world that marriage is obsolete and that any sensible person can live and love better without it.

Some of the fire-breathing dragon ladies who have given women's lib an undeservedly bad name urge single women not to marry and married ones to desert their husbands forthwith. Kate Millet, the movement's leading theoretician, expects marriage to wither away after women achieve full equality. Dr. Roger Egeberg, an Assistant Secretary of HEW, urged Americans in 1969 to reconsider their inherited belief that everyone ought to marry. And last August, Mrs. Rita Hauser, the U.S. representative to the UN Human Rights Commission, said that the idea that marriage was primarily for procreation had become outmoded and that laws banning marriage between homosexuals should be erased from the books.

So much for the voices of prophecy. Are there, in fact, any real indications of a mass revolt against traditional marriage? There certainly seem to be. For one thing, in 1969 there were 660,000 divorces in America—an all-time record—and the divorce rate seems certain to achieve historic new highs in the next few years. For another thing, marital infidelity seems to have increased markedly since Kinsey's first surveys of a generation ago and now is tried, sooner or later, by some 60 percent of married men and 30 to 35 percent of married women in this country. But in what is much more of a departure from the past, infidelity is now tacitly accepted by a fair number of the spouses of the unfaithful. For some couples it has become a shared hobby; mate-swapping and group-sex parties now involve thousands of middle-class marriages. Yet another indication of change is a sharp increase not only in the number of young men and women who, dispensing with legalities, live together unwed but also in the *kind* of people who are doing so; although common-law marriage has long been popular among the poor, in the past few years it has become widespread—and often esteemed—within the middle class.

An even more radical attack on our marriage system is the effort of people in hundreds of communes around the country to construct "families," or group marriages, in which the adults own everything in common, and often consider that they all belong to one another and play mix and match sexually with total freedom. A more complete break with tradition is being made by a rapidly growing percentage of America's male and female homosexuals, who nowadays feel freer than ever to avoid "cover" marriages and to live openly as homosexuals. Their lead is almost certain to be followed by countless others within the next decade or so as our society grows ever more tolerant of personal choice in sexual matters.

Nevertheless, reports of the death of marriage are, to paraphrase Mark Twain, greatly exaggerated. Most human beings regard whatever they grew up with as right and good and see nearly every change in human behavior as a decline in standards and a fall from grace. But change often means adaptation and evolution. The many signs of contemporary revolt against marriage have been viewed as symptoms of a fatal disease, but they may, instead, be signs of a change from an obsolescent form of marriage—patriarchal monogamy—into new forms better suited to present-day human needs.

Marriage as a social structure is exceedingly plastic, being shaped by the interplay of culture and of human needs into hundreds of different forms. In societies where women could do valuable productive work, it often made sense for a man to acquire more than one wife; where women were idle or relatively unproductive—and, hence, a burden—monogamy was more likely to be the pattern. When women had means of their own or could fall back upon relatives, divorce was apt to be easy; where they were wholly dependent on their husbands, it was generally difficult. Under marginal and primitive living conditions, men kept their women in useful subjugation; in wealthier and more leisured societies, women often managed to acquire a degree of independence and power.

For a long while, the only acceptable form of marriage in America was a life-long one-to-one union, sexually faithful, all but indissoluble, productive of goods and children and strongly husband-dominated. It was a thoroughly functional mechanism during the 18th and much of the 19th centuries, when men were struggling to secure the land and needed women who would clothe and feed them, produce and rear children to help them, and obey their orders without question for an entire lifetime. It was functional, too, for the women of that time, who, uneducated, unfit for other kinds of work and endowed by law with almost no legal or property rights, needed men who would support them, give them social status and be their guides and protectors for life.

But time passed, the Indians were conquered, the sod was busted, towns and cities grew up, railroads laced the land, factories and offices took the place of the frontier. Less and less did men need women to produce goods and children; more and more, women were educated, had time to spare, made their way into the job market—and realized that they no longer had to cling to their men for life. As patriarchalism lost its usefulness, women began to want and demand orgasms, contraceptives, the vote and respect; men, finding the world growing ever more impersonal and cold, began to want wives who were warm, understanding, companionable and sexy.

Yet, strangely enough, as all these things were happening, marriage not only did not lose ground but grew more popular, and today, when it is under full-scale attack on most fronts, it is more widespread than ever before. A considerably larger percentage of our adult population was married in 1970 than was the case in 1890; the marriage rate, though still below the level of the 1940s, has been climbing steadily since 1963.

The explanation of this paradox is that as marriage was losing its former uses, it was gaining new ones. The changes that were robbing marriage of practical and life-affirming values were turning America into a mechanized urban society in which we felt like numbers, not individuals, in which we had many neighbors but few lifelong friends and in which our lives were controlled by remote governments, huge companies and insensate computers. Alone and impotent, how can we find intimacy and warmth, understanding and loyalty, enduring friendship and a feeling of personal importance? Why, obviously, through loving and marrying. Marriage is a microcosm, a world within which we seek to correct the shortcomings of the macrocosm around us. Saint Paul said it is better to marry than to burn; today, feeling the glacial chill of the world we live in, we find it better to marry than to freeze.

The model of marriage that served the old purposes excellently serves the new ones poorly. But most of the contemporary assaults upon it are not efforts to destroy it; they are efforts to modify and remold it. Only traditional patriarchal marriage is dying, while all around us marriage is being reborn in new forms. The marriage of the future already exists: we have merely mistaken the signs of evolutionary change for the stigmata of necrosis.

Divorce is a case in point. Far from being a wasting illness, it is a healthful adaptation, enabling monogamy to survive in a time when patriarchal powers, privileges and marital systems have become unworkable; far from being a radical change in the institution of marriage, divorce is a relatively minor modification of it and thoroughly supportive of most of its conventions.

Not that it seemed so at first. When divorce was introduced to Christian Europe, it appeared an extreme and rather sinful measure to most people; even among the wealthy—the only people who could afford it—it remained for centuries quite rare and thoroughly scandalous. In 1816, when president Timothy Dwight of Yale thundered against the "alarming and terrible" divorce rate in Connecticut, about one of every 100 marriages was being legally dissolved. But as women began achieving a certain degree of emancipation during the 19th Century, and as the purposes of marriage changed, divorce laws were liberalized and the rate began climbing. Between 1870 and 1905, both the U.S. population and the divorce rate more than doubled; and between then and today, the divorce rate increased over four times.

And not only for the reasons we have already noted but for yet another: the increase in longevity. When people married in their late 20s and marriage was likely to end in death by the time the last child was leaving home, divorce seemed not only wrong but hardly worth the trouble; this was especially true where the only defect in a marriage was boredom. Today, however, when people marry earlier and have finished raising their children with half their adult lives still ahead of them, boredom seems a very good reason for getting divorced.

Half of all divorces occur after eight years of marriage and a quarter of them after 15—most of these being not the results of bad initial choices but of disparity or dullness that has grown with time.

Divorcing people, however, are seeking not to escape from marriage for the rest of their lives but to exchange unhappy or boring marriages for satisfying ones. Whatever bitter things they say at the time of divorce, the vast majority do remarry, most of their second marriages lasting the rest of their lives; even those who second marriages fail are very likely to divorce and remarry again and, that failing, yet again. Divorcing people are actually marrying people, and divorce is not a negation of marriage but a workable cross between traditional monogamy and multiple marriage; sociologists have even referred to it as "serial polygamy."

Despite its costs and its hardships, divorce is thus a compromise between the monogamous ideal and the realities of present-day life. To judge from the statistics, it is becoming more useful and more socially acceptable every year. Although the divorce rate leveled off for a dozen years or so after the postwar surge of 1946, it has been climbing steadily since 1962, continuing the long-range trend of 100 years, and the rate for the entire nation now stands at nearly one for every three marriages. In some areas, it is even higher. In California, where a new ultraliberal law went into effect in 1970, nearly two of every three marriages end in divorce—a fact that astonishes people in other areas of the country but that Californians themselves accept with equanimity. They still approve of, and very much enjoy, being married; they have simply gone further than the rest of us in using divorce to keep monogamy workable in today's world.

Seen in the same light, marital infidelity is also a frequently useful modification of the marriage contract rather than a repudiation of it. It violates the conventional moral code to a greater degree than does divorce but, as practiced in America, is only a limited departure from the monogamous pattern. Unfaithful Americans, by and large, neither have extramarital love affairs that last for many years nor do they engage in a continuous series of minor liaisons; rather, their infidelity consists of relatively brief and widely scattered episodes, so that in the course of a married lifetime, they spend many more years being faithful than being unfaithful. Furthermore, American infidelity, unlike its European counterparts, has no recognized status as part of the marital system; except in a few circles, it remains impermissible, hidden and isolated from the rest of one's life.

This is not true at all levels of our society, however: Upper-class men—and, to some extent, women—have long regarded the discret love affair as an essential complement to marriage, and lower-class husbands have always considered an extracurricular roll in the hay important to a married man's peace of mind. Indeed, very few societies have ever tried to make both husband and wife sexually faithful over a lifetime: the totally monogamous ideal is statistically an abnormality. Professors Clellan Ford and Frank Beach state in *Patterns of Sexual Behavior* that less than 16 percent of 185 societies studied by anthropologists had formal restrictions to a single mate—and, of these, less than a third wholly disapproved of both premarital and extramarital relationships.

Our middle-class, puritanical society, however, has long held that infidelity of any sort is impossible if one truly loves one's mate and is happily married, that any deviation from fidelity stems from an evil or neurotic character and that it inevitably damages both the sinner and the sinned against. This credo drew support from earlier generations of psychotherapists, for almost all the adulterers they treated were neurotic, unhappily married or out of sorts with life in general. But it is just such people who seek psychotherapy; they are hardly a fair sample. Recently, sex researchers have examined the unfaithful more representatively and have come up with quite different findings. Alfred Kinsey, sociologist Robert Whitehurst of Indiana University, sociologist John Cuber of Ohio State University, sexologist/therapist Dr. Albert Ellis and various others (including myself), all of whom have made surveys of unfaithful husbands and wives, agree in general that:

• Many of the unfaithful—perhaps even a majority—are not seriously dissatisfied with their marriages nor their mates and a fair number are more or less happily married.

• Only about a third—perhaps even fewer—appear to seek extramarital sex for neurotic motives; the rest do so for nonpathological reasons.

• Many of the unfaithful—perhaps even a majority—do not feel that they, their mates nor their marriages have been harmed; in my own sample, a tenth said that their marriages had been helped or made more tolerable by their infidelity.

It is still true that many a "deceived" husband or wife, learning about his or her mate's infidelity, feels humiliated, betrayed and unloved, and is filled with rage and the desire for revenge; it is still true, too, that infidelity is a cause in perhaps a third of all divorces. But more often than not, deceived spouses never know of their mates' infidelity nor are their marriages perceptibly harmed by it.

The bulk of present-day infidelity remains hidden beneath the disguise of conventional marital behavior. But an unlettered minority of husbands and wives openly grant each other the right to outside relationships, limiting that right to certain occasions and certain kinds of involvement, in order to keep the marital relationship all important and unimpaired. A few couples, for instance, take separate vacations or allow each other one night out alone per week, it being understood that their extramarital involvements are to be confined to those times. Similar freedoms have been urged by radical marriage reformers for decades but have never really caught on, and probably never will, for one simple reason: What's out of sight is not necessarily out of mind. What husband can feel sure, despite his wife's promises, that she might not find some other man who will make her dream come true? What wife can feel sure that her husband won't fall in love with some woman he is supposed to be having only a friendly tumble with?

But it's another matter when husband and wife go together in search of extramarital frolic and do their thing with other people, in full view of each other, where it is free of romantic feeling. This is the very essence of marital swinging, or, as it is sometimes called, comarital sex. Whether it consists of a quiet mate exchange between two couples, a small sociable group-sex party or a large orgiastic rumpus, the premise is the same: As long as the extramarital sex is open, shared and purely recreational, it is not considered divisive of marriage.

So the husband and wife welcome the babysitter, kiss the children good night and drive off together to someone's home, where they drink a little and make social talk with their hosts and any other guests present, and then pair off with a couple of the others and disappear into bedrooms for an hour or so or undress in the living room and have sex in front of their interested and approving mates.

No secrecy about that, certainly, and no hidden romance to fear; indeed, the very exhibitionism of marital swinging enforces its most important ground rule—the tacit understanding that participants will not indulge in emotional involvements with fellow swingers, no matter what physical acts they perform together. Though a man and a woman make it with each other at a group-sex party, they are not supposed to meet each other later on; two swinging couples who get together outside of parties are disapprovingly said to be going steady. According to several researchers, this proves that married swingers value their marriages: They want sexual fun and stimulation but nothing that would jeopardize their marital relationships. As sociologists Duane Denfeld and Michael Gordon of the University of Connecticut straight-facedly write, marital swingers "favor monogamy and want to maintain it" and do their swinging "in order to support and improve their marriages."

To the outsider, this must sound very odd, not to say outlandish. How could anyone hope to preserve the warmth and intimacy of marriage by performing the most private and personal sexual acts with other people in front of his own mate or watching his mate do so with others?

Such a question implies that sex is integrally interwoven with the rest of one's feelings about the mate—which it is—but swingers maintain that it can be detached and enjoyed apart from those feelings, without changing them in any way. Marital swinging is supposed to involve only this one segment of the marital relationship and during only a few hours of any week or month; all else is meant to remain intact, monogamous and conventional.

Experts maintain that some people swing out of neurotic needs; some have sexual problems in their marriages that do not arise in casual sexual relationships; some are merely bored and in need of new stimuli; some need the ego lift of continual conquests. But the average swinger, whatever his (or her) motive, normal or pathological, is apt to believe that he loves his spouse, that he has a pretty good marriage and that detaching sex—and sex alone—from marital restrictions not only will do the marriage no harm but will rid it of any aura of confinement.

In contrast to this highly specialized and sharply limited attitude, there seems to be a far broader and more thorough rejection of marriage on the part of those men and women who choose to live together unwed. Informal, nonlegal unions have long been widespread among poor blacks, largely for economic reasons, but the present wave of such unions among middle-class whites has an ideological basis, for most of those who choose this arrangement consider themselves revolutionaries who have the guts to pioneer in a more honest and vital relationship than conventional marriage. A 44-year-old conference leader, Theodora Wells, and a 51-year-old psychologist, Lee Christie, who live together in Beverly Hills, expounded their philosophy in the April 1970 issue of *The Futurist:* " 'Personhood' is central to the living-together relationship; sex roles are central to the marriage relationship. Our experience strongly suggests that personhood excites growth, stimulates openness, increases joyful satisfactions in achieving, encompasses rich, full sexuality peaking in romance. Marriage may have the appearance of this in its romantic phase, but it settles down to prosaic routine. . . . The wife role is diametrically opposed to the personhood I want. I [Theodora] therefore choose to live with the man who joins me in the priority of personhood."

What this means is that she hates homemaking, is career oriented and fears that if she became a legal wife, she would automatically be committed to traditional female roles, to dependency. Hence, she and Christie have rejected marriage and chosen an arrangement without legal obligations, without a head of the household and without a primary money earner or primary homemaker—though Christie, as it happens, does 90 percent of the cooking. Both believe that their freedom from legal ties and their constant need to rechoose each other make for a more exciting, real and growing relationship.

A fair number of the avant-garde and many of the young have begun to find this not only a fashionably rebellious but a thoroughly congenial attitude toward marriage; couples are living together, often openly, on many a college campus, risking punishment by college authorities (but finding the risk smaller every day) and bucking their parents' strenuous disapproval (but getting their glum acceptance more and more often).

When one examines the situation closely, however, it becomes clear that most of these marital Maoists live together in close, warm, committed and monagamous fashion, very much like married people; they keep house together (although often dividing their roles in untraditional ways) and neither is free to have sex with anyone else, date anyone else nor even find anyone else intriguing. Anthropologists Margaret Mead and Ashley Montagu, sociologist John Gagnon and other close observers of the youth scene feel that living together, whatever its defects, is actually an apprentice marriage and not a true rebellion against marriage at all.

Dr. Mead, incidentally, made a major public pitch in 1966 for a revision of our laws that would create two kinds of marital status: individual marriage, a legal but easily dissolved form for young people who were unready for parenthood or full commitment to each other but who wanted to live together with social acceptance; and parental marriage, a union involving all the legal commitments and responsibilities—and difficulties of dissolution—of marriage as we presently know it. Her suggestion aroused a great deal of public debate. The middle-aged, for the most part, condemned her proposal as being an attack upon and a debasement of marriage, while the young replied that the whole idea was unnecessary. The young were right: They were already creating their own new marital folkway in the form of the close, serious but informal union that achieved all the goals of individual marriage except its legality and acceptance by the middle-aged. Thinking themselves rebels against marriage, they had only created a new form of marriage closely resembling the very thing Dr. Mead had suggested.

If these modifications of monogamy aren't quite as alarming or as revolutionary as they seem to be, one contemporary experiment in marriage *is* a genuine and total break with Western tradition. This is group marriage—a catchall team applied to a wide variety of polygamous experiments in which small groups of adult males and females, and their children, live together under one roof or in a close-knit settlement, calling themselves a family, tribe, commune or, more grandly, intentional community and considering themselves all married to one another.

As the term intentional community indicates, these are experiments not merely in marriage but in the building of a new type of society. They are utopian minisocieties existing within, but almost wholly opposed to, the mores and values of present-day American society.

Not that they are all of a piece. A few are located in cities and have members who look and act square and hold regular jobs; some, both urban and rural, consist largely of dropouts, acidheads, panhandlers and petty thieves; but most are rural communities, have hippie-looking members and aim at a self-sufficient farming-and-handicraft way of life. A very few communes are politically conservative, some are in the middle and most are pacifist, anarchistic and/or New Leftist. Nearly all, whatever their national political bent, are islands of primitive communism in which everything is collectively owned and all members work for the common good.

Their communism extends to—or perhaps really begins with—sexual collectivism. Though some communes consist of married couples who are conventionally faithful, many are built around some kind of group sexual sharing. In some of these, couples are paired off but occasionally sleep with other members of the group; in others, pairing off is actively discouraged and the members drift around sexually from one partner to another—a night here, a night there, as they wish.

Group marriage has captured the imagination of many thousands of college students in the past few years through its idealistic and romantic portrayal in three novels widely read by the young—Robert Heinlein's *Stranger in a Strange Land* and Robert Rimmer's *The Harrad Experiment* and *Proposition 31*. The underground press, too, has paid a good deal of sympathetic attention—and the establishment press a good deal of hostile attention—to communes. There has even been, for several years, a West Coast publication titled *The Modern Utopian* that is devoted, in large part, to news and discussions of group marriage. The magazine, which publishes a directory of intentional communities, recently listed 125 communes and the editor said, "For every listing you find here, you can be certain there are 100 others." And an article in *The New York Times* last December stated that "nearly 2000 communes in 34 states have turned up" but gave this as a conservative figure, as "no accurate count exists."

All this sometimes gives one the feeling that group marriage is sweeping the country; but, based on the undoubtedly exaggerated figures of *The Modern Utopian* and counting a generous average of 20 people per commune, it would still mean that no more than 250,000 adults—approximately one tenth of one percent of the U.S. population—are presently involved in group marriages. These figures seem improbable.

Nevertheless, group marriage offers solutions to a number of the nagging problems and discontents of modern monogamy. Collective parenthood—every parent being partly responsible for every child in the group—not only provides a warm and enveloping atmosphere for children but removes some of the pressure from individual parents; moreover, it minimizes the disruptive effects of divorce on the child's world. Sexual sharing is an answer to boredom and solves the problem of infidelity, or seeks to, by declaring extramarital experiences acceptable and admirable. It avoids the success-status-possession syndrome of middle-class family life by turning toward simplicity, communal ownership and communal goals.

Finally, it avoids the loneliness and confinement of monogamy by creating something comparable to what anthropologists call the extended family, a larger grouping of related people living together. (There is a difference, of course: In group marriage, the extended family isn't composed of blood relatives.) Even when sexual switching isn't the focus, there is a warm feeling of being affectionally connected to everyone else. As one young woman in a Taos commune said ecstatically, "It's really groovy waking up and knowing that 48 people love you."

There is, however, a negative side: This drastic reformulation of marriage makes for new problems, some of them more severe than the ones it has solved. Albert Ellis, quoted in Herbert Otto's new book, *The Family in Search of a Future*, lists several categories of serious difficulties with group marriage, including the near impossibility of finding four or more adults who can live harmoniously and lovingly together, the stubborn intrusion of jealousy and love conflicts and the innumerable difficulties of coordinating and scheduling many lives.

Other writers, including those who have sampled communal life, also talk about the problems of leadership (most communes have few rules to start with; those that survive for any time do so by becoming almost conventional and traditional) and the difficulties in communal work sharing (there are always some members who are slovenly and lazy and others who are neat and hard-working, the latter either having to expel the former or give up and let the commune slowly die).

A more serious defect is that most group marriages, being based upon a simple, semiprimitive agrarian life, reintroduce old style patriarchalism, because such a life puts a premium on masculine muscle power and endurance and leaves the classic domestic and subservient roles to women. Even a most sympathetic observer, psychiatrist Joseph Downing, writes, "In the tribal families, while both sexes work, women are generally in a service role. . . . Male dominance is held desirable by both sexes."

Most serious of all are the emotional limitations of group marriage. Its ideal is sexual freedom and universal love, but the group marriages that most nearly achieve this have the least cohesiveness and the shallowest interpersonal involvements; people come and go, and there is really no marriage at all but only a continuously changing and highly unstable encounter group. The longer-lasting and more cohesive group marriages are, in fact, those in which, as Dr. Downing reports, the initial sexual spree "generally gives way to the quiet, semipermanent, monogamous relationship characteristic of many in our general society."

Not surprisingly, therefore, Dr. Ellis finds that most group marriages are unstable and last only several months to a few years; and sociologist Lewis Yablonsky of California State College at Hayward, who has visited and lived in a number of communes, says that they are often idealistic but rarely successful or enduring. Over and above their specific difficulties, they are utopian—they seek to construct a new society from whole cloth. But all utopias thus far have failed; human behavior is so incredibly complex that every totally new order, no matter how well planned, generates innumerable unforeseen problems. It really is a pity; group living and group marriage look wonderful on paper.

All in all, then, the evidence is overwhelming that old-fashioned marriage is not dying and that nearly all of what passes for rebellion against it is a series of patchwork modifications enabling marriage to serve the needs of modern man without being unduly costly or painful.

While this is the present situation, can we extrapolate it into the future? Will marriage continue to exist in some form we can recognize?

It is clear that, in the future, we are going to have an even greater need than we now do for love relationships that offer intimacy, warmth, companionship and a reasonable degree of reliability. Such relationships need not, of course, be heterosexual. With our increasing tolerance of sexual diversity, it seems likely that many homosexual men and women will find it publicly acceptable to live together in quasi-marital alliances.

The great majority of men and women, however, will continue to find heterosexual love the preferred form, for biological and psychological reasons that hardly have to be spelled out here. But need heterosexual love be embodied within marriage? If the world is already badly over-populated and daily getting worse, why add to its burden—and if one does not intend to have children, why seek to enclose love within a legal cage? Formal promises to love are promises no one can keep, for love is not an act of will; and legal bonds have no power to keep love alive when it is dying.

Such reasoning—more cogent today than ever, due to the climate of sexual permissiveness and to the twin technical advances of the pill and the loop—lies behind the growth of unwed unions. From all indications, however, such unions will not replace marriage as an institution but only precede it in the life of the individual.

It seems probable that more and more young people will live together unwed for a time and then marry each other or break up and make an-other similar alliance, and another, until one of them turns into a formal, legal marriage. In 50 years, perhaps less, we may come close to the Scan-dinavian pattern, in which a great many couples live together prior to marriage. It may be, moreover, that the spread of this practice (will de-crease the divorce rate among the young, for many of the mistakes that are recognized too late and are undone in divorce court will be recog-nized and undone outside the legal system, with less social and emo-tional damage than divorce involves.)

If, therefore, marriage continues to be important, what form will it take? The one truly revolutionary innovation is group marriage—and, as we have seen, it poses innumerable and possibly insuperable practical and emotional difficulties. A marriage of one man and one woman in-volves only one interrelationship, yet we all know how difficult it is to find that one right fit and to keep it in working order. But add one more person, making the smallest possible group marriage, and you have three relationships (A-B, B-C and A-C); add a fourth to make two couples and you have six relationships; add enough to make a typical group marriage of 15 persons and you have 105 relationships.

This is an abstract way of saying that human beings are all very dif-ferent and that finding a satisfying and workable love relationship is not easy, even for a twosome, and is impossibly difficult for aggregations of a dozen or so. It might prove less difficult, a generation hence, for chil-dren brought up in group-marriage communes. Such children would not have known the close, intense, parent-child relationships of monogamous marriage and could more easily spread their affections thinly and un-demandingly among many. But this is mere conjecture, for no communal-marriage experiment in America has lasted long enough for us to see the results, except the famous Oneida Community in Upstate New York; it endured from 1848 to 1879, and then its offspring vanished back into the surrounding ocean of monogamy.

Those group marriages that do endure in the future will probably be dedicated to a rural and semiprimitive agrarian life style. Urban communes may last for some years but with an ever-changing membership and a lack of inner familial identity; in the city, one's work life lies outside the group, and with only emotional ties to hold the group together, any dissension or conflict will result in a turnover of membership. But while agrarian communes may have a sounder foundation, they can never become a mass movement; there is simply no way for the land to support well over 200,000,000 people with the low-efficiency productive methods of a century or two ago.

Agrarian communes not only cannot become a mass movement in the future but they will not even have much chance of surviving as islands in a sea of modern industrialism. For semiprimitive agrarianism is to marginal, so backbreaking and so tedious a way of life that it is unlikely to hold most of its converts against the competing attractions of conventional civilization. Even Dr. Downing, for all his enthusiasm about the "Society of Awakening," as he calls tribal family living, predicts that for the foreseeable future, only a small minority will be attracted to it and that most of these will return to more normal surroundings and relationships after a matter of weeks or months.

Thus, monogamy will prevail; on this, nearly all experts agree. But it will almost certainly continue to change in the same general direction in which it has been changing for the past few generations: namely, toward a redefinition of the special roles played by husband and wife, so as to achieve a more equal distribution of the rights, privileges and life expectations of man and woman.

This, however, will represent no sharp break with contemporary marriage, for the marriage of 1971 has come a long way from patriarchy toward the goal of equality. Our prevalent marital style has been termed companionship marriage by a generation of sociologists: in contrast to 19th Century marriage, it is relatively egalitarian and intimate, husband and wife being intellectually and emotionally close, sexually compatible and nearly equal in personal power and in the quantity and quality of labor each contributes to the marriage.

From an absolute point of view, however, it still is contaminated by patriarchalism. Although each partner votes, most husbands (and wives) still think that men understand politics better; although each may have had similar schooling and believes both sexes to be intellectually equal, most husbands and wives still act as if men were innately better equipped to handle money, drive the car, fill out tax returns and replace fuses. There may be something close to equality in their homemaking, but nearly always it is his career that counts, not hers. If his company wants to move him to another city, she quits her job and looks for another in their new location; and when they want to have children, it is seldom questioned that he will continue to work while she will stay home.

With this, there is a considerable shift back toward traditional role assignments: He stops waxing the floors and washing dishes, begins to speak with greater authority about how their money is to be spent, tells her (rather than consults her) when he would like to work late or take a business trip, gives (or withholds) his approval of her suggestions for parties, vacations and child discipline. The more he takes on the airs of his father, the more she learns to connive and manipulate like her mother. Feeling trapped and discriminated against, resenting the men of the world, she thinks she makes an exception of her husband, but in the hidden recesses of her mind he is one with the others. Bearing the burden of being a man in the world, and resenting the easy life of women, he thinks he makes an exception of his wife but deep-down classifies her with the rest.

This is why a great many women yearn for change and what the majority of women's liberation members are actively hammering away at. A handful of radicals in the movement think that the answer is the total elimination of marriage, that real freedom for women will come about only through the abolition of legal bonds to men and the establishment of governmentally operated nurseries to rid women once and for all of domestic entrapment. But most women in the movement, and nearly all those outside it, have no sympathy with the anti-marriage extremists; they very much want to keep marriage alive but aim to push toward completing the evolutionary trends that have been under way so long

Concretely, women want their husbands to treat them as equals; they want help and participation in domestic duties; they want help with child rearing; they want day-care centers and other agencies to free them to work at least part time, while their children are small, so that they won't have to give up their careers and slide into the imprisonment of domesticity. They want an equal voice in all the decisions made in the home—including job decisions that affect married life; they want their husbands to respect them, not indulge them; they want, in short, to be treated as if they were their husbands' best friends—which, in fact, they are, or should be.

All this is only a continuation of the developments in marriage over the past century and a quarter. The key question is: How far can marriage evolve in this direction without making excessive demands upon both partners? Can most husbands and wives have full-time uninter-rupted careers, share all the chores and obligations of homemaking and parenthood and still find time for the essential business of love and com-panionship?

From the time of the early suffragettes, there have been women with the drive and talent to be full-time doctors, lawyers, retailers and the like, and at the same time to run a home and raise children with the help of housekeepers, nannies and selfless husbands. From these examples, we can judge how likely this is to become the dominant pattern of the future. Simply put, it isn't, for it would take more energy, money and good luck than the great majority of women possess and more skilled helpers than the country could possibly provide. But what if child care were more efficiently handled in state-run centers, which would make the totally egalitarian marriage much more feasible? The question then becomes: How many middle-class American women would really prefer full-time work to something less demanding that would give them more time with their children? The truth is that most of the world's work is dull and wearisome rather than exhilarating and inspiring. Women's lib leaders are largely middle-to-upper-echelon professionals, and no wonder they think every wife would be better off working full time—but we have yet to hear the same thing from saleswomen, secretaries and bookkeepers.

Married women *are* working more all the time—in 1970, over half of all mothers whose children were in school held jobs—but the middle-class women among them pick and choose things they like to do rather than *have* to do for a living: moreover, many work part time until their chil-dren have grown old enough to make mothering a minor assignment. Accordingly, they make much less money than their husbands, rarely ever rise to any high positions in their fields and, to some extent, play certain traditionally female roles within marriage. It is a compromise and, like all compromises, it delights no one—but serves nearly everyone bet-ter than more clear-cut and idealistic solutions.

Though the growth of egalitarianism will not solve all the problems of marriage, it may help solve the problems of a bad marriage. With their increasing independence, fewer and fewer wives will feel compelled to remain confined within unhappy or unrewarding marriages. Divorce, therefore, can be expected to continue to increase, despite the offsetting effect of extramarital liaisons. Extrapolating the rising divorce rate, we can conservatively expect that within another generation, half or more of all persons who marry will be divorced at least once. But even if di-vorce were to become an almost universal experience, it would not be the *antithesis* of marriage but only a part of the marital experience; most people will, as always, spend their adult lives married—not continuously in a single marriage, but segmentally, in two or more marriages. For all the dislocations and pain these divorces cause, the sum total of emotional satisfaction in the lives of the divorced and remarried may well be greater than their great-grandparents were able to achieve.

Marital infidelity, since it also relieves some of the pressures and discontents of unsuccessful or boring marriages—and does so in most cases without breaking up the existing home—will remain an alternative to divorce and will probably continue to increase, all the more so as women come to share more fully the traditional male privileges. Within another generation, based on present trends, four of five husbands and two of three wives whose marriages last more than several years will have at least a few extramarital involvements.

Overt permissiveness, particularly in the form of marital swinging, may be tried more often than it now is, but most of those who test it out will do so only briefly rather than adopt it as a way of life. Swinging has a number of built-in difficulties, the first and most important of which is that the avoidance of all emotional involvement—the very key stone of swinging—is exceedingly hard to achieve. Nearly all professional observers report that jealousy is a frequent and severely disruptive problem. And not only jealousy but sexual competitiveness: Men often have potency problems while being watched by other men or after seeing other men outperform them. Even a regular stud, moreover, may feel threatened when he observes his wife being more active at a swinging party than he himself could possibly be. Finally, the whole thing is truly workable only for the young and the attractive.

There will be wider and freer variations in marital styles—we are a pluralistic nation, growing more tolerant of diversity all the time—but throughout all the styles of marriage in the future will run a predominant motif that has been implicit in the evolution of marriage for a century and a quarter and that will finally come to full flowering in a generation or so. In short, the marriage of the future will be a heterosexual friendship, a free and unconstrained union of a man and a woman who are companions, partners, comrades and sexual lovers. There will still be a certain degree of specialization within marriage, but by and large, the daily business of living together—the talk, the meals, the going out to work and coming home again, the spending of money, the lovemaking, the caring for the children, even the indulgence or nonindulgence in outside affairs—will be governed by this fundamental relationship rather than by the lord-and-servant relationship of patriarchal marriage. Like all friendships, it will exist only as long as it is valid; it will rarely last a

lifetime, yet each marriage, while it does last, will meet the needs of
the men and women of the future as no earlier form of marriage could
have. Yet we who know the marriage of today will find it relatively familiar, comprehensible—and very much alive.

------

*"There is no question that sex-role and
parental-role rigidities are in the process
of diminishing, and new dimensions of
flexibility are making their appearance in
marriage and the family."*

HAS MONOGAMY FAILED?

by Herbert A. Otto

Never before in the history of Western civilization has the institution
of marriage been under the searching scrutiny it is today. Never before
have so many people questioned the cultural and theological heritage
of monogamy—and set out in search of alternatives. The American family
of the 1970s is entering an unprecedented era of change and transition,
with a massive reappraisal of the family and its functioning in the offing.

The U.S. statistic of one divorce per every four marriages is all too
familiar. Other figures are even more disquieting. For example, a recent
government study revealed that one-third of all first-born children in
the United States from 1964 through 1966 were conceived out of wedlock, thereby forcing many hasty marriages that might not have occurred
otherwise. Some marriage specialists estimate that anywhere from 40 to
60 per cent of all marriages are at any given time "subclinical." The
couples involved could materially benefit from the help of a marriage
counselor, but they never reach a clinic. Divorce is still the most widely
accepted means of coping with a marriage beset by problems. Relatively
few couples having marital difficulties are aware of available marriage

counseling services or utilize them. Divorce today is very much a part of the social fabric, and some sociologists refer to a "divorce culture." It is safe to say that most men, women, and children in this country have been touched by the divorce experience—either in their own families, or among friends and close acquaintances.

The other day a good friend, senior executive of a large company and in his early forties, dropped by for a visit. He told me he had been thinking of divorce after sixteen years of marriage. The couple have a boy, twelve, and two girls, one of whom is ten, the other eight. "We've grown apart over the years, and we have nothing in common left anymore other than the children. There are at least twenty years of enjoying life still ahead of me. I was worried about the children until we discussed it with them. So many of their schoolmates have had divorced parents or parents who had remarried, they are accustomed to the idea. It's part of life. Of course, if the older ones need help, I want them to see a good psychiatrist while we go through with this. My wife is still a good-looking woman, younger than I, and probably will remarry. I'm not thinking of it now, but I'll probably remarry someday." This situation illustrates an attitude and the climate of the times. Divorce has become as much an institution as marriage.

Paradoxically, the high divorce rate can be viewed as both a symptom of the failure of monogamy and an indication of its success. A large majority of men and women remarry within four years after their divorce. As Dr. Bernard Steinzor points out in his latest book, *When Parents Divorce,* "divorce has become an expression of the increasing personal freedom afforded the average citizen." It is a fact that the average citizen continues to pursue personal freedom within the frame-work of marriage. Serial monogamy or progressive monogamy is today so widespread that it has arrived as an alternative structure. According to one analyst, we are close to the day when 85 percent of all men and women reaching the age of sixty-five will have been remarried at least once. I am reminded of a cartoon that appeared in *The New Yorker* some time ago: A young couple is shown leaving what is identified by a sign as the home of a justice of the peace. The bride, dressed in the latest mod fashion, turns brightly to her young man and says, "Darling! Our first marriage!"

The full-scale emergence of serial monogamy has been accompanied by an explosive upswing of experimentation with other alternative structures. Begun by the under-thirty generation and hippie tribal families, the 1960s have seen the growth of a new commune movement. This movement has started to attract significant segments of the older, established population. For example, I recently conducted a weekend marathon in Chicago—under the auspices of the Oasis Center—that was open to the public. Seven out of thirty-six participants were members of communes. Three of the seven were successful professional men in their mid-forties. Another participant, a college professor in his early thirties, mentioned that he had been a member of a commune composed of several psychiatrists, an engineer, a teacher, and a chemist. When I visited New York following the Chicago weekend, a senior editor of a large publishing house casually mentioned that he and some friends were in the process of organizing a commune. They were looking for a large brownstone close to their offices.

The commune movement even has its own journal, *Modern Utopian*. Issued by the Alternatives Foundation of Berkeley, California, it is in its fourth year of publication. In 1969, this journal published the first comprehensive directory of intentional or utopian communes in the United States and the world. The addresses of close to two hundred intentional communities in this country are given. (It has been estimated that there are four to six times this number of communes in the United States.) California leads the *Modern Utopian* directory with more than thirty listed. New York has twenty-eight and Pennsylvania thirteen, with communes listed from thirty-five other states. Half a dozen books that I know of are currently in preparation on the commune movement.

Communes of various types exist, varying from agricultural subsistence to religious. To provide a base for economic survival, many of the communes furnish services or construct marketable products such as hammocks or wooden toys for preschoolers. Others operate printing presses or schools. Most communes not located in cities raise some of their own food. Relatively rare is the commune that is self-supporting solely on the basis of its agricultural operation. Sizes vary with anywhere from twelve persons or fewer to a hundred persons or more as members of an intentional community. The educational and vocational backgrounds of members also vary widely. The young people and school dropouts are currently being joined by a growing number of "Establishment dropouts." Many of these are people who have made successful contributions in their chosen vocations or professions and have grown disillusioned, or who are seeking to explore new life-styles.

Communes often have their beginnings when several persons who know each other well, like each other, and have similar values decide to live together. Sometimes a commune is formed around a common interest, craft, or unifying creative goal. Political views or convictions may also play a role in the formation of a commune. There are a number of peace-movement and radical communes; sometimes these are composed of political activists, and sometimes of people who see the commune movement as a "radical approach to revolution." Members of one such group, the Twin Oaks community in Virginia, think of themselves as a post-revolutionary society. As detailed in *Modern Utopian,* this "radical commune" was organized as the result of a university conference:

> Twin Oaks was started by a group of people who met while attending an "academic" conference during 1966 at Ann Arbor, Michigan, on the formation of a Walden II community. One of the Twin Oakers related how this conference resulted in a very elaborate, academic type plan on how to get a Walden II community going. But when the conference was over, the professors all returned to their teaching posts, and nobody had any idea where they could get the several million dollars that the plan called for to start the thing. So eight people decided to start right away with whatever resources they could get together. . . .
>
> For while Twin Oaks was designed to be a living experiment in community, it also aims to stimulate others to do the same. As one member said, "We generally hold to the opinion that people who *don't* start communities (or join them) are slightly immoral." It's all part of the revolution being over—they define revolution as a "radical restructuring" of society, both economic and, more important, cultural. (But maybe you can't really separate the two.) One member summed up a desirable post-revolutionary society as: "A society that creates people who are committed to non-aggression; a society of people concerned for one another; a society where one man's gain is not another man's loss; a society where disagreeable work is minimized and leisure is valued; a society in which people come first; an economic system of equality; a society which is constantly trying to improve in its ability to create happy, productive, creative people."

The personal property a member brings to a commune remains his, although he may be expected to share it when needed. Some purists object that, since members do not donate personal property for the benefit of the group, the current social experiments should not be referred to as "communes." Obviously, the term has acquired a new meaning and definition. The emphasis today is on the exploration of alternate models for togetherness, the shaping of growing dynamic environments, the exploration of new life-styles, and the enjoyment of living together.

A number of communes are deliberately organized for the purpose of group marriage. The concept of group marriage, however, differs widely. Some communes exclusively composed of couples have a living arrangement similar to the "big family" or group family that originated in Sweden in 1967. These married couples share the same home, expenses, household chores, and the upbringing of the children. Infidelity is not encouraged. Other group-marriage communes tolerate or encourage the sharing of husbands and wives. On the other end of the group-marriage continuum are communes such as The Family near Taos, New Mexico. This group of more than fifty members discourages pairing—"Everyone is married to everyone. The children are everyone's."

The life-span of many communes is relatively short due to four major disintegrative pressures that fragment intentional communities. Disagreement over household chores or work to be performed is a major source of disruption. When members fail to fulfill their obligations, disillusionment and demoralization often set in. Closely related are interpersonal conflicts, frequently fueled by the exchange of sex partners and resultant jealousy. Drugs do not seem to create a major problem in most communes, as there is either a permissive attitude or drug use is discouraged or forbidden. A small number of religious/mystical communes use drugs for sacramental purposes and as a means of communion.

The problems associated with economic survival generate considerable pressure. A final strong force that contributes to the collapse of communes stems from the hostility of surrounding communities. There are innumerable instances of harassment by neighbors, strangers, civil authorities, and police. The persistent and violent nature of this persecution is probably traceable to deep-seated feelings of threat and outrage when the neighboring communities discover a group in their midst suspected of having unorthodox living arrangements. These pervasive feelings of resistance and anger (which may be partially subconscious) are conceivably engendered in many persons by what they perceive to be a threat to the existing family structure.

The weight of tradition and the strong imprinting of parental and familial models assure that for some time to come the overwhelming bulk of the population will opt for something close to the family structures they have known. In view of this strong thrust, it is all the more surprising that preventive programs (other than didactic approaches) that center on the strengthening of the family are almost unknown. Also sadly lacking is massive federal support for programs designed to help marriages and families beset by problems. A network of federally supported marriage-counseling clinics making marital and premarital counseling services available throughout every state in the Union could accomplish a great deal toward reducing marital unhappiness and divorce.

Present-day medical science widely recommends that we have an annual physical check-up as a means of prevention. In a similar manner, annual assessment and evaluation should be available to couples interested in developing and improving their marriages. The goal would be to identify, strengthen, and develop family potential *before* crises arise, with the main focus on helping a family achieve an even more loving, enjoyable, creative, and satisfying marriage relationship. The plan of a marriage and family potential center was developed in 1967 and 1968 by a colleague, Dr. Lacey Hall, and myself during my stay in Chicago. The project was supported by the Stone Foundation, but, owing to a number of complex reasons, the program was never fully implemented. As a part of the work in Chicago, and also under the auspices of the National Center for the Exploration of Human Potential, a number of "More Joy in Your Marriage" groups and classes have been conducted and have shown considerable promise as a preventive approach.

Another highly promising field of inquiry is the area of family strengths. Little or no research and conceptualization had been done in relation to this area until the work of the Human Potentialities Research Project at the University of Utah, from 1960 through 1967. Paradoxically, family counseling and treatment programs have been offered for decades without a clearly developed framework of what was meant by family strengths, or what constitutes a "healthy family." In spite of extensive efforts to obtain foundation or government support for this research, no financial support was forthcoming. Ours remains a pathology-oriented culture saddled with the bias that the study of disorganization, illness, and dysfunction is the surest road to understanding the forces that go into the making of health and optimum functioning.

The emergence of alternative structures and the experimentation with new modes of married and family togetherness expresses a strong need to bring greater health and optimum functioning to a framework of interpersonal relationships formerly regarded as "frozen" and not amenable to change. There is no question that sex-role and parental-role rigidities are in the process of diminishing, and new dimensions of flexibility are making their appearance in marriage and the family. It is also evident that we are a pluralistic society with pluralistic needs. In this time of change and accelerated social evolution, we should encourage innovation and experimentation in the development of new forms of social and communal living. It is possible to invent and try out many models without hurting or destroying another person. Perhaps we need to recognize clearly that the objective of any model is to provide an atmosphere of sustenance, loving, caring, and adventuring. This makes growth and unfoldment possible.

It is in this light that the attention of an increasing number of well-known humanistic psychologists has been drawn to the institution of marriage. A new recognition of the many dimensions and possibilities of monogamy is beginning to emerge. For example, Dr. Jack Gibb and Dr. Everett Shostrom have each been conducting a series of couples groups at Growth Centers designed to revitalize and deepen love in the marital relationship.

Another eminent psychologist and author, Dr. Sidney Jourard, suggests that we "re-invent marriage" by engaging in "serial polygamy to the same person." He points out that many marriages pass through a cycle of gratifying the needs of both partners, and are experienced as fulfilling until an impasse is reached. One partner or the other finds continuation in that form intolerable, and the marriage is usually legally dissolved at that point. He believes it is possible for the couple at this juncture to struggle with the impasse and to evolve a new marriage with each other, one that includes change, yet preserves some of the old pattern that remains viable. This is the second marriage that, whatever form it takes, will also reach its end. There may then again be a time of estrangement, a period of experimentation, and a remarriage in a new way—and so on for as long as continued association with the same spouse remains meaningful for both partners.

One of the originators of the group marathon technique, Dr. Frederick Stoller, has another interesting proposal to add new dimensions to marriage and family relationships. He suggests an "intimate network of families." His intimate network consists of a circle of three or four families who meet together regularly and frequently, share in reciprocal fashion any of their intimate secrets, and offer one another a variety of services. The families do not hesitate to influence one another in terms of values and attitudes. Such an intimate family network would be neither stagnant nor polite, but would involve an extension of the boundaries of the immediate family.

Another possibility to introduce new elements of growth and creativity to monogamy is contained in my own concept of the "new marriage," i.e., marriage as a framework for developing personal potential. This concept is based on the hypothesis that we are all functioning at a small fraction of our capacity to live fully in its total meaning of loving, caring, creating, and adventuring. Consequently, the actualizing of our potential can become the most exciting adventure of our lifetime. From this perspective, any marriage can be envisioned as a framework for actualizing personal potential. Thus, marriage offers us an opportunity to grow, and an opportunity to develop and deepen the capacity for loving and caring. Only in a continuing relationship is there a possibility for love to become deeper and fuller so that it envelops all of our life and extends into the community. However, growth, by its very nature, is not smooth and easy, for growth involves change and the emergence of the new. But growth and the actualization of personal potential are also a joyous and deeply satisfying process that can bring to marriage a *joie de vivre,* an excitement, and a new quality of zest for living.

There are a number of characteristics that form a unique Gestalt and distinguish the new marriage from contemporary marriage patterns:

● There is a clear acknowledgment by both partners concerning the *personal relevance* of the human potentialities hypothesis: that the healthy individual is functioning at a fraction of his potential.

● Love and understanding become dynamic elements in the actualization of the marital partners' personal potential.

● Partners in the new marriage conceive of their union as an evolving, developing, flexible, loving relationship.

● In the new marriage there is planned action and commitment to achieve realization of marriage potential.

● The new marriage is here-and-now oriented and not bound to the past.

● There is clear awareness by husband and wife that their interpersonal or relationship environment, as well as their physical environment, directly affects the actualization of individual potential.

● There is clear recognition by spouses that personality and the actualization of human potential have much to do with the social institutions and structures within which man functions. The need for institutional and environmental regeneration is acknowledged by both partners as being personally relevant, leading to involvement in social action.

● Husband and wife have an interest in exploring the spiritual dimensions of the new marriage.

Since it is often difficult for two people to actualize more of their marriage potential by themselves, participants in the new marriage will seek out group experiences designed to deepen their relationship and functioning as a couple. Such experiences are now being offered at Growth Centers that have sprung up in many parts of the United States. Extension divisions of institutions of higher learning and church organizations are also increasingly offering such group experiences. Based on my many years of practice as marriage counselor, it has long been my conclusion that every marriage needs periodic rejuvenation and revitalization. This is best accomplished in a couples group that focuses on the development of greater intimacy, freedom, joy, and affection.

The challenge of marriage is the adventure of uncovering the depth of our love, the height of our humanity. It means risking ourselves physically and emotionally; leaving old habit patterns, and developing new ones; being able to express our desires fully, while sensitive to the needs of the other; being aware that each changes at his own rate, and unafraid to ask for help when needed.

Has monogamy failed? My answer is "no." Monogamy is no longer a rigid institution, but instead an evolving one. There is a multiplicity of models and dimensions that we have not even begun to explore. It takes a certain amount of openness to become aware on not only an intellectual level but a feeling level that these possibilities face us with a choice. Then it takes courage to recognize that this choice in a measure represents our faith in monogamy. Finally, there is the fact that every marriage has a potential for greater commitment, enjoyment, and communication, for more love, understanding, and warmth. Actualizing this potential can offer new dimensions in living and new opportunities for personal growth, and can add new strength and affirmation to a marriage.

MARRIAGE IN TWO STEPS

by Margaret Mead

The June bride evokes memory pictures of her mother and her mother's mother as just a happy girl, caught between tears and laughter. The newest bridegroom, describing his difficulties, awakens memories of other crises, each story a different one, and yet in its happy outcome the same.

For everyone taking part in a wedding each small event, like the solemn ritual of marriage itself, binds the generations in the shared belief that what has been true and lasting in the past is true and lasting

Reprinted from the *Redbook Magazine* July, 1971, copyright 1971 The McCall Publishing Company.

today and will remain so safely across time. On such occasions sentiment and loving hope for the young couple—these two who are entering the most important relationship of their adult lives—join in renewing our faith in traditional forms. This, we believe, is how families begin.

But in the cool light of everyday experience a different picture emerges. As a society we have moved—and are still moving—a long way from the kinds of marriage our forefathers knew and believed in. We still define marriage as essentially an adult relationship. But now, in a period in which full participation in adult life is increasingly delayed, the age of first marriage for boys as well as girls has been declining steadily. And although people can look forward to longer years of vigorous maturity, young couples are entering parenthood not later than in the past, but even earlier.

We still believe that marriage entails financial responsibility. Yet we indulge in endless subterfuge to disguise the economic dependency of the majority of very young marriages. Significantly, we have devised systems of loans and insurance to ease our financial burden of seeing children through years of higher education. However, we have not invented any form of insurance to cover the care of children born of student marriages, or born to teenage parents who are struggling to find themselves. If we encourage these young marriages, as in fact we do, then we must think more clearly about the long-term economic problems for which we, as parents, may have to take some responsibility.

We still believe that marriage is the necessary prelude to responsible parenthood even though, in every social class, pregnancy is to an increasing extent preceding marriage. We still strongly believe that children born of a marriage should be wanted. In the past, this meant accepting the birth of children no matter what the number and circumstances; but today, with existing methods of conception control, every child could be a chosen child.

We still believe that the continuity of the family, based on marriage, is fundamental to our way of life and to the well-being of every individual child. Yet there is clear evidence of the fragility of marriage ties, especially among very young couples who become parents before they know each other as husband and wife.

The disparities are plain to see and the outlook is unpromising. We might expect this to force us to recognize how great are the discrepancies between our expectations, based on tradition, and what is happening to young American families. The truth is, we have not really faced up to the many conflicts between belief and experience, precept and practice, in our current, muddled style of marriage. It is not enough to

say, "Yes, marriage patterns are changing." What we have not fully
realized is that we do not have to stand by helplessly while change sweeps
over us, destroying our hopes for a better life for our children.

Instead, we can look steadily at the changes that have brought us
where we are.

We can ask, "How can we invest marriage forms with new meaning?"

We can move toward a reconciliation of belief and practice that is
consonant with our understanding of good human relationships.

Of course, there is no simple way of defining the changes that have
already taken place, but two things are crucial in the contemporary attitude—our attitude toward sex and our attitude toward commitment. Today, I am convinced, most Americans have come to regard sex, like eating and sleeping, as a natural activity. We lean toward the belief that
persons who are deprived of sex will be tense and crotchety and perhaps unreliable in their personal relationships. We have come to believe
also that asking physically mature young people to postpone sex until
their middle twenties is neither fair nor feasible. And as we have learned
to deal more evenhandedly with boys and girls, most of us have ceased
to believe in any double standard of morality. This is in keeping with
our belief that sex, like marriage and parenthood, should involve social
equals who are close in age. When the age gap widens—when the man
is much older than the woman or the woman older than the man—we
disapprove. And although we may not express our doubts, we do not
have very high expectations for eventual happiness when two people
must bridge wide differences in upbringing. We believe that young
people should learn about sex together, as equals. But this means that
both are likely to be equally inexperienced. Our emphasis, in the ideal,
is on spontaneity. It is this combination of beliefs, together with our continuing certainty that sex is safe only in marriage, that has fostered—that
has, in fact, forced—our present acceptance of very young marriage.

But in accepting early marriage as the easiest solution to the problem of providing a sex life for everyone, we confront new difficulties.
No matter how many books adolescent boys and girls have read, or how
freely they have talked about sex, they actually know very little about it
and are very likely to bungle their first serious sex relations. Certainly,
this is not new; an unhappy honeymoon all too often has been a haunt-
ing prelude to marriage. What is new is that the young husband and
wife are as yet inexperienced in living through the initial difficulties that
can enter into any important adult relationship of choice. They are, for
example, inexperienced in making friends and living through the give-
and-take that adult friendships require. Young men today rarely know

how to make friends with girls, and girls, looking for mates, are unlikely to be much interested in a man as a friend. Heterosexual friendships therefore are postponed until after marriage, and then entered into only with other married couples. Thus, friendship, which ideally should precede marriage and help the young man and woman better understand the adjustments that any adult relationship requires, now comes too late to help a first marriage.

Inexperience is one hazard. But it becomes especially hazardous because we also believe that no one should be trapped in a final mistake. Individuals as they grow and develop are permitted to change their jobs and occupations, to move from one part of the country to another, to form new associations, and develop new interests that bring them into contact with new people. And as part of our expectation that people change as they grow, most of us have come also to accept the idea of divorce. When a marriage does not work out most of us believe each partner should have another chance to start over again with a different man or a different woman. We believe in commitment, but we do not believe that commitments are irrevocable.

But divorce also is a hazard. It is true that for two adults without children who now find that they cannot carry out a commitment made at an earlier stage of their lives, divorce can be an end and a beginning; but because of the role children play in the present style of marriage, divorce becomes a widespread hazard. For whereas in the past a man, and especially a woman, might marry in order to have children, now having a child validates marriage. Pregnancy often precedes marriage, and even where it does not, the style is to have a child quickly. It is as if having a child sets the seal of permanence on a marriage that is in truth far from permanent, and that, at this stage, is still in the making.

The child thus becomes a symbol. This use of a child is out of keeping with our belief that each person should be valued as an individual for his own sake. And when the marriage breaks down, the child is sacrificed to the changed needs of the man and woman, who are acting not as parents but as husband and wife. The child—a person in his own right, growing toward the future—stands as a symbol of an unreal past.

Perhaps we can catch a glimpse of what we might make of marriage and parenthood if we think in terms of a new pattern that would both give young couples a better chance to come to know each other, and give children a better chance to grow up in an enduring family. Through what steps might this be accomplished?

It should be said at once that changes as important as those involved in creating a new style of marriage can never be brought about through the actions of a few people, or even all the members of a single group. In a democracy as complex as ours, in which one must always take into account a great diversity of religious, regional, class, and national styles, success will depend on contributions made by all kinds of people. Many ideas will arise out of discussions in the press, from the pulpits of many churches, on television, in the agencies of government, in the theater, and in community organizations. Some will come from those whose work brings them face to face with the failures of the present system and who are aware of the urgent need for new forms. Some will be shaped by the actual experiments in which lively, imaginative young people are engaging. And still others will arise out of the puzzlement and questions of the people who listen to the suggestions made by all those who are trying to become articulate about the issues. Out of all these discussions, carried on over a period of time, there will, I hope, evolve the kind of consensus that will provide the basis for a new marriage tradition. We are still a long way from the point at which we can consider the new tradition in such pragmatic terms as its formal social framework—in law and religious practice. No one, it should be clear, can write a prescription or make a blueprint for a whole society.

What I am doing here is advancing some ideas of my own as one contribution to an ongoing discussion. First I shall outline the goals that I personally hope we may reach.

I should like to see us put more emphasis upon the importance of human relationships and less upon sex as a physical need. That is, I would hope that we could encourage a greater willingness to spend time searching for a congenial partner and to enjoy cultivating a deeply personal relationship. (Sex would then take its part within a more complex intimacy and would cease to be sought after for itself alone.)

I should like to see children assured of a lifelong relationship to both parents. This, of course, can only be attained when parents themselves have such a relationship. I do not mean that parents must stay married. As long as early marriage remains a practice, it must be assumed that some marriages—perhaps many marriages—will break down in the course of a lifetime of growth, mobility, and change. But I should like to see a style of parenthood develop that would survive the breaking of the links of marriage through divorce. This would depend on a mutual recognition that co-parenthood is a permanent relationship. Just as brother and sister are irrevocably related because they share the same parents, so also parents are irrevocably related because they share the same child. At present, divorce severs the link between the adult partners and each, in some fashion, attempts—or sometimes gives up the attempt—to keep a separate contact with the children, as if this were now a wholly individual relationship. This need not be.

Granting the freedom of partners to an uncongenial marriage to seek a different, individual commitment within a new marriage, I would hope that we would hold on to the ideal of a lifetime marriage in maturity. No religious group that cherishes marriage as a sacrament should have to give up the image of a marriage that lasts into old age and into the lives of grandchildren and great-grandchildren as one that is blessed by God. No wholly secularized group should have to be deprived of the sense that an enduring, meaningful relationship is made by the acceptance, approval, and support of the entire society as witnesses.

At the same time, I believe, we must give greater reality to our belief that marriage is a matter of individual choice, a choice made by each young man and woman freely, without coercion by parents or others. The present mode of seeking for sex among a wide range of partners casually, and then, inconsistently, of accepting marriage as a form of "choice" arising from necessity, is a deep denial of individuality and individual love. In courtship, intensity of feeling grows as two people move toward each other. In our present system, however, intensity of feeling is replaced by the tensions arising from a series of unknown factors: Will pregnancy occur? Is this the best bargain on the sex market? Even with sexual freedom, will marriage result? Today true courtship, when it happens, comes about in spite of, not because of, the existing styles of dating and marrying.

These goals—individual choice, a growing desire for a lifelong relationship with a chosen partner, and the desire for children with whom and through whom lifelong relationships are maintained—provide a kind of framework for thinking about new forms of marriage. I believe that we need two forms of marriage, one of which can (though it need not) develop into the other, each with its own possibilities and special forms of responsibility.

The first type of marriage may be called an *individual marriage* binding together two individuals only. It has been suggested that it might be called a "student" marriage, as undoubtedly it would occur first and most often among students. But looking ahead, it would be a type of marriage that would also be appropriate for much older men and women, so I shall use the term *individual marriage*. Such a marriage would be a licensed union in which two individuals would be committed to each other as individuals for as long as they wished to remain together, but not as future parents. As the first step in marriage, it would not include having children.

In contrast, the second type of marriage, which I think of as *parental marriage,* would be explicitly directed toward the founding of a family. It would not only be a second type but also a second step or stage, following always on an individual marriage and with its own license and ceremony and kinds of responsibility. This would be a marriage that looked to a lifetime relationship with links, sometimes, to many people.

In an individual marriage, the central obligation of the boy and girl or man and woman to each other would be an ethical, not an economic one. The husband would not be ultimately responsible for the support of his wife; if the marriage broke up, there would be no alimony or support. The husband would not need to feel demeaned if he was not yet ready, or was not able, to support his wife. By the same token, husband or wife could choose freely to support the other within this partnership.

Individual marriage would give two very young people a chance to know each other with a kind of intimacy that does not usually enter into a brief love affair, and so it would help them to grow into each other's life—and allow them to part without the burden of misunderstood intentions, bitter recriminations, and self-destructive guilt. In the past, long periods of engagement, entered into with parental consent, fulfilled at least in part the requirement of growing intimacy and shared experience. But current attitudes toward sex make any retreat to this kind of relationship impossible. In other societies, where parents chose their children's marriage partners, the very fact of meeting as strangers at the beginning of a lifelong relationship gave each a high sense of expectancy within which shared understanding might grow. But this is impossible for us as an option because of the emphasis on personal choice and the unwillingness to insist on maintaining a commitment that has failed.

Individual marriage in some respects resembles "companionate marriage" as it was first discussed in the 1920's and written about by Judge Ben Lindsey on the basis of his long experience in court with troubled young people. This was a time when very few people were ready as yet to look ahead to the consequences of deep changes in our attitude toward sex and personal choice. Today, I believe, we are far better able to place young marriage within the context of a whole lifetime.

Individual marriage, as I see it, would be a serious commitment, entered into a public, validated and protected by law and, for some, by religion, in which each partner would have a deep and continuing concern for the happiness and well-being of the other. For those who found happiness it could open the way to a more complexly designed future.

Every parental marriage, whether children were born into it or adopted, would necessarily have as background a good individual marriage. The fact of a previous marriage, individual or parental, would not alter this. Every parental marriage, at no matter what stage in life, would have to be preceded by an individual marriage. In contrast to individual marriage, parental marriage would be hard to contract. Each partner would know the other well, eliminating the shattering surprise of discovery that either one had suffered years of mental or physical illness, had been convicted of a serious crime, was unable to hold a job, had entered the country illegally, already had children or other dependents, or any one of the thousand shocks that lie in wait for the person who enters into a hasty marriage with someone he or she knows little about. When communities were smaller, most people were protected against such shocks by the publication of the banns. Today other forms of protection are necessary. The assurance thus given to parents that their son or daughter would not become hopelessly trapped into sharing parenthood with an unsuitable mate also would serve as a protection for the children not yet born.

As a couple prepared to move from an individual to a parental marriage they also would have to demonstrate their economic ability to support a child. Instead of falling back on parents, going deeply into debt, or having to ask the aid of welfare agencies, they would be prepared for the coming of a child. Indeed, both might be asked to demonstrate some capacity to undertake the care of the family in the event one or the other became ill. Today a girl's education, which potentially makes her self-sustaining, is perhaps the best dowry a man can give his son-in-law so he will not fall prey to the gnawing anxiety of how his family would survive his death. During an individual marriage, designed to lead to parental marriage, a girl, no less than a boy, might learn a skill that would make her self-supporting in time of need.

Even more basic to the survival of a marriage, however, is the quality of the marriage itself—its serenity, its emotional strength, its mutuality. Over long years we have acquired a fund of experience about good marriages through the inquiries made by adoption agencies before a child is given permanently to adoptive parents. Now, if we wished to do so, we could extrapolate from this experience for the benefit of partners in individual marriages but not yet joined in parenthood and for the benefit of infants hoped for but not yet conceived. And in the course of these explorations before parental marriage the ethical and religious issues that sometimes are glossed over earlier could be discussed and, in a good relationship, resolved. Careful medical examinations would bring to light present or potential troubles, and beyond this, would help the couple to face the issue: What if, in spite of our desire for a family, having a child entails a serious risk to the mother, or perhaps the child? What if, in spite of a good prognosis, we, as a couple, cannot have a child? And then, even assuming that all such questions have been favorably resolved, it must not be forgotten that in all human relationships there are imponderables—and the marriage will be tested by them.

As a parental marriage would take much longer to contract and would be based on a larger set of responsibilities, so also its disruption would be carried out much more slowly. A divorce would be arranged in a way that would protect not only the two adults but also the children for whose sake the marriage was undertaken. The family, as against the marriage, would have to be assured a kind of continuity in which neither parent was turned into an angry ghost and no one could become an emotional blackmailer or be the victim of emotional blackmail.

Perhaps some men and women would choose to remain within individual marriage, with its more limited responsibilities; having found that there was an impediment to parental marriage, they might well be drawn into a deeper individual relationship with each other. And perhaps some who found meaningful companionship through parenthood would look later for more individualized companionship in a different kind of person.

By dignifying individual relationships for young people we would simultaneously invest with new dignity a multitude of deeply meaningful relationships of choice throughout life. First and foremost, we would recognize parenthood as a special form of marriage. But we would also give strong support to marriage as a working relationship of husband and wife as colleagues, and as a leisure relationship of a couple who have not yet entered into or who are now moving out of the arduous years of multiple responsibilities.

By strengthening parenthood as a lasting relationship we would keep intact the link between grandparents, parents, and children. Whether they were living together or were long since divorced, they would remain united in their active concern for their family of descendants. The acceptance of the two kinds of marriage would give equal support, however, to the couple who, having forgone a life with children, cherish their individual marriage as the expression of their love and loyalty.

The suggestion for a style of marriage in two steps—individual marriage and marriage for parenthood—has grown out of my belief that clarification is the beginning of constructive change. Just as no one can make a blueprint of the future, so no one can predict the outcome of a new set of principles. We do know something about the unfortunate direction in which contemporary marriage is drifting. But we need not simply continue to drift. With our present knowledge, every child born can be a child wanted and prepared for. And by combining the best of our traditions and our best appraisal of human relations, we may succeed in opening the way for new forms of marriage that will give dignity and grace to all men and women.

When Alix Shulman and her husband decided their household burdens were unfairly divided, they developed a new arrangement. Some readers may find their "contract" upsetting; others may see it as a way of making married partners feel truly equal.

A CHALLENGE TO EVERY MARRIAGE

by Alix Kates Shulman

When my husband and I were first married, a decade ago, keeping house was less a burden than a game. We both worked full-time in New York City, so our small apartment stayed empty most of the day and taking care of it was very little trouble. Twice a month we'd spend Saturday cleaning and doing our laundry at the laundromat. We shopped for food together after work, and though I usually did the cooking, my husband was happy to help. Since our meals were simple and casual, there were few dishes to wash. We occasionally had dinner out and usually ate breakfast at a diner near our offices. We spent most of our free time doing things we enjoyed together, such as taking long walks in the evenings and spending weekends in Central Park. Our domestic life was beautifully uncomplicated.

When our son was born, our domestic life suddenly became *quite* complicated; and two years later, when our daughter was born, it became impossible. We automatically accepted the traditional sex roles that society assigns. My husband worked all day in an office; I left my job and stayed at home, taking on almost all of the burdens of housekeeping and child raising.

When I was working I had grown used to seeing people during the day, to having a life outside the home. But now I was restricted to the company of two demanding preschoolers and to the four walls of an apartment. It seemed unfair that while my husband's life had changed little when the children were born, domestic life had become the only life I had.

I tried to cope with the demands of my new situation, assuming that other women were able to handle even larger families with ease and still find time for themselves. I couldn't seem to do that.

We had to move to another apartment to accommodate our larger family, and because of the children, keeping it reasonably neat took several hours a day. I prepared half a dozen meals every day for from one to four people at a time—and everyone ate different food. Shopping for this brood—or even just running out for a quart of milk—meant putting on snowsuits, boots and mittens; getting strollers or carriages up and down the stairs; and scheduling the trip so it would not interfere with one of the children's feeding or nap or illness or some other domestic job. Laundry was now a daily chore. I seemed to be working every minute of the day—and still there were dishes in the sink; still there wasn't time enough to do everything.

Even more burdensome than the physical work of housekeeping was the relentless responsibility I had for my children. I loved them, but they seemed to be taking over my life. There was nothing I could do, or even contemplate, without first considering how they would be affected. As they grew older just answering their constant questions ruled out even a private mental life. I had once enjoyed reading, but now if there was a moment free, instead of reading for myself, I read to them. I wanted to work on my own writing, but there simply weren't enough hours in the day. I had no time for myself; the children were always *there*.

As my husband's job began keeping him at work later and later—and sometimes taking him out of town—I missed his help and companionship. I wished he would come home at six o'clock and spend time with the children so they could know him better. I continued to buy food with him in mind and dutifully set his place at the table. Yet sometimes whole weeks would go by without his having dinner with us. When he did get home the children often were asleep, and we both were too tired ourselves to do anything but sleep.

could introduce
to the top
is
interest somewhat longer
with attention sp―

We accepted the demands of his work as unavoidable. Like most couples, we assumed that the wife must accomodate to the husband's schedule, since it is his work that brings in the money.

As the children grew older I began free-lance editing at home. I felt I had to squeeze it into my "free" time and not allow it to interfere with my domestic duties or the time I owed my husband—just as he felt he had to squeeze in time for the children during weekends. We were both chronically dissatisfied, but we knew no solutions.

After I had been home with the children for six years I began to attend meetings of the newly formed Women's Liberation Movement in New York City. At these meetings I began to see that my situation was not uncommon: other women too felt drained and frustrated as housewives and mothers. When we started to talk about how we would have chosen to arrange our lives, most of us agreed that even though we might have preferred something different, we had never felt we had a choice in the matter. We realized that we had shipped into full domestic responsibility simply as a matter of course, and it seemed unfair.

When I added them up, the chores I was responsible for amounted to a hectic 6 A.M. to 9 P.M. (often later) job, without salary, breaks or vacation. No employer would be able to demand these hours legally, but most mothers take them for granted—as I did until I became a feminist.

For years mothers like me have acquiesced to the strain of the preschool years and endless household maintenance without any real choice. Why, I asked myself, should a couple's decision to have a family mean that the woman must immerse years of her life in their children? And why should men like my husband miss caring for and knowing their children?

Eventually, after an arduous examination of our situation, my husband and I decided that we no longer had to accept the sex roles that had turned us into a lame family. Out of equal parts love for each other and desperation at our situation, we decided to re-examine the patterns we had been living by, and starting again from scratch, to define our roles for ourselves.

We began by agreeing to share completely all responsibility for raising our children (by then aged five and seven) and caring for our household. If this new arrangement meant that my husband would have to change his job or that I would have to do more free-lance work or that we would have to live on a different scale, then we would. It would be worth it if it could make us once again equal, independent and loving as we had been when we were first married.

Simply agreeing verbally to share domestic duties didn't work, despite our best intentions. And when we tried to divide them "spontaneously" we ended up following the traditional patterns. Our old habits were too deep-rooted. So we sat down and drew up a formal agreement, acceptable to both of us, that clearly defined the responsibilities we each had.

It may sound a bit formal, but it has worked for us. Here it is:

MARRIAGE AGREEMENT

I. Principles

We reject the notion that the work which brings in more money is more valuable. The ability to earn more money is a privilege which must not be compounded by enabling the larger earner to buy out of his/her duties and put the burden either on the partner who earns less or on another person hired from outside.

We believe that each partner has an equal right to his/her own time, work, value, choices. As long as all duties are performed, each of us may use his/her extra time any way he/she chooses. If he/she wants to spend it making money, fine. If he/she wants to spend it with spouse, fine, If not, fine.

As parents we believe we must share all responsibility for taking care of our children and home—not only the work but also the responsibility. At least during the first year of this agreement, *sharing responsibility* shall mean dividing the *jobs* and dividing the *time.*

In principle, jobs should be shared equally, 50-50, but deals may be made by mutual agreement. If jobs and schedule are divided on any other than a 50-50 basis, then at any time either party may call for a re-examination and redistribution of jobs or a revision of the schedule. Any deviation from 50-50 must be for the convenience of both parties. If one party works overtime in any domestic job, he/she must be compensated by equal extra work by the other. The schedule may be flexible, but changes must be formally agreed upon. The terms of this agreement are rights and duties, not privileges and favors.

II. Job Breakdown and Schedule

(A) Children

1. Mornings: Waking children; getting their clothes out; making their lunches; seeing that they have notes, homework, money, bus passes, books; brushing their hair; giving them breakfast (making coffee for us). Every other week each parent does all.

2. Transportation: Getting children to and from lessons, doctors, dentists (including making appointments), friends' houses, park, parties,

movies, libraries. Parts occurring between 3 and 6 P.M. fall to wife. She must be compensated by extra work from husband (see 10 below). Husband does all weekend transportation and pickups after 6.

3. Help: Helping with homework, personal problems, projects like cooking, making gifts, experiments, planting; answering questions; explaining things. Part occurring between 3 and 6 P.M. fall to wife. After 6 P.M. husband does Tuesday, Thursday and Sunday; wife does Monday, Wednesday and Saturday. Friday is free for whoever has done extra work during the week.

4. Nighttime (after 6 p.m.): Getting children to take baths, brush their teeth, put away their toys and clothes, go to bed; reading with them; tucking them in and having nighttime talks; handling if they wake or call in the night. Husband does Tuesday, Thursday and Sunday. Wife does Monday, Wednesday and Saturday. Friday is split according to who has done extra work during the week.

5. Babysitters: Getting babysitters (which sometimes takes an hour of phoning). Babysitters must be called by the parent the sitter is to replace. If no sitter turns up, that parent must stay home.

6. Sick care: Calling doctors; checking symptoms; getting prescriptions filled; remembering to give medicine; taking days off to stay home with sick child; providing special activities. This must still be worked out equally, since now wife seems to do it all. (The same goes for the now frequently declared school closings for so-called political protests, whereby the mayor gets credit at the expense of the mothers of young children. The mayor closes only the schools, not the places of business or the government offices.) In any case, wife must be compensated (see 10 below).

7. Weekends: All usual child care, plus special activities (beach, park, zoo). Split equally. Husband is free all Saturday, wife is free all Sunday.

(B) Housework

8. Cooking: Breakfast; dinner (children, parents, guests). Breakfasts during the week are divided equally; husband does all weekend breakfasts (including shopping for them and dishes). Wife does all dinners except Sunday nights. Husband does Sunday dinner and any other dinners on his nights of responsibility if wife isn't home. Whoever invites guests does shopping, cooking and dishes; if both invite them, split work.

9. Shopping: Food for all meals, housewares, clothing and supplies for children. Divide by convenience. Generally, wife does local daily food shopping; husband does special shopping for supplies and children's things.

10. Cleaning: Dishes daily; apartment weekly, biweekly or monthly. Husband does dishes Tuesday, Thursday and Sunday. Wife does Mon-

day, Wednesday and Saturday. Friday is split according to who has done extra work during week. Husband does all the house cleaning in exchange for wife's extra child care (3 to 6 daily) and sick care.

11. Laundry: Home laundry, making beds, dry cleaning (take and pick up). Wife does home laundry. Husband does dry-cleaning delivery and pickup. Wife strips beds, husband remakes them.

Our agreement changed our lives. Surprisingly, once we had written it down, we had to refer to it only two or three times. But we still had to work to keep the old habits from intruding. If it was my husband's night to take care of the children, I had to be careful not to check up on how he was managing. And if the babysitter didn't show up for him, I would have to remember it was *his* problem.

Eventually the agreement entered our heads, and now, after two successful years of following it, we find that our new roles come to us as readily as the old ones had. I willingly help my husband clean the apartment (knowing it is his responsibility) and he often helps me with the laundry or the meals. We work together and trade off duties with ease now that the responsibilities are truly shared. We each have less work, more hours together and less resentment.

Before we made our agreement I had never been able to find the time to finish even one book. Over the past two years I've written three children's books, a biography and a novel and edited a collection of writings (all will have been published by spring of 1972). Without our agreement I would never have been able to do this.

At present my husband works a regular 40-hour week, and I write at home during the six hours the children are in school. He earns more money now than I do, so his salary covers more of our expenses than the money I make with my free-lance work. But if either of us should change jobs, working hours or income, we would probably adjust our agreement.

Perhaps the best testimonial of all to our marriage agreement is the change that has taken place in our family life. One day after it had been in effect for only four months our daughter said to my husband, "You know, Daddy, I used to love Mommy more than you, but now I love you both the same."

Romance, Love part TWO and Intimacy

Our society has placed a very high emphasis on romantic love, a form of love dating back to the early part of the thirteenth century. Romantic love has influenced our society, largely through the mass media, to such an extent that romantic expectations have penetrated the popular societal attitude toward marriage, sex, and family life. What is love? Is love, as Americans define it, common in all human societies? Is intimacy necessary? Why are people so easily disappointed and disenchanted with marriage, especially when so often their self-defined reasons for marriage were to experience love and intimacy? What is the relationship between expectation and socialization? Are we a society that has allowed itself to become excessively and unrealistically socialized regarding the things love can do for two people? Do we worship love? De we earnestly believe that the so-called "chemistry of attraction" or the "electric spark" of infatuation is necessary for a paired relationship to endure? Is love a requirement for intimacy or are there other factors more important than love?

Clark Vincent in his article "When Married Love is Disappointing" is concerned chiefly with persons who marry while quite young. Many couples begin their marriage with sexual expectations and misunderstandings that are virtually guaranteed to cause trouble. The author points to the fact that our culture conditions sexual immaturity. Boys, for example, are taught not only to "score" but to win by conquering and pretending. Girls are socialized to attract. Until very recently the classical female picture of courtship has been him chasing her until she catches him. Vincent reminds the reader that couples who love and respect each other can learn how to play together, how to have fun together and how to rediscover each other's evolving, changing personality.

In Krich and Blum's "Marriage and the Mystique of Romance," the authors help the reader to view realistically the nature of romantic expectations. Most persons enter the marriage relationship with expectations of themselves and their mates that neither could possibly meet. When we don't receive what we expect in life, we are disappointed. If persons are reasonably secure as individuals and bring a sense of wholeness to the marriage relationship, they are more likely to constructively handle the disappointment of marriage. Even though marriage is disappointing for a variety of reasons, persons can use disappointment well if it leads them to investigate what their marriage really offers.

If the unwillingness or the inability to disclose oneself cheats persons of love, the inability to sustain intimate relationships also keeps persons from knowing themselves and others more deeply. Allen and Martin provide one type of guide for determining one's intimacy quotient. "What's Your Intimacy Quotient?" raises questions to which the reader can respond concerning how well he has fared in (and what he has learned from) his interpersonal relationships from infancy through adulthood. The article is also an indication of what risks one may be willing to take in relationships with others. The quiz is scored, and the reader has one indication of some possible strengths and weaknesses in his ability to form more intimate relationships.

What is the fear that cheats us of our love potential? In the article "The Fear That Cheats Us of Love" Jourard and Whitman state that the failure to disclose ourselves to others cheats us of love. Even though we cannot tell the people we know and love everything we think or feel, we err in the masks that we wear much of the time. Such lack of self-disclosure prevents children from knowing their parents; parents don't know their children, and many husbands and wives are often strangers to each other. Our own self-deceptions and our uncertainties about our roles as men and women confuse us about how to communicate with those we love. Jourard states that the most important reason for self-disclosure is that without it we cannot truly love. How can I love a person I don't know? How can the other person love me if he doesn't know me?

*Neither sexual nor romantic pleasures
need fade after the wedding, says an
experienced marriage counselor. Even if
things have begun to go wrong, here are
some realistic remedies.*

WHEN MARRIED LOVE
IS DISAPPOINTING

by Clark Vincent, Ph.D.

There has been in recent years a marked increase in the number of
youthful marriages. Many of these marriages are sound and happy, for
a husband and wife, though young, may still have the maturity and experience to adapt very well to married life. But not all young couples do.
In fact, for a generation so often spoken of in terms of its "sexual revolution" it is surprising to me and to many other marriage counselors how
many newlyweds begin their marriages with sexual expectations and misunderstandings that are virtually guaranteed to cause trouble. Almost
all these young people enter marriage expecting, as they should, a full,
exciting and meaningful sex life. Most of them believe, in fact, that sex
will be the most important area of their marriage. A great number of
husbands and wives unfortunately, all too soon are disillusioned. The
disappointment can come quickly, as it sometimes does to extremely inhibited people who naively assume that their sexual fears will disappear
automatically in the marriage bed and their sexual ignorance be overcome by that best of all teachers, experience. But bad experience can
be a bad teacher. Maladroit and fearful love-making has led many a
young wife to conclude, "If this is what it's all about, the hell with it."
One can go through married life—although in a somewhat limited fashion
—without ever discovering what the shouting was about. Disillusionment
can come also to people who enter marriage believing themselves to
be both sexually knowledgeable and sexually experienced. Typical of this
sort of disillusioned young person is a 19-year-old bride of six months
who complained to me, "Before we got married all he wanted was sex.
Now he spends more time with his car than with me." It is not unusual

in young marriages for sexual interest to go into a severe decline. "We've been married for five years now, and sex gets worse instead of better," a 26-year-old wife told me. "The whole thing is a drag. I love my husband, but he no longer turns me on. When we were dating, I'd tremble if he simply touched me. Now . . . well, I have orgasms, but it's strange—they're orgasms without passion." Any woman probably can have an orgasm if she and her husband use the "right" techniques. But when a woman talks about being "turned on," she is referring to totality of feelings: the giving and receiving of pleasure, the body-and-soul experience of being female. The essence of sexual union is not orgasm; it is pleasure. And there is as much variety of sexual pleasure as there are individual human beings.

Why, then, do people who love each other, and who know that they once wanted each other intensely, so often find that marriage ends their passion? Is it possible to avoid these lifeless marriages?

To answer the second question first: It should be possible to create a sexual relationship that not only will last but will grow—physically, emotionally and spiritually—over the years. It may be difficult for a young couple to believe that the quality of sex can improve over a lifetime; yet this is the affirmation of many married couples in their 60s and 70s. But the young couple may be thinking primarily in terms of quantity and duration—how often, how prolonged—whereas the older couples are talking about quality. It is as if many young people have somehow been taught that the pleasure of eating is to eat a lot and often, and have no idea that the quality of the cooking can make a difference.

The concept of sexual quality, however, is one that countless young married people are unaware of. Before marriage the question of sexual quality rarely comes up. At that point all sex is pleasurable because it is at least exciting. Whether the actual sexual performance is good, bad or indifferent, someone has pursued—and caught—someone. There is an element of danger in it. One is dealing with big emotions, daring oneself to touch and be touched. One has secrets and there are strategies to be planned. For the man, if the girl will only give in, he will have "scored." For the girl, to be so desired is thrilling in itself—and if she plays her cards right, she can trade sexual favors and promises for love, for security, for marriage. It is a game, and a fascinating one.

In a society such as ours, in which the forms and rituals of seduction are a major theme of our literature, our films and even our advertising, it is only natural that virtually everyone is expert at playing the game. And the game, when played to its fullest, seems to promise that this wonderful sexuality, this astonishing feeling that flows between a man and woman who are courting each other passionately, will become a permanent part of marriage.

Unfortunately, this doesn't happen. Courtship and marriage are very different. Courtship is one of the most romantic dramas most people act out in their lifetime. And sex in courtship, therefore, is colored with romance and novelty.

With marriage the courtship adventure changes. The source of much of the high drama is gone. When a couple marry, society officially licenses them to have sexual intercourse. Society *expects* them to do so and would consider it strange if they did not. Now, for the first time, sex becomes sanctioned, and thereby loses the thrill of forbidden fruit. Many people are not prepared to devote the creative thought that is necessary if legal, marital sex is to have adventure and drama.

It often can be helpful for these people, however, if they realize that there is no one to blame for the problems they are facing and that, far from being unusual, these problems are widespread in our society. If a husband suddenly appears cold, thoughtless, unimaginative or even sexually boring, it is probably not because of some flaw in his character (as often seems to be the case). Instead it may be a result of the way he and millions of other young men were raised. Our society produces many adults who are far better adapted to the rituals of courtship than to those of marriage. Thus at the time of marriage a good deal of sexual maturing still must be done.

There are many reasons for this sexual immaturity. Some fairly universal attitudes within our society lead young people into marriage with childish sexual expectations and attitudes that may work well in courtship, but are guaranteed to fail in marriage. Boys, for example, are taught that throughout life their status will depend on how competent, competitive and goal-directed they are. They quickly learn that to achieve respect in terms of schoolwork, sports and career they must be—or appear to be—winners.

In sexual matters this need to appear to be a winner means that a boy, in order to achieve status with his friends, must seem to have more sexual experience and sexual knowledge than he really may possess. Since he must not admit ignorance, the facts of life he trades in the locker room with his equally inexpert friends tend to be incorrect. In general, the boys' sexual ideal is a sexual athlete. They believe wild and totally false erotic adventure stories, and to gain status they sometimes make up false stories of their own. They do not necessarily see sex as an act of love. Thus by the time they have reached an age where they begin courtship they have a surface overlay of apparent sexual sophistication—and practically no solid understanding of human sexuality.

In the excitement of dating and courtship, a young man's failure to really understand his girl's sexual needs can pass unnoticed. But early in marriage this ignorance can begin to cause trouble. Many a young man has been taught to go after what he wants, get it quickly and efficiently and then turn his mind to something else.

That formula may work in the business world, but when he is making love to his wife it is a disaster. A young wife usually does not respond well to her husband's view that "now that we're married we don't have to go through all the romantic talk and buildup." She responds very badly to his casual way of making love, in which he arrives at orgasm with athletic enthusiasm and great speed. And she reacts with fury if he turns over and goes to sleep once he has finished with her. Her angry or cold responses often baffle him.

Quite obviously, such a young man needs some simple facts about female sexuality. But here too, what society has taught him about the male role makes it very difficult for him to get those facts. Since it is vital to his own self-esteem as a man to believe that he knows everything important about sex, he is unlikely to look into a book or a magazine for sexual instruction (as a woman might do, since her self-image does not depend on being an expert). Similarly, a woman who before marriage accepted her husband as the sex expert he seemed to be has difficulty admitting to herself that she was wrong. And she tells herself that since her husband is experienced, he obviously is doing the right things; therefore something must be wrong with her.

Many aspects of the young wife's upbringing also impinge on the couple's ability to make a good sexual adjustment. Today, as for countless generations in the past, most young women are raised to believe that their main—in fact, their only—sexual role is to attract. The classic female picture of courtship (he chases her until she catches him) is still considered the ideal almost everywhere in our society. A young woman who had delighted in such a courtship can find herself totally depressed after marriage when her husband ceases to chase.

Whereas a woman's gauge of self worth rises or falls according to how attractive she feels a man's feelings of selfworth are gauged by his accomplishments. This, of course, includes proving that he can persuade an attractive girl to marry him; he often devotes huge amounts of time and creative energy to reaching that goal. But once married, as most young wives know all too well, many young husbands begin to spend more time, energy and creativity proving themselves in areas outside the marriage. The goals of earning money, gaining promotions and winning new titles and responsibilities can grow ever more important, until they leave little time and creative thought for the romantic aspects of a man's relationship with his wife.

This in no way means that his marriage has grown less important to him. It means, rather, that his entire practical life situation has changed. The drive to find a permanent sexual partner, one of the strongest drives known to mankind, has now been satisfied and is being replaced by drives to make his wife, his home and of course, himself secure. Practical matters that never crossed the mind of a bachelor suddenly assume importance. To be a man now means more than making love to a woman; it means assuming real responsibilities. And for many men in our society, this means a lifelong attempt to surpass themselves.

It may be a flaw in our social structure (and many intelligent people believe it is) that men feel driven to struggle endlessly for greater success, but it is a fact of life in millions of homes. And this struggle can send a man home at the end of a frustrating day longing more to relax than to play the passionate lover.

Getting married also changes the physical realities of life for young women. The most intense changes, of course, come with pregnancy and childbirth. A girl who previously had thought her energy was limitless often learns on having a baby that a lot of the time she is exhausted. Usually she discovers that she is not the perfect mother she had fantasied she would be and sometimes she misses her old job, her old freedom. It is a time when a woman can find herself intensely in need of her husband's reassurance.

But this is just the time that many a new husband becomes most obsessed with struggling toward new and higher goals. Not realizing that his wife, like every new mother, has an increased need for attention, a young husband can be quite surprised to find that the new efforts he is putting in "for his family's sake" seem so little appreciated. And if his wife does not understand the degree to which the setting of new goals is universal for males, she may interpret her husband's lessened attention and fewer compliments to mean that he has ceased to love her or that she is failing as a woman. She can easily grow to think of his work as a rival. In time her jealous reactions, complaints and demands for attention will begin to interfere with his progress; she will become less a helpmate than a burden.

This failure to understand each other's real needs is most greatly noticed, of course, in bed. A man and a woman who once approached each other with delight may come together after marriage with resentment.

Their sex drives may be perfectly healthy but their expression of these drives becomes stale.

There are many ways in which failure to understand the physical, emotional and social differences between men and women can lead to chronic problems in a marriage. To take only one example, a young wife is often disturbed by the fact that her husband, though in a bad mood, may nevertheless be interested in sex. The young wife knows that she does not operate that way. In general she is more interested in sex when she is "up" psychologically. So after a bad day for both of them, or after a quarrel, she is incapable of understanding how he could possibly want her or be attracted to her. She concludes that all he wants is physical release, which she translates to mean, "He's using me." Actually his interest in sex is in keeping with the desire of most young men to prove themselves sexually when they have proved themselves in no other way during the day. If all else goes wrong, making love to his wife enables a man once again to feel like an adult male.

Although it does not solve problems to be told that other people have the same or even worse ones, there is often an advantage in being able to see one's personal shortcomings in a more impersonal perspective. If a young wife can stand off and realize that a sex problem is not the result of some flaw in her husband's drives or in her own attractiveness, she can begin trying to solve it. And sexual disappointment occurs so often in the early years of marriage for so many couples that one generally can rest assured that it does not mean the marriage is loveless and doomed.

What, though, can be done about it?

The first sensible move is for the couple to discuss what is happening to them. Admittedly this can be a touchy matter. To inform one's husband that he has failed as a lover is not marvelously tactful. To leave a magazine on the bedside table propped open to an article on the art of love-making is to do not much of anything. Men are likely to ignore such articles and to feel that nothing a "sex expert" may suggest applies to them.

But a husband and wife should be able to discuss almost anything having to do with sex. Many young wives consider it next to impossible to raise such a discussion. It conflicts with their early training that the woman's sexual role is passive. And to that we can say only that the subject must be raised anyway. No woman is such a good actress that she can constantly hide her sexual dissatisfaction, and no man can feel truly masculine if he cannot satisfy his wife sexually.

Even in an honest discussion, however, both young people should try as much as possible not to damage the other's self-esteem. Nothing a husband says should make his wife feel unattractive and nothing a wife says should make her husband feel like a failure. A man whose wife helps him feel attractive and male (which involves acknowledging that he already has a great deal of sexual expertise) usually will have very few objections to learning how he can better satisfy her.

But most young couples never get beyond discussing sex as they discussed it before they were married, when the question was "Should we or shouldn't we?" (After marriage the question becomes "When should we?") They avoid talking about the feelings, fantasies and hang-ups that worry and excite them.

There are certain common-sense truths about communication. The more a couple know about any subject, the more likely they are to talk about it. Although many people feel that "studying" human sexuality takes the romance out of it, it is not the truth. Learning about sex actually takes the fear out of sex. And the study of our own sexual nature goes far beyond knowing an admirable variety of positions for making love.

We are what we are, and we feel what we feel because of deep psychological drives, powerful social forces and the teachings (some sensible, some not) of our elders. Any academic course one takes in human behavior, or any well-written novel one reads, invariably leads to insights about one's mate and one's self. And all sexual insights are valuable subjects of discussion between man and wife.

Thousands of "experts" have written on the art of love-making, and their advice invariably includes the notion that it can be an endlessly creative act. That may sound like a joke, for physically there are a limited number of things one can do in making love. But with very few notes in the scale, new songs are written every day.

There is no single right time to make love, there is no rule book that explains which sexual act should come before which and there is no sexual act that isn't fit for experimentation.

A husband and wife can fall easily into a habitual sex routine and later wonder why love-making no longer thrills them. But few wives would expect their husbands to enjoy the same dinner evening after evening. And it may very well be up to a wife to find new menus, or to ask if her husband has any suggestions. It may also be up to her to make clear that she is not limited sexually—that she is happy to try whatever he may enjoy.

If a woman learns to make her own wants known—nonverbally as well as verbally—it may lead to her husband's doing the same. Love-making, like gourmet cooking, involves a never-ending exploration of subtleties.

Throughout this article we've been assuming that the young couples under discussion do love each other and do want an improved sexual relationship. It is unfortunate that many who do love, and love deeply, believe in shielding the person they love from knowing the ways in which the loved one has failed. A cultural paradox intensifies this situation; men feel that to suffer in silence is a sign of masculine strength; women see suffering in silence as a sign of feminine strength.

The reality is that silent suffering can be the opposite of strength. Each person simply may be afraid of the consequences of expressing displeasure. Each is afraid of the other's reaction. But if love is present, the truth, even if it is unpleasant, often binds a couple more closely together.

The fact that one can feel love and express it in words and deeds does not guarantee that one will also find it easy to express it sexually. All anyone can know about the man who takes his wife flowers is that he likes to take her flowers. What else he may like about her, or she about him, no one can tell. Do they enjoy making love as much as the seemingly unromantic couple down the street? Who knows?

One can develop all sorts of comfortable ways of life that may look extremely uncomfortable to an outsider. It is conceivable that a husband can work 12 hours a day and Saturdays without in any way disturbing his affectionate relationship with his understanding wife.

But for most people there does indeed appear to be a relationship between the creative efforts put into a marriage and the rewards the marriage provides. Some young marriages run into difficulty because without ever realizing it, both partners fail in creative effort.

In fitting everything into a day one must budget time, money and energy. Domestic conversations can become problem-oriented and limited to the baby's rash, the leaky faucet, the bills. Some couples can live for years literally without discussing anything deeper than how the day went.

One can also, without noticing, get out of the habit of having fun together. When other couples are always along, which is a habitual social pattern in some marriages, young husbands and wives do not realize that the actual fun comes from the good talk, the laughs, the flirtation with someone other than one's spouse. Such evenings can be delightful, but if they leave no time for evenings of talk, pleasure and ease between husband and wife, it is surely a clue that the relationship somehow needs revitalizing.

Probably every couple, whether married for two, 12 or 20 years, need to get away together periodically without their children and without their friends. They must plan dates just for the pleasure of being alone. On these occasions, all talk of nagging daily problems must be eliminated. There are couples who may find that without the day-to-day problems to discuss, they have nothing to say to each other. These couples should consider seriously where their marriage has led them; they need dramatic changes in their way of life.

But (and I must stress that this can work only for a couple who love and respect each other) any couple can relearn how to play together, how to have fun together and how to rediscover each other's evolving, changing personality. Many couples say they cannot afford to do this. The reality is, however, that if their marital and sexual relationship is at all important to them, they cannot afford *not* to have such time together.

Dating and having fun, revitalizing a stale relationship, will not solve serious sexual problems and incompatibilities. But it can set a climate, put one in the frame of mind to ask, as one asked when romance was new. "What can I do to make you happy?" As a contemporary poet puts it. "In the end the love you take is equal to the love you make."

Before a husband and wife can find satis-
faction together they must first understand
that they cannot expect to feel happier
as a married couple than they did when
they were single.

MARRIAGE AND
THE MYSTIQUE OF ROMANCE

by Aron Krich with Sam Blum

Marriage is always a disappointing experience.

If that sounds harsh and unpleasant, let me point out immediately that I believe marriage has more possibilities than ever before for the

Reprinted from *Redbook Magazine*, November, 1970. Copyright © 1970 The McCall Publishing Company.

fulfillment of a couple. Mankind appears to have a built-in need for permanent relationships of deep intimacy. And that's what marriage is— or should be. Nevertheless, failure to realize that at least some aspects of marriage will always be disappointing plays an important part, I believe, in the high rate at which young couples divorce.

As a psychotherapist who specializes in marital therapy, I help individuals whose marriages have become too uncomfortable to go on with unless there is a change. And very often the first change required is that one partner—or both—acknowledge that marriage is not what he had thought, or hoped, or even prayed, it would be. But often it is difficult for people to recognize their own disappointments.

Disappointment is a strange emotion. Although we experience disappointment as often as we do anger, anger has been written about at great length in the psychological literature whereas disappointment is virtually ignored. It is very seldom even talked about. Disappointment is, in fact, almost a taboo subject in our society. Consider the fact that as children most of us were taught to be "good losers." When our best efforts failed or when our fondest dreams were dashed, we were expected to control our emotions, or at least not show them. A good sport, we were told, shrugs off disappointment with a grin. Showing disappointment seemed to embarrass our elders, so it embarrassed us too. And many of us worked at hiding this emotion, even from ourselves.

Most of us did our best, for example, not to dwell on the disappointments of the past; and we tried not to get too excited about the future, for that would be courting disappointment. But none of this worked, because disappointment strikes anyway, more often than not in unexpected ways. By denying disappointment, all we do is shut out our awareness of the real cause of our pain.

It is rare, therefore, that a patient will come to me complaining of disenchantment with marriage. More often the original complaint concerns how disagreeably the other partner is behaving. A common first complaint may be that the husband is "stingy—unwilling to part with a dollar." In such a case, of course, the husband's complaint is that his wife seems to think he's Aristotle Onassis.

But beneath the surface complaint one often finds the real problem is that both partners' secret dreams have been shattered. The wife who complains of her husband's stinginess is not always disturbed about the things she's unable to buy; what is breaking her heart is that she dreamed of marrying a man who would *want* to give her the things that might please her. The husband may be equally disturbed. He had pictured marriage as the joining of two people in a loving partnership and now it seems that his wife wants to bleed the assets of that partnership for her own pleasures.

This sort of problem can be dealt with. In marriage counseling people can be helped to understand, for example, that they come from different families and therefore have different pictures of what marriage should be. If they were very impressed with their childhood homes they may now be disappointed in any behavior that differs from their father's or mother's.

On the other hand, they may have been hoping that their own marriage would be very different from their parents', and any echo of their parents' attitudes is extremely distressing.

But many couples, once they accept the fact that marriage has not turned out as they'd hoped, can at least defuse their arguments. The husband probably will always tend to resent what he considers his wife's expensive tastes; the wife always will resent what she considers her husband's cheapness. But if there is basic good will in the marriage, both can learn to accept these disappointments. They can make clear to each other just how far against their own natures they feel they should go; each can adjust and learn to take the other's upsetting qualities with a certain amount of humor.

I am not saying that disappointments in marriage are always tolerable. Marriage counselors frequently see disappointments so real and severe that no normal person could or should live with them.

Many people—especially when they marry young—find themselves tied to someone who is incapable of filling the role of husband or wife. I don't feel that all marriages are worth saving; I don't believe in marital martyrdom that brings pleasure to no one.

In the majority of cases, however, it would be tragic if a couple's problems led them to divorce. It is sad to see a couple go through a painful divorce because they were unprepared for the run-of-the-mill disenchantment of marriage.

Every married couple must learn to face disappointment, but they also must learn to distinguish between disappointments that grow out of reasonable expectations and disappointments that grow out of unrealistic fantasies. It is reasonable, for example, to expect to enjoy sex; if sex is not pleasurable in a marriage, that is certainly a disappointment. But it is no reason to give up the enjoyment of sex as a goal. On the other hand, the unrealistic fantasy of many courting couples is that a good sex life will make up for any other marital hardships. The realization that sex is not that powerful a force can be a great disappointment, but one to which the couple will have to adjust.

Recognizing unrealistic expectations, however, is not as easy to do as it may sound. Most of us believe that we have come to marriage realistically, prepared to give and take. But in actuality we often have unrealistic, romantic expectations that we hide from ourselves.

There are two main forces that create unrealistic, romantic expectations. The first is social: We as a society retain a concept of romantic love that has no place in marriage, and in fact cannot exist in marriage. The well-known psychoanalyst Lawrence Kubie has said bluntly, "The romantic Western tradition . . . institutionalizes and beautifies a neurotic state of obsessional infatuation." In other words, one certainly can love and cherish one's husband or wife, but to remain madly, jealously, selfishly, worshipfully in love would be to perpetuate a temporary state of lunancy.

The second force is personal: Each of us comes into marriage with unresolved problems. The degree to which we believe in romantic tradition combined with the severity of our neurotic needs determines how well or how poorly we react to the disappointments inherent in marriage.

In the normal adolescent pattern, boys and girls are burdened with guilt and doubts about themselves. When they date, however, they begin to gain assurance about their own worth. In time some boy thinks some girl is wonderful and she thinks he's wonderful too. As the romance intensifies, the boy and girl decide to cast in their lots together. They get married.

But human nature being what it is, one or the other eventually becomes convinced that he actually is wonderful and begins to look at his partner with critical eyes. "Have I made a mistake?" he will ask. "Couldn't a wonderful person like me do better?" At this point both partners will be somewhat disappointed; their love has proved imperfect.

In actuality, however, this disappointment scenario, which almost everyone plays out, is useful. The quarrels usually end with a reconciliation that temporarily revives the couple's original closeness. And at the same time such quarrels reveal each person's less attractive angers and needs, and this relieves the tension of trying to keep each other on a pedestal.

It is disappointing indeed to have to reveal that you are not really so very wonderful, and to realize that the person you married isn't so astonishingly wonderful either. But in this fashion married love gradually replaces romantic love. It may be disenchanting to give up a fantasy, but it is reassuring to replace it with something solid.

If we ourselves are fairly solid people, we can accept our romantic disappointments and turn our major attention to the fulfilling tasks, the everyday pleasures and the unexpected delights of marriage. For some couples this disillusionment means the collapse of everything important.

Impossibly romantic fantasies tend to grow out of childhood disappointments. If a girl has grown up vaguely discontented with herself and her way of life, for example, she can begin to pin her hopes on eventual marriage. Whether she says it aloud to her friends or secretly into her pillow or only tucks it into the back of her mind, very often the thought is there: Someday he'll come along, the man who will make everything all right, the man who will make me happy. Men go through similar fantasies.

These fantasies are not sick. The dream of a love so perfect that it will wipe out the disappointments of the past probably is shared by every human being in those periods of adolescence when one wonders who one is and if one is worth loving at all. But if one relies on such fantasies coming true, one must be disappointed.

For marriage will not make an unhappy person happy. Marriage is the relationship that most adults find conducive to attaining satisfaction from life, but marriage in itself does not create happiness.

Millions of people react with distress when they realize that marriage has not eased their discomforts and discontents. When they do not live "happily ever after" and life continues to look raw and real, they assume that they must have been mistaken in their choice of a mate.

Under the circumstances they frequently don't know whom to be angry at—themselves for not having waited or their spouse for having fallen short of their dreams.

Such disenchantment can set in very quickly. A letdown occurs sooner or later after most weddings. There are good reasons for this. The courtship was probably exciting. When the wedding day comes, it is full of tension and importance. But once the party is over, where are you? You're married, like everyone else. You may try to keep the excitement of the courtship and wedding alive throughout the honeymoon and beyond, but this attempt must fail in time. Excitement eventually gives way to routine, and when it does, there comes unavoidable disappointment. One's reaction to that disappointment depends very much on one's inner strengths. Most people get through this time more or less easily, but I remember a woman I worked with some years ago who had an especially difficult time. In her case, disappointment set in immediately after the wedding. She found herself weeping the moment she was alone with her husband. The wedding had been so beautiful, she said, that she couldn't stand the idea that it was over so fast. Twenty-two years of preparation for an hour of glory!

But there were more complicated aspects to her problem. She had been brought up in a rather emotionless home. As a child she had hungered for her parents' love, and had learned to derive what pleasure she

marriage is usually not a method to feeling secure as human beings worth long

could from occasional praise for "doing things right." Now she had put months of preparation into the wedding and it had gone perfectly. Once it was over, her most intense (though subconscious) craving was to go home with her parents and again try to reap the reward of their praise. She expected the mere ceremony of marriage to alter this need. Of course, it did not.

Her case is extreme; few wives feel so heartbroken on their wedding day. But it is a good example of an expectation many people have: that the love of a husband or wife will make them feel, for the first time in their lives, secure human beings who are worth loving.

Marriage *can* add to one's feeling of self-worth if one enters it feeling worth loving in the first place. But the love of a husband or wife cannot make up for the love one failed to get as a child. Countless people approach marriage counselors complaining of the inadequacy of their spouse's love, when actually no amount of love would be enough to make them feel good about themselves.

The "rescue fantasy" is another marital pitfall most marriage counselors are familiar with. A woman (or man) who feels worthless seeks out someone to whom she (or he) can be important. A woman, for example, may choose to marry someone who truly is in need of psychiatric help. But she is convinced that love alone can heal, and she stakes her future on it. She is determined to transform—through love, understanding and faith—a man whom most people in their right minds would avoid: an alcoholic, a drug addict, a schizophrenic, a chronic failure, a depressive. Ninety-nine times out of 100, needless to say, the rescuer is lucky not to go down with the ship and is left totally distraught.

When anything that needs to be "cured" is the basis for a marriage, it promptly infects the marriage itself. This does not mean that there is no hope for a marriage in which the rescue fantasy has played a part. What needs to be acknowledged is that both partners need help. If husband and wife have good will toward each other, both can enter therapy; thus the whole constellation of their symptoms can be treated at once. It would not really work, for example, to relieve an alcoholic of his need to drink without also relieving his wife of her need to rescue a sick man. It often turns out that she fears his getting better. If he were healthy, why would he need her?

No less complicated are the disappointments of people who count on making small changes in their mates. Frequently a marriage can begin to founder because of a husband's or wife's inability to make trivial adjustments. Soon after a marriage a wife may discover that her husband is sloppy—the sort of man who has had a lifelong habit of throwing his socks into a corner of the bedroom. If this drives his wife to distraction, he may be able to mend the worst of his ways. But then again he may wonder why such small things should matter. "If she really loved me," he tells himself, "she would accept me as I am." His wife, meanwhile, is telling herself, "If he really loved me, he'd change."

In other words, battles that begin with this sort of triviality often have nothing at all to do with who should pick up the socks. Really at stake is the question of what both husband and wife expect from love. This is an important area of disappointment in married life. In courtship the words "I love you"—which usually mean "I think you're wonderful"—are taken for granted. They are good words to trade, for the fact that someone wonderful thinks you are wonderful makes you feel and act more wonderful still. But when said during courtship the words "I love you" are more a magical incantation than a statement of fact.

For example, "I love you" may mean "I desire you" or "I want you to desire me." It may mean "I accept you as you are" or it may be a plea: "Please take me as I am." It may even mean "I'll give you a chance to become what I want you to become." Perhaps it means "I feel guilty about you and want to correct the wrongs you have suffered from others," or, on the other hand, "I want you to feel guilty about *me* and correct the wrongs I have suffered at the hands of others." Two people rarely mean the same thing when they say, "I love you." In the reality of married life one comes face to face with what the other actually meant. And that confrontation can be seriously disappointing.

It appears to be even more painful to discover that one's own picture of what loving should be is something that one simply cannot sustain. That is the most difficult kind of disappointment to overcome in marriage counseling. Long after the counselor thinks that his patient has absorbed a number of insights he will hear the patient say again, "But I just don't love him." And the counselor must try to work out once more how his patient expected love to feel.

Did love mean that one would never again want other people? Well, one can love and still want other people.

Did it mean that the other person would seem endlessly fascinating? After a while in marriage one does know most of the other person's opinions and all his good stories.

Often the patient was simply expecting to feel in marriage a way in which no one can feel; and there is not enough room here—nor would there be in a book—to list the ways in which people can feel let down in marriage. In the past, marriage counselors encountered many a wife who complained that she was not loved but was a sexual object. Her husband, at the same time, complained of feeling unloved because his wife reacted coldly to his loving embrace. Marriage was not living up to the fantasy of either. We counselors hear fewer such stories now, because most women have grown to expect not only sex but also sexual fulfillment. Therefore we more often encounter the case of the wife disappointed because her husband is failing *her* in bed.

New possibilities for disappointment in marriage spring up all the time, since more seems to be expected of marriage today than ever before. Marriage should provide a background for the acting out of necessary social roles or a practical arrangement for moving with calm and security through parenthood. But too many couples view marriage instead as an arrangement to increase their personal happiness. This idea is purely a concept of modern Western civilization, and it actually prevents a couple from using their marriage as the base from which to seek happiness.

Many husbands and wives are increasingly caught up in weighing how much they give against how much they get; they are ceaselessly seeking out each other's motivations and investigating each other's emotions; they are quick to permit themselves to feel shortchanged or betrayed.

In a reaction against isolation and competitiveness of the modern world, many people today enter into marriage in search of total intimacy. They pledge to be open on all matters, to tell each other everything. But all too often they find that this does not bring them the emotional fulfillment they seek. The attempt to tell "everything" and get into each other's mind is likely to fail, for it overburdens the relationship to treat one's husband or wife as an alter ego.

I therefore differ with many marriage counselors of the all-you-have-to-do-is-communicate-your-true-feelings-to-have-a-perfect-home-life   school. Of course each must communicate to the other knowledge and feelings that might help the relationship. But an astonishing number of people enter into marriage convinced that their life together will thrive on a diet of total confession and uncontrolled emotion.

I understand and respect the longing for openness and intimacy. But if two people begin married life with a mutual wish to merge, it seems inevitably to lead to trouble. For two people cannot become one person; it is difficult enough to go through life carrying one's self.

Marriage is, after all, a living arrangement—and a necessary one. Most human beings need a stable family environment. They have helpless infants who need warmth, comfort and security. Marriage brings rewards of sex and companionship. In marriage one moves through life with some security from isolation and aloneness.

Although I insist to my patients and must insist here that in a successful marriage "romance must go." I'm not totally unromantic. There are beautiful moments in marrriage that, like disappointment, often are unexpected. There are sudden upsurges of closeness; there are warm feelings of understanding and support. There are poetic and deeply meaningful moments made up of new ingredients that can't be named ahead of time. But we have no possibility of experiencing such moments if we are nursing the bitterness of past disappointments.

To be open to new delights we must face and bury old disappointments, always asking ourselves if the pain we feel does not come from expecting something that our mates, our children, our homes simply cannot provide us with. If we trust our mates to do what they reasonably can to meet the needs they are able to meet, we are much less likely to be disappointed with them and with ourselves. We can use disappointment well if it leads us to investigate what our marriage really offers.

Test your capacity to experience the
pleasure of genuine closeness.

WHAT'S YOUR INTIMACY QUOTIENT?

by Gina Allen and Clement Martin, M.D.

Psychologists have variously and gloomily diagnosed our society as neurotic, emotionally plagued, armored, flattened, one-dimensional, contactless, repressed, robotic and addicted to game playing. These are ways of saying that intimacy is lacking in human relationships—that it is the missing link between our rationality and our emotions, between men and women, between love and sex. Without a sense of intimacy, interpersonal contact becomes a worrisome job of guarding our psychic territory against invaders: Any stranger undergoes a lengthy interrogation through the bars of a high iron gate before he gains entrance, and few pass the test. Both male supremacy and women's lib are products of this

rupture in our consciousness, which can turn love into an infantile dependency trip and sex into a track-and-field event (in which either con-
testant could be replaced by a copulating machine and the partner would
never notice the difference).

Intimacy is the venturous, unarmed encounter between two equally
vulnerable people. It is so soft that many men fear it as a threat to their
masculinity, yet it is incredibly hard in the quantity of sheer courage
required to risk the possibility of a surprise attack with one's defenses
down. Beyond ideas of softness or hardness, intimacy is—psychologists
are beginning to suspect—a biological necessity. Behavioral scientists have
discovered that without close emotional contact, even well-fed babies
and animals can die—from sensory starvation. The parade of neurotic
and psychosomatic problems in our adult population (and a majority
have at least one symptom of major stress, according to a U.S. Public
Health survey) suggests that while lack of intimacy may not kill grown
men and women as quickly as it can kill infants, it deprives them of the
learning experiences needed to mature in personality and to cope with
emotional stresses that slowly grind them down—death on the install-
ment plan.

This quiz measures your capacity for intimacy—how well you have
fared in (and what you have learned from) your interpersonal relationships from infancy through adulthood. In a general way, it also measures
your sense of security and self-acceptance, which gives you the courage
to expose yourself to the ego hazards of intimacy—to risk the embarrass-
ment of proffering love or friendship or respect and getting no response.
Some are blessed with this ability; some acquire it through experience
and maturity; others, not even comprehending it, or too fearful of it,
survive behind a facade they continually seek to strengthen but can never
quite make shatterproof. The insight this test should provide can be useful in two ways. It can alert you to weaknesses that may be reducing your
performance in bed or in business or in any other area of life. It can also
help predict the kind of person with whom you are potentially compatible, socially or sexually, for this is one area of interpersonal relationships
where opposites do not necessarily attract. A person of high intimacy
capacity can discomfort someone of low capacity who is fearful to respond. The farther the first advances, the farther the other retreats. But
those of similar capacities, whether high or low, will tend to make no
excessive demands on each other and for that reason, will find themselves
capable of an increasingly intimate and mutually fulfilling relationship.

Consider this a bonus: When two people take the test and afterward
compare their answers, the quiz provides not only a comparison of in-

timacy potentials but the chance to know each other better—which automatically increases the intimacy of a relationship.

The questions can be answered easily. If your response is yes or mostly
yes, place a plus ($+$) in the box following the question. If your response
is no or mostly no, place a minus ($-$) in the box. If you honestly can't
decide, place a zero in the box. But try to enter as few zeros as possible.
Even if a particular question doesn't apply to you, try to imagine yourself in the situation described and answer accordingly. Don't look for
and significance in the number or the frequency of your plus and minus
answers, because the test has been set up so that they do not mean good
and bad.

At the end of the quiz, each of its sections will be discussed in terms
of the different areas of attitudes and behavior and of how the answers
provide an index to your potential for intimacy.

1. Do you have more than your share of colds? ☐
2. Do you believe that emotions have very little to do with physical
   ills? ☐
3. Do you often have indigestion? ☐
4. Do you frequently worry about your health? ☐
5. Would a nutritionist be appalled by your diet? ☐
6. Do you usually watch sports rather than participate in them? ☐
7. Do you often feel depressed or in a bad mood? ☐
8. Are you irritable when things go wrong? ☐
9. Were you happier in the past than you are right now? ☐
10. Do you believe it possible that a person's character can be read or
    his future foretold by means of astrology, *I Ching*, tarot cards or
    some other means? ☐
11. Do you worry about the future? ☐
12. Do you try to hold in your anger as long as possible and then some-
    times explode in a rage? ☐
13. Do people you care about often make you feel jealous? ☐
14. If your intimate partner were unfaithful one time, would you be
    unable to forgive and forget? ☐
15. Do you have difficulty making important decisions? ☐
16. Would you abandon a goal rather than take risks to reach it? ☐
17. When you go on a vacation, do you take some work along? ☐
18. Do you usually wear clothes that are dark or neutral in color? ☐
19. Do you usually do what you feel like doing, regardless of social
    pressures or criticism? ☐
20. Does a beautiful speaking voice turn you on? ☐

21. Do you always take an interest in where you are and what's happening around you? ☐
22. Do you find most odors interesting rather than offensive? ☐
23. Do you enjoy trying new and different foods? ☐
24. Do you like to touch and be touched? ☐
25. Are you easily amused? ☐
26. Do you often do things spontaneously or impulsively? ☐
27. Can you sit still through a long committee meeting or lecture without twiddling your thumbs or wriggling in your chair? ☐
28. Can you usually fall asleep and stay asleep without the use of sleeping pills or tranquilizers? ☐
29. Are you a moderate drinker rather than either a heavy drinker or a teetotaler? ☐
30. Do you smoke not at all or very little? ☐
31. Can you put yourself in another person's place and experience his emotions? ☐
32. Are you seriously concerned about social problems even when they don't affect you personally?
33. Do you think most people can be trusted?
34. Can you talk to a celebrity or a stranger as easily as you talk to your neighbor? ☐
35. Do you get along well with salesclerks, waiters, service-station attendants and cabdrivers? ☐
36. Can you easily discuss sex in mixed company without feeling uncomfortable? ☐
37. Can you express appreciation for a gift or a favor without feeling uneasy? ☐
38. When you feel affection for someone, can you express it physically as well as verbally?
39. Do you sometimes feel that you have extrasensory perception? ☐
40. Do you like yourself? ☐
41. Do you like others of your own sex? ☐
42. Do you enjoy an evening alone? ☐
43. Do you vary your schedule to avoid doing the same things at the same times each day? ☐
44. Is love more important to you than money or status? ☐
45. Do you place a higher premium on kindness than on truthfulness? ☐
46. Do you think it is possible to be too rational? ☐
47. Have you attended or would you like to attend a sensitivity or encounter-group session? ☐
48. Do you discourage friends from dropping in unannounced? ☐

49. Would you feel it a sign of weakness to seek help for a sexual problem? ☐

50. Are you upset when a homosexual seems attracted to you? ☐

51. Do you have difficulty communicating with someone of the opposite sex? ☐

52. Do you believe that men who write poetry are less masculine than men who drive trucks? ☐

53. Do most women prefer men with well-developed muscles to men with well-developed emotions? ☐

54. Are you generally indifferent to the kind of place in which you live? ☐

55. Do you consider it a waste of money to buy flowers for yourself or for others? ☐

56. When you see an art object you like, do you pass it up if the cost would mean cutting back on your food budget? ☐

57. Do you think it pretentious and extravagant to have an elegant dinner when alone or with members of your immediate family? ☐

58. Are you often bored? ☐

59. Do Sundays depress you? ☐

60. Do you frequently feel nervous? ☐

61. Do you dislike the work you do to earn a living? ☐

62. Do you think a carefree hippie life style would have no delights for you? ☐

63. Do you watch TV selectively rather than simply to kill time? ☐

64. Have you read any good books recently? ☐

65. Do you often daydream? ☐

66. Do you like to fondle pets? ☐

67. Do you like many different forms and styles of art? ☐

68. Do you enjoy watching an attractive person of the opposite sex? ☐

69. Can you describe how your date or mate looked the last time you went out together? ☐

70. Do you find it easy to talk to new acquaintances? ☐

71. Do you communicate with others through touch as well as through words? ☐

72. Do you enjoy pleasing members of your family? ☐

73. Do you avoid joining clubs or organizations? ☐

74. Do you worry more about how you present yourself to prospective dates than about how you treat them? ☐

75. Are you afraid that if people knew you too well they wouldn't like you? ☐

76. Do you fall in love at first sight? ☐

77. Do you always fall in love with someone who reminds you of your parent of the opposite sex? ☐

78. Do you think love is all you presently need to be happy? ☐

79. Do you feel a sense of rejection if a person you love tries to preserve his or her independence? ☐

80. Can you accept your loved one's anger and still believe in his or her love? ☐

81. Can you express your innermost thoughts and feelings to the person you love? ☐

82. Do you talk over disagreements with your partner rather than silently worry about them? ☐

83. Can you easily accept the fact that your partner has loved others before you and not worry about how you compare with them? ☐

84. Can you accept a partner's disinterest in sex without feeling rejected? ☐

85. Can you accept occasional sessions of unsatisfactory sex without blaming yourself or your partner? ☐

86. Should unmarried adolescents be denied contraceptives? ☐

87. Do you believe that even for adults in private, there are some sexual acts that should remain illegal? ☐

88. Do you think that hippie communes and Israeli kibbutzim have nothing useful to teach the average American? ☐

89. Should a couple put up with an unhappy marriage for the sake of their children? ☐

90. Do you think that mate swappers necessarily have unhappy marriages? ☐

91. Should older men and women be content not to have sex? ☐

92. Do you believe that pornography contributes to sex crimes? ☐

93. Is sexual abstinence beneficial to a person's health, strength, wisdom or character? ☐

94. Can a truly loving wife or husband sometimes be sexually unreceptive? ☐

95. Can intercourse during a woman's menstrual period be as appealing or as appropriate as at any other time? ☐

96. Should a woman concentrate on her own sensual pleasure during intercourse rather than pretend enjoyment to increase her partner's pleasure? ☐

97. Can a man's efforts to bring his partner to orgasm reduce his own pleasure? ☐

98. Should fun and sensual pleasure be the principal goals in sexual relations? ☐

99. Is pressure to perform well a common cause of sexual incapacity? ☐

100. Is sexual intercourse for you an uninhibited romp rather than a demonstration of your sexual ability? ☐

MOOD AND PSYCHOSOMATICS
(Questions 1-8)

Because the mind is part of the body, anything that affects one also affects the other. Signals are exchanged between the two not only via the central nervous system but also by chemical messages carried through the blood stream. So just as a headache can affect a person's mood, emotional problems can manifest themselves as a headache or make him more susceptible to colds or even more serious illnesses, such as heart disease or cancer, in subtle psychosomatic ways that science does not yet fully understand. Questions 1 through 8 deal with those aspects of your feelings and physiology that most reflect your degree of emotional adjustment and your ability to cope with stress. In this section, the more minus answers, the better.

The physical system most closely tuned to the emotions is the alimentary, because a child's first gratifications and frustrations are centered on eating, digesting and eliminating. Therefore, digestive problems, from heartburn to hyperacidity to ulcers, are frequently psychosomatic in origin. Studies carried out at the Chicago Institute for Psychoanalysis found that these afflictions occur most often in people whose dependencies and ego needs come into conflict with their adult desire to be independent and self-sufficient. These psychosomatic symptoms or ailments demonstrate an inability to express emotions and to willingly accept certain needs and conflicts as normal and inevitable.

Even when illnesses are genuinely organic in origin or the result of bad nutrition and health habits, the effect still is to dull a person's ability to cope with stress, to interact with others and to enjoy his surroundings. Sometimes these "real" health problems are themselves a defense against intimacy. A person who has little love for himself may use health neglect as a form of self-punishment; the consequent health problems—being chronically run-down, overweight or whatever—make him unattractive to others and thereby spare him the anxieties of close interpersonal interaction. Not only can he blame his insularity on the fact that he feels bad or is unappealing to others but he can, like a hypochondriac who incessantly complains about his health, secure from others a certain amount of attention and sympathy that he identifies as love.

The interdependence of mental and physical well-being is experienced by everyone during periods of depression. The best cure for the blues is activity. A brisk walk or a game of tennis or handball gives the body

and, with it, the mind a quick pick-me-up. But the blues can also produce such physical lethargy that a depressed person can't even force
himself to physical exertion. In some, a mild, unrecognized depression,
with its accompanying sluggishness, becomes a way of life.

If the depressed person tends to retreat into a lethargic melancholy
that depresses those around him, the irritable person, or the one with a
trigger temper, tries to manipulate others by threat of emotional or even
physical outbursts. Both types are difficult, sometimes impossible, to live
with.

THE BURDEN OF BEING INDEPENDENT
(Questions 9-19)

In the same way that many of our psychosomatic and physical ailments arise from the conflict between the wish to remain a dependent
child with no responsibilities and the need to mature into a self-sufficient,
responsible, independent adult, so do many of our other physical and
psychological needs. Questions 9 through 19 deal with these competing
adult-child needs and, except for question 19, minus answers suggest a
favorable resolution of the conflict.

The person who has not adequately resolved his adult-child conflict
often sees the past as a happier time than the present; he also tries to
derive a sense of strength and security from any number of sources outside himself—booze, drugs, astrology, religion, a spouse, sympathetic
friends. By indulging his dependencies, he also evades assuming personal
responsibility when things go wrong—as they invariably do, simply because those people or things he has put in charge of his life can't really
run it for him. When his crutches let him down, he probably doesn't
openly express his anger, however, for that could cost him his support.
He can't lash out at his wife or his friends; they might withdraw. He
can't even blame alcohol or drugs for the problems these may be creating;
logic would dictate that he give them up. So he bottles up his feelings
of hostility and frustration until he explodes in anger, usually over some
trifle.

A person so dependent on others tends toward jealousy and possessiveness, denying others any expression of individuality or personal interests that can be construed as competing with his own needs or caus-
ing neglect of them. Such smothering often causes the smothered one to
seek relief through solitude or even infidelity, which is never forgiven
nor forgotten but used to stoke the fires of resentment that the betrayed
calls love. Though he constantly professes love, he has not enough even

for himself, much less for anyone else, and his possessiveness eventually strangles any love that others have for him.

The independent, coping adult takes responsibility for his own life, accepts his fallibility and possesses the self-confidence to make a mistake —even a serious one—and not write himself off as a failure. He does not overly worry that he may make a bad decision and will even gamble in reaching toward his goals. Yet he is not so future oriented that he can't enjoy the present. He works hard when he works, then leaves his job at the office, or wherever, when it's time to play.

In general, the truly independent person is secure enough to dress as he likes, live as he likes and shrug off criticism that his own code or conscious tells him is unwarranted. Most important, he is secure enough to respect the rights and differences of others and not feel threatened.

AWARENESS: THOSE WHO HAVE EYES TO SEE
(Questions 20-30)

"Lose your mind—come to your senses," Fritz Perls used to tell his students. And that's what should happen when two people make love— perceive feelings, ideas and sensations that cannot be communicated visually nor verbally. Unfortunately, too many people are sensually blind and deaf and cannot, like truly intimate beings, readily exchange those subtle feelings and emotions for which there are no words. Questions 20 through 30 explore your capacity to not just see and hear but to perceive and feel and respond to others as well as to your surroundings. Here, hopefully, your answers are pluses.

If you turn on to all kinds of sights, sounds, feels, tastes, odors and places, you probably have a high capacity for intimacy simply because your senses are so highly tuned. Or, to put it another way, your senses are highly tuned because you're not afraid to be intimate. You respond to the tone of a person's voice knowing, intuitively, that it usually communicates his inner feelings of either calm or stress more faithfully than does his outward appearance or composure. You utilize your other senses likewise to experience and "get close to" things, familiar or unfamiliar, because your curiosity level sufficiently exceeds your anxiety level that you're not afraid a new sensation will be unpleasant.

Take, for example, the sense of smell. Most humans left it behind when our species stopped navigating on all fours, using our noses to warn us of danger or lead us to food and water and sex. Uptight people may have a highly developed sense of smell, but it's likely to be one that rejects most human and organic odors because of personal inhibitions against the intimacy these suggest. And if the sense of smell is deficient, the sense of taste usually suffers: either from disuse of that sense or from suppression of it through inhibitions. People who find Indian food "smelly" or oral sex "dirty" are usually those who associate the distinctive tastes and odors with activities forbidden in childhood. Such people are rarely adventurous either in bed or in life and find it difficult to engage in intimate relationships that may expose their inhibitions to sensory stimuli that cause them anxiety.

Also unadventurous, and certainly not sensual, are people who abhor being touched. They probably become the museum curators who put DO NOT TOUCH signs on every piece of sculpture or artwork. Touchers are the people who disobey the signs; they want to experience something more fully than sight alone allows. They also, within reasonable limits, don't take anything too seriously—especially themselves. They are amused by unexpected happenings that would be threatening to others. They can laugh when a joke is on *them*. They consider an unexpected adventure more fun than proceeding according to some well-defined plan and, because they find it so easy to relate to the moment in which they are living, they can turn boredom into relaxation and fatigue into pleasant drowsiness the minute they fall into bed.

The kind of people who sense subtle things easily and eagerly are almost never heavy drug users, drinkers or smokers. At the same time, they aren't teetotalers, either—people so rigid and so fearful of even slightly altering their state of consciousness that they can't allow themselves to take a smoke or a coke or a social drink if the occasion seems to warrant. Sensuous people distinguish themselves by their lack of need for artificial stimulants or drugs to free them of their inhibitions. They are stimulated by reality; they are by nature uninhibited. And this capacity to enjoy other people, things and themselves gives them a high potential for intimacy.

EMPATHY VERSUS SYMPATHY
(Questions 31-39)

Sympathy is cheap. Anyone who drives past a serious car accident and sees injured people being cared for can sympathize with their misfortune: At the very least, you think, "Those unfortunate people—thank God it's not me." But the far greater accomplishment is to encounter another human being under less spectacular circumstances and be able to literally feel his distress in such a way that you are genuinely able to understand what he's saying, what he's doing, how he is trying to cope with some emotional crisis that doesn't have the institutionalized quality of a car wreck. Questions 31 through 39 test your ability to put yourself in another person's place—emotionally, not just intellectually—and honestly share whatever feelings are affecting him at a given moment. Here, the plus answers count.

Ordinary sympathy includes strong elements of superiority or judgment on the part of the sympathizer. Empathy does not; it is simple understanding and sharing. It is, moreover, a prerequisite to intimacy, creating the ability to accept strangers trustingly, to understand problems one has never personally faced and to withhold judgment out of simple respect for other people's differences and weaknesses. This has nothing to do with extrasensory perception—if anything, it should be called supersensory perception—but the person capable of deep empathy may wonder at times if he *is* picking up some kind of telepathic communications, because he's so perceptive to the unexpressed thoughts, feelings and needs of family, friends and lovers.

SELF-IMAGE AND SELF-ESTEEM
(Questions 40-42)

These three questions should provide good clues to your real feelings about yourself and the way you view life in general. Hopefully, the view is positive—and your answers are pluses.

If you find yourself unlovable, you can expect others to find you that way, too. For the most part, people will accept your evaluation of yourself and react to you accordingly. That may make them unloving in your eyes, so you build more barriers against them—an activity they view as hostile. Perceiving their reactions, you likewise find them hostile and decide the world is a cold, unfriendly place. An entirely different cycle of interactions is set in motion if you are able to love yourself. Then others see you as lovable and offer you affection. Surrounded by love instead of barriers, you find the world a warm, accepting place.

Some people understand this in theory but apply it too narrowly. They like themselves, they insist. But if at the same time a man says he doesn't enjoy other men and a woman declares that she can't abide the company of females, there is reason to suspect that they don't really accept themselves, either.

Another test of how well you really like yourself is whether or not you enjoy spending time in your own company. The person who can't spend a pleasant evening alone doesn't really care much for himself. "The ability to be alone is the condition for the ability to love," says

Erich Fromm. It's not love but dependency when someone needs another simply to escape feelings of loneliness.

CHILD, PARENT AND ADULT
(*Questions 43-50*)

The transactional analysts divide the self into three major components
—the child, the parent and the adult—in a useful way that helps people
understand the emotional conflicts that everyone experiences and must
try to reconcile. For practical purposes, the distinctions are probably
more valid and comprehensible than Freud's id, ego and superego and
are more easily applied to the day-to-day reality of living and interacting
with other people. Questions 43 through 50 give some indication of
whether an individual is primarily controlled by his inhibited, critical
"parent," who represents parental and social conditioning; by his insecure but satisfaction-seeking "child," who demands both pleasure and
support; or by his "adult," the sensibly rational element in his personality that tries to mediate between his immediate desires and his long-
range best interests. Ideally, the adult, mature by virtue of experience
and good judgment, dominates the other elements of personality *most
of the time* but still gives each other element its due. Your degree of
maturity, or "adultness," is indicated in this section by the number of
plus answers to questions 43 through 47 and minus answers to questions
48 through 50.

When the parent is in charge, a person may appear to be functioning
efficiently, but there is little joy or spontaneity in his life. The parent
continually cautions the unruly child to reason and to think and to ignore
his cravings and emotions. The rise in popularity of sensitivity or encounter groups in recent years is a sign that we realize this and that
we're looking for ways to strengthen the adult-oriented child within
us. At his best, the child in our natures is spontaneous, feeling and outgoing. At his worst, he is dedicated to instant gratification, regardless of
the effects on other people or of the long-range consequences to himself.

Most of the time, the child within us is a little frightened. He sees the
unexpected, even the unexpected arrival of friends, as a threat to his
safely ordered world. He panics easily. This reaction reinforces his fears
and also the fears of the child-dominated adult, who then concludes
that he is inadequate and unable to cope.

Since the child, conditioned by the parent, may feel that sex is a forbidden pleasure, people are often beset by sexual problems; it is the
adult in a person that recognizes these for what they are and seeks pro-

fessional help, since the child may think that unsatisfactory sex, or none at all, is an appropriate punishment for unquenchable sexuality.

Nowhere is the child in our sexual attitudes more evident than in a fear of homosexuals, for few of us have learned to handle our own personality components that we associate with the other sex—and with homosexuality. Women are frightened of their aggressive impulses, men of their desires for dependence. Both wonder if these secret, hidden feelings are abnormal and can be detected by other people they've been taught to believe are abnormal also. To keep such fears controlled, we ostracize those who arouse them—and thereby diminish our capacity to love.

GAMES PEOPLE PLAY
(Questions 51-53)

We shortchange our love lives when we try to relate to each other as actors playing traditional masculine and feminine roles instead of interacting as real, live, distinctive individuals. Questions 51 through 53 attempt to gauge the extent to which you communicate openly and honestly without either assuming or assigning protective roles that can only prevent intimacy in relationships. Here, the more minus answers, the better.

Roles are not conducive to communication and without communication, there can be no intimacy. "The aggressive male and the dependent woman relationship is bound to explode or erode," warns sex therapist Dr. Alex Runciman of Santa Monica, California. The trouble, in the words of Cool Hand Luke, is the failure to communicate. This is the chief complaint unhappily married wives most often present to marriage counselors, and it is also a frequent factor in sexual incapacity. For sex is a type of communication, and partners who can't talk or touch or express their fears and feelings to each other are almost certain to experience sexual difficulties sooner or later. For this reason, the first effort by most sex therapists is to re-establish, or strengthen, a couple's capacity to communicate. Dr. Runciman tells of one couple who returned in frustration after flunking their first assignment—to simply get reacquainted. "No wonder we can't fuck!" the husband cried. "We can't even shake hands!" That insight alone was an important first step toward sexual recovery.

Fortunately, there are indications, verified by surveys, that the traditional sex roles are on their way out. Men now often tell researchers that they are looking for women who are intelligent, athletic, adventurous and independent—qualities that weren't considered very feminine just a few years ago. And women, more and more, are looking for men who are communicative, sensitive, educated and intelligent—not the aggressive "strong, silent type" of olden days.

WHAT YOU DO IS WHAT YOU ARE
(Questions 54-62)

A person's day-to-day behavior is largely predetermined by childhood training, psychological experiences and acquired attitudes. It is the you that other people know. But behavior also works the other way—it can shape a person's feelings and attitudes, a fact that the behavioral psychologists have used with some success in the treatment of personality problems, emotional disorders, even serious mental illness and drug addiction. They've found that when an irrational person is coached to *act* rational, he actually becomes more rational; that when a person *acts* as if he had no dependency on drugs, the dependency is reduced. The fearful person loses much of his anxiety merely by putting on a brave front, and the depressed person can suddenly find himself happy by acting happy. Questions 54 through 62 give some indication of how uptight you are in certain areas that later portions of this analysis will deal with more specifically. Plus answers here suggest that your behavior is not working very well as a problem-solving device but is being dictated by your problems.

Behavior manipulation and behavioral response are major elements in daily living. Parents manipulate children by rewarding desired behavior to reinforce it and by withholding rewards to discourage behavior they consider bad. Adults use similar tactics on each other, but usually in an unconscious way that too often backfires. When a woman suspects her husband of infidelity, actual or only wishful, she may shower him with attention in an effort to keep his love—and find that she has only aggravated the problem. He probably feels a sense of guilt already and her increased affection increases his guilt. Because he doesn't like feeling guilty, he resents all the more her implicit demands for a response that he will not or cannot provide voluntarily. Or we have the woman who simply feels neglected, gives up trying to win love and approval with constructive behavior and settles for the angry attention elicited by nagging. If her husband tries to deal with this phenomenon by ignoring it, the nagging increases in volume and duration until a response—any response—has been obtained.

We also reinforce our *own* behavior, sometimes consciously, sometimes not. At the end of the day, we take a drink because we've worked hard and earned it or because everything has gone wrong and we deserve it. In this way, habits are built, day by day, that both reflect and affect the personality of the individual. For instance, if a person lives in disorder, it can mean he habitually ignores his surroundings by way of surviving in them—to the point where this has become his style of life.

Quite different is the person who guiltlessly pampers himself. He buys flowers, or whatever, because they delight him; occasionally he treats himself to luxuries at the expense of necessities and he will likely accord the same treatment to others simply to please them, not to impress them. The key word here is guiltlessly; it distinguishes between self-pampering for pleasure and self-indulgence out of need.

A person can escape boredom even when alone for long periods if he has developed the habit of pleasing himself. He's not dependent on others to amuse him nor to structure his time. He looks forward to Sundays, not as dull days when he has difficulty finding something to do but as weekly gifts of time to spend for his own satisfaction. He is the opposite of the Sunday neurotic who works weekends at home mainly to escape the guilt of relaxation, which he equates with sloth and laziness.

The typical Sunday neurotic doesn't enjoy his work any more than he enjoys his free time, but he absolutely loathes those people who seem to live without working and obviously do not share his value system nor sense of priorities. He is wrathful toward welfare recipients and angry toward ambitionless street people and hippies. Far from occasionally envying those who enjoy an apparently carefree life, he is psychologically threatened by their very existence. Compulsive workers who cannot enjoy periods of complete nonproductivity feel like martyrs to their careers, families or other obligations. The chief difference is that their kind of martyrdom demands equivalent suffering from everyone else. To say the least, such people are not sufficiently satisfied with themselves to make good intimate partners, except, possibly, for other masochists.

PLAYFULNESS AND CREATIVITY
(Questions 63-69)

"All work and no play makes Jack a dull boy," as the old saying goes. But it's probably more accurate to say that Jack was a dull boy to begin with and, lacking imagination and creativity, he finds it easier to work than to let himself go in what his work ethic tells him would be a wasteful orgy of conversation, creativity and imaginative flights of fancy. If he is to permit himself any relaxation, it must be passive receptivity to some form of entertainment that demands no active participation and permits him, temporarily, to simply turn his mind off for the purposes of recharging his physical and mental batteries. Questions 63 through 69 measure your ability to indulge in things that should, at least, be pleasurable relaxation and pleasantly intimate encounters. In this section, plus answers are good signs.

Television, many have noted, is one of our more effective methods of birth control. It *can* provide as many new ideas as a book or a newspaper or provide topics of lively conversation. But for too many people, it merely substitutes for interpersonal intimacy and dialog by providing a source of passive concentration until the eyelids grow heavy and the long day ends. Again, TV itself is not the villain. It just works out that creative, imaginative people tend to find as much or more in books and magazines to satisfy their appetite for new knowledge that, to them, is as entertaining as a situation comedy or the late-night talk shows.

The point is that communicative people are usually creative people (and vice versa) who search for new information they can assimilate and then use in conversation with others. They even find daydreaming pleasantly productive: They use their fantasies not only to generate new ideas but to plan things and alter their moods.

In general, creative people are curious, cognizant and adventurous. They fondle pets, touch statuary, marvel at the ordinary and accept the unusual. In short, they explore and search for novelty and uniqueness and refuse to categorize people simply as rich, poor, liberal, conservative, male, female. As a result, they have a wide variety of enthusiasms as well as friends, and their success with the opposite sex often astounds their associates. "What does she see in him?" envious males ask one another as he leaves with the girl the rest were watching. But it wasn't what she saw in him, it was what he saw in her that made the difference. For he didn't see her as "a cute chick" or "a great bod" but as a unique and appealing person, and this feeling was successfully communicated. This is such an unusual and flattering way for a woman to be approached that her response is almost always warm. The same goes for men, whom most women treat initially as just another representative of the male sex.

But it's not just at the first meeting that the sensitive person appreciates being appreciated as an individual. This kind of creative seeing is even more important after 20 years of looking at each other. That's because partners imprint each other when they fall in love, and if a couple never bothers to update the original impression, except critically, the original imprint is lost over the years. As the silver wedding anniversary approaches, he looks at her and wonders what he is doing married to a girdled, graying mother of three who is always too tired to go to the club. And she looks at this balding, paunchy, plodding business-man and wonders what became of the gallant who once made her shiver with romantic excitement.

Such disillusionment doesn't occur between creative, intimate part-ners. In the beginning, their imprints on each other were more than skin-deep. And because they never expected themselves to stay the same forever, they kept seeing and communicating with each other and re-newing the imprint. They never wake up to find themselves well-acquainted strangers. Rather, for them, the original intimacy and love remain and serve to continuously strengthen their relationship.

GOOD-NEIGHBOR POLICIES
(Questions 70-75)

Because life, at least a full life, requires close and frequent contact with other human beings, the ability to comfortably interact with casual acquaintances and total strangers is an important trait in anyone's char-acter. Questions 70 through 75 provide clues to the positive or negative behavior patterns you have cultivated in dealing with others. The first three answers are, hopefully, pluses; the second three, minuses.

The person who feels he has no talent for playing the piano usually doesn't try; he can still enjoy music by listening to records or attending a concert. But the person who feels he has no talent for interpersonal relationships doesn't have such options, because the quality of his life depends heavily on his ability to interact with others. Too many indi-viduals experience difficulty meeting new people or feel uncomfortable around strangers and conclude that sociality is a gift bestowed on some people but not on others. They make the best of the situation by adopt-ing standardized and safe (which usually means agreeable but distant) behavior responses toward others. Situation A calls for one response, situation B another, and so on, until some novel and unexpected type of encounter leaves them helplessly lacking a same, preprogramed plan of behavior. So they avoid meeting new people, dislike shaking hands—touching or being touched—and keep interpersonal contacts to a mini-mum simply to minimize the chance of being caught with their responses down.

This is the wrong policy. What the socially inept person most needs is practice. That's what the socially adept person has been doing, inten-tionally or not, all his life. He began learning to please members of the opposite sex by pleasing those in his own family. He has practiced re-lating to store clerks, people at bus stops, cabdrivers and waitresses,

that they may be having a particularly harried day and allow-
s, or that they seem in unusually good spirits and would welcome letting someone know. He collects their smiles, laughter and casual
flirting as signs of his progress. In short, he *works* at interpersonal relationships, rejecting the propaganda that advises him constantly that all
he needs to be popular is the right deodorant, mouthwash, automobile
or clothing. He knows that he can't compensate for personality deficiencies with either chemicals or possessions, but he can overcome them
with personal insight put into constant practice.

LOVE VERSUS NEED
(*Questions 76-85*)

That pleasant tingling sensation and feeling of warmth and euphoria
that rushes through the body when one receives an enthusiastically romantic response may be love; but too often it is nothing more than a
feeling of great psychological relief that a strong need is being or is
about to be satisfied. Thus, the feeling of love is easily confused with the
need for love. Questions 76 through 85 attempt to determine your real
motives when you feel that you love someone. The first four questions
should have minus answers; on the others, plus answers are a good sign
that your feelings are expressive, not exploitative.

People who fall in love at first sight are rarely interested in establishing an emotionally intimate relationship. More likely, they have just
laid eyes on a person who conforms closely enough to their physical
ideal and who seems malleable enough to be changed, with a little effort,
into Miss or Mr. Right. In many cases, Miss or Mr. Right reminds this
person of a childhood love—an older sister or brother or a parent—someone so thoroughly known and predictable that he or she represents no
threat of displaying individuality for which one might have to make
allowances. In almost every case, however, Miss or Mr. Right will not
and cannot make the changes this kind of love demands; and if, to retain
affection or secure a wedding band, the loved one tries to fake it, soon
enough the façade will collapse of its own weight and leave standing
there Miss or Mr. Wrong.

People without parental hang-ups or illusions of changing someone,
who marry out of a genuine mutual attraction, can still come to grief if
they expect too much of love and of their loved one and abdicate responsibility for their own happiness. Any two people who think that love
conquers all are in for an unpleasant surprise. They can become too close
to allow each other breathing room, too mutually dependent to allow

each other bad moods, depressions or expressions of personal weakness. And when one or the other turns out to be a little clautrophobic and reverses the struggle in a lifesaving maneuver toward independence, the other only clings more tightly. The result is hostility on both sides an emotion that the lovers often consider the antithesis of love. It isn't. Love is a complex combination of emotions that includes hostility, hate, envy, anger and other feelings we've been taught to deplore. Only when we understand that all these feelings are components of love can we handle the situation when a stress symptom surfaces. If we don't understand this, then we leap to the conclusion that love is dead in the face of anger or rejection and either bury it prematurely or repress the unacceptable emotion. In either case, love loses, for a relationship that ignores honest antagonisms only generates the explosive components of a time bomb that will eventually explode with great destructiveness.

Partners who never fight aren't really intimate; those who are intimate constantly make adjustments and only the most minor of these are made without some conflict and compromise. But they resolve these conflicts immediately and honestly, without silently waiting for one or the other to capitulate or for time to simply bury the problem. On the flip side of this relationship are those love partners who make conflict a way of life. If there is nothing to quarrel about at a particular moment, they can always dig up former loves or grudges, so that each can exhume an old jealousy or complaint. (Best of all is the one-time infidelity that can be flaunted to trigger a hostile reaction and a resentful response.)

Sex is always fertile ground for conflict. Even with the best-matched partners, desire for sex doesn't always coincide, any more than does desire for food, recreation or sleep. Differences in the latter threaten no one's ego, but differences in sexual appetite are frequently taken as rejection by the one who makes the advance. More often sexual disinterest represents inhibitions or fears on the part of the partner or simple, old-fashioned fatigue that hasn't the slightest interpersonal significance unless one insecure partner has his or her antennae out to pick up signals of rejection. In a secure relationship, neither feels the need to project blame for sexual disappointments on the other nor feels that occasional sexual incapacity or disinterest means anything more than tiredness, too much partying or too many emotional distractions left over from the day. These are problems only when chronic, because sex, like everything else in life, has its routine ups and downs. Indeed, it's when sex seems unappealing that the truly intimate couple can give each other the psycological support and nondemanding physical caresses that permit sex to blossom again.

SEX BEHAVIOR: GOOD AND BAD
(*Questions 86-100*)

In some ways, this is the most important section of the quiz, for personality strengths and weaknesses tend to reveal themselves more acutely in sexual attitudes than in any other area of life. This is because sex demands so much personal involvement and because we place so much importance on it in passing judgment on others and on ourselves. Questions 86 through 100 measure your sexual inhibitions and the extent to which you allow your sexuality to give you (and others) pleasure, not just fulfillment of physiological and psychological needs. Minus answers to questions 86 through 93 mean your sexual attitudes are liberal; plus answers from question 94 on indicate that you use sex in a productive way not only to enjoy yourself but to enhance the intimacy of a mature and loving relationship.

Significantly, sex is the only natural physiological function surrounded by legal taboos, which illustrates the extent to which our culture has viewed sexuality as something dangerous and menacing. Not only do our laws generally deny sexual expression to all but the married, they often reinforce this policy by legally restricting the distribution of contraceptive information and devices. Implicit in these laws is the idea that the danger of pregnancy will deter people from engaging in sexual relations, as though sex, in itself, were a national peril. The same premise is reflected in most of our state sex laws, which try—unsuccessfully, to be sure—to dictate the sexual activities even of married people in the privacy of their own bedrooms. Most states not only prescribe severe penalties for "unnatural" sex acts but deny women the right to terminate unwanted pregnancies that result from "natural" copulation.

So the divorce rate soars as we struggle to preserve, by law and by social pressure, an ancient concept of the patriarchal nuclear family that quite possibly could stand some updating. For instance, various experiments in communal living show the traditional nuclear family to be more of an old rural and agrarian survival device than a modern-day necessity. Desirable? Possibly, especially when it serves the needs and interests of those committed to the nuclear family as an ideal. But, at the same time, the evidence is virtually indisputable that children fare better either in a communal environment or with a single parent than when unhappy partners in an unworkable marriage attempt to preserve their union at all costs because they think they owe it to their offspring.

In its present form, marriage leaves increasingly large numbers of people with no approved sexual outlets, thus promoting jealousy and friction. Even for the congenially married, advancing age can be a frus-

trating time because of the myth that people should—and usually do—
retire from sex the minute they go on Social Security. Some defy this
rule by going on a promiscuous rampage in their middle years in an effort
to have all the fun they can before it's too late. The myth of a sexless
old age is one reason divorce after 20 years or more of marriage is so
common and so often inspired by anxieties rather than actual incompatibility.

Of course, disrupting a marriage in the middle years of life can make
the myth a reality; people without partners (whether old or young or in
between) simply have less opportunity for sexual fulfillment and often
find themselves—women, especially—suppressing their own natural and
virtually lifelong sex drives merely for lack of an alternative. Other harmful myths are that pornography leads to sex crimes, that sexual self-restraint
either is healthful or preserves sexual ability longer, that intercourse during menstruation is either unhealthy or inappropriate.

This last notion is an unfortunate prejudice stemming from ancient
superstitions. There is nothing "unclean" about a menstruating woman,
and some not only want an orgasmic experience at this time but need
it for physical comfort. Many of the causes of distress that are labeled
premenstrual tension are duplicates of the female pelvic state during
sexual arousal immediately before climax. Just as orgasm can accommodate pelvic needs in the one instance, so it sometimes can in the other.

But if orgasm is considered a necessity for men, it continues to be regarded by many people as a luxury for women, whose greatest pleasure
is supposed to come from giving pleasure to their partners. Even "J"
advises "the sensuous woman" to play Sarah Bernhardt in bed and fake
orgasm. Such selflessness may seem commendable, but Masters and Johnson learned in their research that the woman who tries to give pleasure
"by the numbers" cannot become immersed in the mounting sensuous
stimuli that should also bring her to orgasm. This not only limits her own
sexual pleasure but can be disturbing to her partner if he happens to be
likewise acting the part of a noninvolved spectator. At least it is disturbing to Dr. David Reuben, the man who knows "everything you always wanted to know about sex," for he goes to a good deal of trouble
telling men how to detect a counterfeit climax.

Why would a woman try to fake an orgasm and a man try to find
her out? Because, for too many people, performance means more than
pleasure. The man's role in sexual athletics demands that *he* bring *her*
to orgasm; and if she fakes it, he must conclude he wasn't "good" enough
and the show was hers. Similarly, if a man doesn't become wildly aroused

and reach a stupefying climax, some women regard this as evidence that they lack sexual virtuosity.

Rather a competitive picture of what should be the most intimate of human involvements, isn't it? She pretending a pleasure she doesn't experience, he performing valiantly, and then playing detective to find out whether or not he has truly earned another gold star for manliness. Orgasm that happens as a part of physical communication between intimate partners is an ecstatic experience, but it loses much of its magic and luster, and sometimes becomes impossible to achieve, when it is the sole goal of sexual activity.

The pressure to *perform* well is a factor in almost every case of sexual inadequacy. It is such an important factor that Masters and Johnson find the elimination of this pressure an important first step in treating all sexual incapacity.

Couples who would avoid sexual troubles and keep the joy in their lovemaking would do well to concentrate on pleasure rather than performance—the moment-by-moment sensual delights that their physical closeness brings. Orgasm can be a high point in that pleasure. But since orgasm cannot be forced nor willed, it can become an elusive goal. Wiser to heed the words of Dallas therapist Dr. Emma Lee Doyle, who advises: "Take down your sexual goal posts and enjoy the whole ball game, for time-outs, water breaks and even penetrations can be fun."

Now for the scoring.

Questions   1-18, count your minuses ___
Questions 19-47, count your pluses   ___
Questions 48-62, count your minuses ___
Questions 63-72, count your pluses   ___
Questions 73-79, count your minuses ___
Questions 80-85, count your pluses   ___
Questions 86-93, count your minuses ___
Questions 94-100, count your pluses ___
                              Total ___

Subtract from this total *half* the number of zero answers to obtain your corrected total.

If your corrected total score is under 30, you have a shell like a tortoise and tend to draw your head in at the first sign of psychological danger. Probably life handed you some bad blows when you were too young to fight back, so you've erected strong defenses against the kind of intimacy that could leave you vulnerable to ego injury. If you scored between 30 and 60, you're about average, which shows you have potential. You've erected some strong defenses, but you've matured enough, and have had enough good experiences, that you're willing to take a few chances with other human beings, confident that you'll survive regardless. Any score over 60 means you possess the self-confidence and sense of security not only to run the risks of intimacy but to enjoy it. This could be a little discomforting to another person who doesn't have your capacity or potential for close interpersonal relationships, but you're definitely ahead in the game and you can make the right person extremely happy just by being yourself. If your score approaches 100, you're either an intimate Superman or you are worried too much about giving right answers, which puts you back in the under-30 category.

In wanting to make others like us, we may be making it impossible for them to love us, says a psychologist who believes that if we wish to be loved, we must first prove that we have the courage to be known.

THE FEAR THAT CHEATS US OF LOVE

by Sidney M. Jourard, Ph.D., with Ardis Whitman

If we want to be loved, we must disclose ourselves. If we want to love someone, he must permit us to know him. This would seem to be obvious. Yet most of us spend a great part of our lives thinking up ways to avoid becoming known.

Indeed, much of human life is best described as impersonation. We are role players, every one of us. We say that we feel things we do not feel. We say that we did things we did not do. We say that we believe things we do not believe. We pretend that we are loving when we are full of hostility. We pretend that we are calm and indifferent when we actually are trembling with anxiety and fear.

We not only conceal ourselves; we also usually assume that the other person is in hiding. We are wary of him because we take it for granted that he too will frequently misrepresent his real feelings, his intentions or his past, since we so often are guilty of doing those very things ourselves.

As a therapist and research psychologist I often meet people who believe that their troubles are caused by things outside themselves—by another person, bad luck or some obscure malaise—when in fact they are in trouble because they are trying to be loved and seeking human response without letting others know them. For example, a husband and wife may come to me with a problem they think is purely sexual in origin but instead it turns out to be a frustration that has arisen because these two people can't communicate with each other.

Of course we cannot tell even the people we know and love everything we think or feel. But our mistakes are nearly always in the other direction. Even in families—good families—people wear masks a great deal of the time. Children don't know their parents; parents don't know their children. Husbands and wives are often strangers to each other.

One has only to think of the astronomical rate of divorce and of the contemporary conflict between parents and children, one has only to hear the anxiety and pain expressed in the therapist's office when these closest of all relationships are touched upon, to know that it is possible to be involved in a family for years, playing one's role nicely and never getting to know the other members of the family—who also are playing roles.

A few years ago a colleague and I devised a questionnaire with which we sought to find out what people were willing to disclose to others. We discovered that even with those they cared about most, people shared little of their true feelings or their most profound longings and beliefs; revealed little of what they really thought on such touchy subject as sex, self-image, religion.

Why is this so? For a great variety of reasons, some obvious, some not; some sensible, some profoundly harmful. But the most important reason springs from the very nature of the human enterprise itself. Paradoxically, we fail to disclose ourselves to other people because we want so much to be loved.

Because we feel that way, we present ourselves as someone we think can be loved and accepted, and we conceal whatever would mar that image. If we need to believe that we are without hostile impulses, that we are morally superior to other people, we won't give anything away that spoils that image.

Another reason we hide is to protect ourselves from change. Change is frightening to most people. Here is a young bride, for example, who returns from her honeymoon still lost in the romantic haze of being in love, blissfully happy and convinced that this is the way it is always going to be. But what happens?

One day her husband comes home, troubled over some problem at work, and broods in silence or snaps at her irritably. She in turn finds that getting meals and cleaning house—even when they're done for the chosen beloved—are not all that satisfying. Her feelings are changing. But instead of facing the fact that nothing in life stands still, she tries to pretend, to herself and to her husband, that she feels exactly as she did before.

The truth is that we want to think of ourselves as *constant*. Once we have formed our image of who and what we are, we proceed to behave as if that were all we ever could be. We "freeze," as though we had taken a pledge to ourselves that even if we did change, we'd try not to notice it.

And we don't want the other person to change either. Once he is labeled husband or child or father or unselfish friend, we have no wish to disturb that image. If something is happening inside him that may make him behave differently toward us, we don't want to hear about it.

Still another reason we don't disclose ourselves is that we were never taught how. On the contrary, unless we were very lucky as children, we were taught more about how to conceal ourselves from other people than about how to disclose ourselves. And we are still playing roles that we adopted almost before we can remember.

As small children we are and we act our real selves. We say what we think; we scream for what we want; we tell what we did. Then quite early we learn to disguise certain facts about ourselves because of the painful consequences to which they lead.

In fact, our own self-deceptions, painfully acquired, are among the strongest factors in our inability to reveal ourselves.

Personal ambition and economic pressures also give us powerful reasons for concealing what we really are. We grow up in a world where it is important to get ahead, and you can't do that without competing with other people. To put it bluntly, we want the job the other person wants, so of course we aren't going to be talking to him very candidly. Nor are we going to be honest with our professional superiors if being so reflects to our discredit. Our society itself exerts pressures on a person to suppress all but those characteristics that are considered acceptable.

All of us hide behind the iron curtain of our public selves. And with our "intimates" we again fail to disclose ourselves because we are so vulnerable to those we love. Under special pressures we might tell the stranger on the train about our longings and lusts and frailties, but how can we talk about them to those we love, who might be hurt by such revelations?

And of course it is true that we should not gratuitously hurt those we love. In the intimacy of daily life we *must* at times hide our feelings. But it is fatally easy to assume from this that we must never tell the truth when it will hurt. Every therapist, for example, is familiar with the man who, because his marriage is profoundly dissatisfying to him, is carrying on an affair. His involvement with another woman may break up his marriage; yet he says that he cannot talk about his basic dissatisfactions with his wife "because it will hurt her"!

Finally, we are uncertain about our roles as men and women, and this uncertainty confuses us about how to communicate with those we love. What is it to be a good husband, a good wife, a good father, a good mother? What is it to be a man, a woman?

If people find it too difficult to impersonate the ideal version of "masculine" and "feminine" current in their time, they will hide their deviant attitudes. I've noticed recently, for example, that women who come for therapy tend to withhold whatever is spontaneous and authentic about themselves if those characteristics do not fit the social role they've been led to believe is appropriate. They try not to sound aggressive, strong, ambitious. They're afraid that even the therapist will reject them.

Men, on the other hand, hide what prevents them from seeming strong and masculine. Our researches showed that in general men tend to disclose considerably less than women do—and are told less. Often fathers seem to be the last to know anything subjective about their children; they talk a lot less about themselves to their sons and daughters than mothers do. All this may be changing for the young; but males 30 and over have been brought up in a world in which they have been taught to hide their feelings of weakness, their fears and their hurts, in order to appear tough, achieving, unsentimental.

If we have such good reasons not to disclose ourselves, why should we? Admittedly there are times when telling everything is unwise and hurtful. Neither can we always avoid playing roles. Often they are inescapable; they must be played or else the social system will not work. We are teachers and businessmen, housewives and mothers; and as responsible people people we often must discipline ourselves to these roles.

Moreover, each person is entitled to be a "self" and entitled to keep that self private when he feels that he is not yet ready to disclose it. Healthy personalities aren't always fully visible. Chronic self-revelation may be idolatrous or even destructive in certain circumstances.

What matters is that we should be able to be private when we wish, when that's meaningful, and to be quite open and transparent when that's appropriate. That is all we should be trying for; but that is a great deal. We are warm, live, human, growing creatures; and when we suppress our identities completely, serious consequences follow.

For there is a limit to intuitive understanding. If we must spend much time together, if our lives are bound together, if we must collaborate for common ends, we are in trouble if we cannot communicate.

Thus a wife who finds her husband silent and preoccupied may believe that there is another woman in his life; a husband who finds his wife unresponsive in bed may blame himself for a problem that is really hers. When our loved ones do disclose themselves, we find all our preconceptions altered, one after another, by the facts as they come forth, since our previous ideas were based on insufficient evidence.

Another reason disclosure is so important is that without it we really cannot know ourselves. Or to put it another way, we learn to deceive ourselves while we are trying to deceive others. For example, if I never express my sorrow, my love, my joy, I'll smother those feelings in myself until I almost forget that they were once part of me.

What is the truth about ourselves? Often we ourselves don't know. But if I feel so safe in your presence that I am willing to try to disclose myself to you, I'll find out about myself just by talking about how I feel and what I need and whether my needs are defensible.

When we cannot communicate we not only fail to have access to our inner selves but we also are under psychic and bodily stress. It's hard work trying not to be known and it brings a lot of patients to doctors and therapists.

Perhaps the most important reason for self-disclosure is that without it we cannot truly love. How can I love a person I don't know? How can the other person love me if he doesn't know me?

Indeed, we often marry strangers. In our society people commonly marry in a romantic haze. They marry an image, not a person—an image spun out of their own needs and fantasies. Often a courtship, instead of being a period of mutual exposure of the self and study of the other, is a period of mutual deception, a period in which the couple construct false public selves. It is not rare for a person to fall in love with, court and marry someone and then, much later, come face to face with that person's real self and wonder, How did I ever get joined with him?

"He changed," a woman complains. Perhaps—but perhaps he never really was the person she thought she loved.

Obviously, it is hard to pick the right husband or wife if our concept of the other person is not accurate. And having picked someone we don't know or understand, how can we behave in loving ways that make him happy? If I care, I care about what he needs, what he is, what he wants, how I am failing him. But I cannot do this unless I know what he needs and what he wants and I cannot know this unless he tells me.

And then how can I feel my love to be real if this person, allegedly so beloved, is not to be trusted with my innermost thoughts and feelings? In my heart I know that if I love someone, I display my love by letting him know me. Loving requires trust and openness one to the other, a metaphoric nakedness. We must drop our defenses.

The inability to communicate is especially dangerous to a close and meaningful sexual relationship. Given a reasonable lack of prudery, a lusty sex life grows best out of a relationship between two persons who can disclose themselves to each other in all areas of their lives without fear of being hurt.

The wife who takes little interest in sex may really be complaining that this man is a stranger who comes to her without disclosure of himself, a stranger with whom she feels no bond. Sex deteriorates when a couple cannot establish a close, mutually revealing, *nonsexual* relationship; the very defenses one uses to keep from being known and possibly hurt by the spouse one cannot understand are the same defenses that impede spontaneity in sex.

Parents and children too need to know each other. Most mothers love their children, but the children may be languishing emotionally because the mother does not know or will not learn what each child needs from her to grow, to become a loving person.

Self-disclosure is as important a part of growing as it is of love, and growth is a part of change. The real self is continually evolving. One's needs, wishes, feelings, values, goals and behavior all change with age and experience.

I think of this illustration, with which the therapist is most familiar: Here is a woman who married at a stage of her life in which she was passive, dependent and easily won by a dominant man whose sense of his own strong identity was reinforced by her helplessness. In time she discovers that she has become more self-reliant; she is less easy to please; she is more able to assert difference.

Now she doesn't know what to do. If she is herself, if she expresses herself, she may make her spouse feel very insecure; so she usually goes on trying to pretend that she is what she was before.

The same thing can happen to the man who falls in love with a dominant woman because he needs to be taken care of. Eventually he may outgrow this need, and then, unless she can change too, they are at an impasse.

But can they change? Of course they can. Often a person imagines that his partner is as immobile as a rock and will always be that way. Having decided this, a husband or wife then digs in for a lifetime of dissatisfaction—or institutes divorce proceedings. But many a spouse, following a bitter divorce, has been dumfounded to discover that the discarded partner *has* changed. The stodgy, unromantic ex-husband has become more attentive to his appearance, more considerate of women, more romantic and impractical; the fretful, nagging wife blooms with good will.

This is certainly evidence that both can change, but it is evidence also that they did not feel free to change while they lived together.

Freedom and the right to grow are a difficult and painful gift for a couple to give each other, but there is no alternative. People outgrow the roles in which they have been cast by their partners, and when they have grown and changed, each must be able to let that fact be known so that the partner he or she loves can take it into account.

This is indeed a frightening prescription, but it's a consoling one too. For if changing and growing are dangerous in marriage, it is equally true that many marriages fail because of a lack of such growing, and many a foundering marriage is saved by an acknowledged change in one or both partners. A great many divorces might be avoided if both partners were willing to disclose to each other what they were thinking and then together "reinvent" their marriage.

I have been making the point that without the ability to disclose ourselves to each other, we are in serious trouble. But what can we do about it?

First of all, we can ask ourselves how many things we feel free to talk about. Can we let it be known that we are full of paradox and contradiction, that we change from day to day, that we are often self-deceived and unable to understand ourselves? Can we say, "I was the one who was wrong" and mean it?

In marriage can we talk freely to our husband or wife about what's bothering us? Can we discuss our sexual longings, needs and disappointments? Can we really *hear* what the other person is saying about these things? As mothers can we really hear our children when they are complaining about us or expressing a need we didn't think they should have? In our perplexing world can we hear and understand people of other generations, backgrounds, races? And make ourselves clear to them?

What we need is to be able to realize what troubles us and what it is in ourselves and in the other person that prevents us from understanding and loving. If we are authentically communicating, we will drop pretense, defenses, duplicity and bad faith. We will stop using our behavior as a gambit designed to disarm the other fellow.

Husbands and wives need tough and candid talk aimed at dispelling misunderstandings. They need to understand how they differ, what they respect or love in each other, what they hold in common—yes, and what enrages them in each other. If we speak honestly, we must be able to say, "What you are doing right now makes me angry."

Complaints are to an interpersonal relationship what pain is to the body—a sign that something is wrong, that something must be done. I often advise quietly martyred patients to learn the art of complaining. For example, a working wife may simmer day after day because when she comes home from work she has to do all the household chores without help from her husband. In time she may stop loving him out of sheer anger and frustration. How much better if she had expressed herself clearly and strongly in the very beginning!

To be sure, it may happen that a person complains on the basis of irrational and unrealistic needs and demands. But it is good to get even these complaints out into the open where husband or wife can rebut or where, at the very least, there will be an impasse and both will see that something must be done.

What is it we must be able to trust the other person to do? To be patient and gentle while we are exploding in wrath? Of course not. What we need is to know that he will neither belittle, betray nor unjustly punish us; that he will respond to us honestly, see us as real and in turn respond to us really and honestly. If we would be trusted, we must be trustworthy, and we demonstrate that first by being honest ourselves and then by being honest in our responses.

It became apparent early in my researches that disclosure begets disclosure and secrecy begets secrecy.

Self-disclosure comes too from a grace that I can only call *flexibility*. We need to abandon our fears that the other person will grow away from us or leave us and replace these fears with a genuine concern for *his* growth and happiness. Husbands and wives often feel they love each other when they mean they want to possess each other. This is not love. People who love each other will be genuinely concerned about each other's welfare. They will actively want the other to grow, even if it shakes their own security.

In fact, a good relationship of any kind is one that can be re-invented if necessary, one that carries within it always the seeds of new growth.

Indeed, I often counsel people whose marriage is at the breaking point but who still find it meaningful to live together to try to invent a new marriage with each other. If necessary, they might try living apart for a while, visiting each other on weekends. They might try lending their children to foster parents or living with another family or going on separate vacations. What is hoped for is that each will find himself married to a new partner he can live with—the old spouse grown in some new dimension.

In any case, courageous self-disclosure is especially needed today in our swiftly moving world, where, in fact, few relationships *can* stand still. More than ever we need to be able to invite disclosure from our changing, wandering children. And more than ever men and women—in marriage and out—need to feel free to talk to each other.

If a man and woman can share new insights, if they can explore them together, if she can tell him that she still feels like a woman and that she still sees him as a man, if he can tell her that he really wants her to be free but he just doesn't want to feel deserted, then they can make it together.

But a word of warning is in order. We can get so uptight about needing to be candid with each other that we probe for disclosure whether it's forthcoming or not. It won't work. Parents should not try to bring an end to the silence a child evidently wants; wives should not go about saying to an abstracted and worrying husband, "What are you thinking about?" Instead, we *invite*. We invite by our own disclosure; we invite by behaving toward others in ways that will satisfy their basic needs.

We have learned the art of communication when we realize that it is not all a matter of words. Obviously we use our bodies when we want to communicate sexually with each other. But touch is a superb means of communication at other times too. Less "civilized" people have long understood this. The most primitive mode of establishing contact with another person is to touch him—to hold his hand, or to hug him.

The trouble is that in America we have many taboos about touching each other. We seem to live as though we had an invisible fence around us. In research I have recently undertaken, I have found that many people literally are almost never touched except in sexual encounter. In the preliminary stages of these studies I watched pairs of people in conversation in coffee shops in San Juan, London, Paris and in my own college town of Gainesville, Florida. I counted the times that one person touched another during a one-hour sitting. The scores were: San Juan, 180; Paris, 110; London, 0; Gainesville, 2.

Yet nonverbal understanding is at least as important as verbal. It can be a way of releasing our real selves when our limited words won't do it.

I remember a case in which a man in his late 20s, very obsessed with his own manliness, consulted me for help when he found he couldn't finish a thesis on which he was working. We proceeded through the beginning stages of therapy swiftly enough and then we reached an impasse of intellectualized chitchat.

During one session when the chitchat died out there was a period of silence, and the patient sat there with a look of desperation on his face. I felt an impulse to take his hand and hold it. In a split second I pondered as to whether I should do such a thing. I did it. I took his hand and gave it a firm squeeze. He grimaced, and with much effort not to do so, he burst into racking sobs. The dialogue proceeded from there.

Human beings appear to have a built-in need for self-disclosure. We want to know the other person is *there;* we want to know what we are thinking by *saying* it and hearing it resonate in the other's response; we want to share.

Presumably we'll never be able to do this fully. There will always be the loneliness of never wholly reaching those we love. Loneliness is not a curable disease for human beings. But we can ameliorate it, and it may indeed be growing less instead of greater. Certainly the young are much more candid about sexual matters, morality, radical politics, the way they think of each other, than people used to be; and they don't have their elders' inability to communicate across national boundaries, sex boundaries, race and class boundaries. Families too may become different, less well defined, less traditional, more open to the world.

In any case we need people, in families and out, who will talk freely enough to help one another explore for new understanding, new ways of living, new ways to love and grow. Self-disclosure is a way of sharing, a way of learning from each other.

Marital THREE
Health

While much of the literature regarding marriage is of a critical nature, it would seem foolish to concentrate on negative analyses without drawing out certain positive principles and premises which, on the basis of experience, seem to produce a state of being which we have chosen to call marital health. What constitutes a healthy marriage? What is the difference between individual fulfillment and marital fulfillment? Does one necessarily depend on the other? What does it mean to "work" at marriage? What may a person or a couple do to enrich their life and their growth together? To what extent are sex-role definitions of behavior preventing people from experiencing a more satisfying existence within the marital dyad? What options are open to couples who want to achieve a more satisfying communication of their deepest feelings, thoughts, frustrations, and joys? What is a good balance between self-sufficiency and interdependence? How important is autonomy to marital growth? Is individual identity desirable in marriage or is it better to cultivate a sense of "couple identity?"

Ivan B. Gendzel in his article "Dependence, Independence, and Interdependence" helps the reader to examine some of the roots of an unhealthy relationship. Even though one is very dependent on others physically and psychologically at birth and during the childhood years, the need to develop independence and increasingly interdependent relationships increases as one enters the adolescent and early adult years. The ability to make it on one's own, not because one has to, but because one wants to is crucial to marital health. The author believes that after marriage is dissolved there is a need to achieve a satisfactory independent state before remarrying. The dependent person needs to achieve a degree and sense of identity and independence before committing himself anew to a dyadic relationship.

Some good marriages apparently fail, according to Richard Farson in his article "Why Good Marriages Fail." Farson states that perhaps good marriages fail precisely because they are good; and because of the heightened expectations present in good marriages, they are often in greater jeopardy than the bad ones. The couples who get in the most trouble are those who know enough to see the things that are wrong with their marriage. Ironically, according to the author, it takes quite a bit of success in a marriage to make that understanding possible.

"Must Marriage Cheat Today's Young Women?" by Philip E. Slater describes the options available to women today that were not present in their mother's generation. Because of traditional roles imposed upon and also chosen by women, the young women of today will need to actively seize the opportunities presenting themselves. Slater's thesis is that women who adopt a traditional role do so gradually and subtly. When this happens the wife is rearing children and being a dutiful wife. Many of these young women have been cheated by choice and not by chance.

Persons frequently search for externals in an attempt to achieve a more desirable marital relationship. John F. Crosby in his article "Making It Together: Growth From Within" indicates some alternatives couples have for revitalizing their marriage. The author invites the reader inside some marital situations, depicting positive and negative ways of building and rebuilding a marital relationship. Crucial questions include: What are both willing to risk in order for the relationship to grow rather than stagnate? What myths concerning marriage and the family are the couple willing to discard in order to more nearly achieve marital fulfillment?

"Understanding the Crises in Men's Lives" by Fredelle Maynard describes the necessity for both husband and wife to put crises in perspective. The same crises affect men and women differently. The author states that if a woman is to cope effectively with the problems of men who are important to her, she needs to understand what precipitates crisis in a man's life and how to react to it. Crises for men usually occur within a competitive framework. Men deeply feel the pressure to "look good" and "measure up" to a standard. For men marriage, career, parenthood, the middle years, and retirement are the chief crises. Maynard states that for both sexes, certain moments in the life cycle bring conflict and anxiety.

*The marriage relationship often can be a
barrier to growth and maturity, with
powerful pressures toward unhealthy
dependence. The breakup of such a marriage offers a priceless opportunity for
one to achieve self-knowledge and the
development of an independence which
can allow one to enter into a new and
healthy interdependence with strength.*

DEPENDENCE, INDEPENDENCE, INTERDEPENDENCE

by Ivan B. Gendzel, M.D.

Man is not an island unto himself, either physically or emotionally. He
is totally dependent at birth, and for a long time thereafter for survival.
Webster's definition of this dependence is: "Unable to exist, sustain oneself, or act suitably or normally, without the assistance and direction
of another or others." In the following discussion I hope to investigate
the various aspects of this concept of dependence, of a similar concept
called independence, and to suggest some definitions of a further concept called interdependence.

The various periods of an individual's life have been defined and
labeled by many behavioral scientists. Chronologically, one progresses
from the neonatal state and infancy through maturity and senility with
appropriate biological definitions of the various phases. Freud, at the
beginning of this century, introduced his ideas of the personality development that occurs during the years of maturation, and paid particular
attention to the early formative years. Eric Erickson in more recent times
has put forth his formulation relating the personal and social interplay,
and outlined eight stages through which a normal person progresses during his development.

Perhaps another way of looking at things might be that during a normal life time and in the usual course of development, the person also

Ivan B. Gendzel, "Dependence, Independence, and Interdependence," *The Single Parent,* January/
February, 1972.

can be conceived of as progressing through the following three stages: dependence, independence and finally interdependence.

Obviously, the newborn is totally biologically dependent upon adults, usually his parents, for those materials that will sustain his physical and emotional life. It has been shown, as for example by the studies of Rene Spitz, that supplying only all of the physical necessities of life does not suffice in maintaining life. He found that a very high percentage of those children who were deprived of adequate emotional nurturing did not survive the first year, and a scant few survived the second year. If the infant is given adequate physical and emotional supplies, then not only may he survive, but he may flourish and develop a basic sense of trust in his environment. This particularly includes his parents and this sense of trust will be important in later years in helping to develop this same sense of trust in himself. Even after he has mastered locomotion, and even has become an active and productive adolescent, he may still remain dependent on his parents or other agencies for financial, and more subtly, for continuing emotional support.

As an example, imagine a physician in training, who may graduate from medical school at the age of 26, and then has to look forward to years of internship and residency training and also some time in the military, during which he may still not be "off on his own." Less and less have young physicians been willing to accept this extraordinary prolonged period of financial dependency without adequate identification, and recent changes have included earlier marriage, demands for higher salaries, an expectation that his wife will work or help support the family while he completes his training, and a greater willingness to enter into long term financial debt in order not to be obligated to one's family. In another example, a 17 year old might rapidly find for himself a satisfying vocation, move out of the parental home, and feel quite ready to strike out "on his own," perhaps even ready for marriage and children. In between these two extremes, most people in our current society do seem to achieve for themselves a sense of emotional and vocational independence.

This stage of independence is the goal then of all these developmental years. It is during this time that a person must somehow experience that he can truly survive as an independent being. Of course, he still has to depend on society to bring the food to the supermarket where he can buy it, and also on an employer or a consuming public to whom he can sell his skills. But he must know somehow that he has something worthwhile and valuable to offer, and that he can "make it on his own." This probably supposes a degree of financial independence, but vastly more important is also an emotional independence.

By this I mean that a person must *know* inside himself, that in spite of who may come and go, he still has the necessary emotional content within to be satisfied alone. If need be, he can spend Saturday night comfortably reading a book, or enjoy a lonesome walk on Wednesday after work. It means that he does not build up unendurable anxieties when faced with the prospect of living by himself and being alone for a while. It does mean that when he learns to care about someone and something, and when this object, either animate or inanimate, is lost, he is not annihilated. He allows himself to experience the loss, but after an appropriate period of mourning for this lost object, he is then able to continue in the path of life and be satisfied, productive, and alone again.

It is during this period of achieving his independence, that his thinking might arrive at the following unstated, but felt formulations: "I know I can make it and probably do pretty well in life. I've learned to care for my own needs. Within reason, I can exist in my present society alone. However, not that I *have* to, but because I *want* to, I feel that I would now like to forsake this independent state and its many advantages, and become more significantly and permanently involved with and committed to other people."

At this time, a meaningful and enduring relationship, of which marriage is just but one example, implies a degree of interdependence. Both partners feel comfortable being able to lean on the other person while knowing that they will be there. It is not a lopsided relationship, where one person does all the leaning against an upright and uninvolved partner. It is not a relationship where two partners lead parallel lives, acknowledging intermittently the existence of the other. And finally, it is not a relationship where the two people need each other so badly that it is almost necessary to be together so that they can breathe together. It is a relationship which is mutual and which very much encourages the sharing of weaknesses and strengths so that the former are lessened and the latter increased, usually well beyond the simple sum of each partner's initial share. It is this interdependent relationship that a person may willingly enter into only after he has adequately achieved his own degree of independence.

All too frequently people move from their dependent state, without fully experiencing the independent state, into the interdependent state of marriage. Perhaps the simplest example is the young girl who moves directly from her parents' home into her husband's home, possibly related to an unwanted pregnancy or to sexual fears and guilt. Only years later does she become dissatisfied and feel cheated and unfulfilled. However, it is not too late even at this time for this young lady, or perhaps not so young lady, to realize that she in actuality has been in a pseudo interdependent state. And perhaps without the necessity of refuting the relationship, she may be able to fill in the bypassed events and mature sufficiently to establish herself as an intact adult. Unfortunately, however, all too often does this result in the dissolution of the marital situation. I might mention that the young girl of today appears less likely to accept marriage as a premature "answer" to her problems, and more likely to seek alternative solutions.

Mention was made before of a lopsided dependent relationship where one person requires the support and enforcement of the other for an adequate sense of identity. It therefore becomes necessary to manipulate this other person so as not to lose him, and to make him do and act in such a way as to fulfill one's dependent needs and wants.

Perhaps a most simple example of this in our modern society is the wife and mother who has not learned to drive, and therefore is unable to accomplish the many activities that require her transportation by car. In a city with adequate public transportation, this may pose no problem at all. But in more suburban and rural areas, this significantly impairs her effectiveness. It has been my experience repeatedly when I encounter a couple where this problem exists, that in various subtle ways, the man has fostered and promoted this specific dependency. Though he may complain about it, he has still allowed this to happen and has not taken sufficient steps in helping to bring it to an end. I can recall one husband who finally had to buy his wife a new car and park it in the driveway where it remained for many months, and the wife finally did get the message that he did not wish to maintain her in this dependent state. To the benefit of them both, and to the benefit of the relationship, she did learn to drive. It is my impression that when one member of a relationship clearly and effectively says "I will not tolerate this unusual and excessive dependence," the other person will get the message. With help and support the dependent couple is then willing and able to give up the less mature ways and grow. What I'm trying to point out is that a lopsided relationship does clearly require the covert cooperation of both members and though this is apparently what both participants may want initially, they find it eventually unsatisfactory and unfulfilling and do complain about it. Though it is possible for marital relationship to be a stimulus for growth and maturity for both partners, it frequently becomes a source of increasing dissatisfaction and greater pressure for change.

It is particularly at this time when the dependent aspects of the relationship are made clear, that new opportunities for growth and development are afforded. As mentioned, the partners may by themselves or with assistance from others change the unsatisfactory aspects of their relationships. At times, this does not appear possible and the relationship is dissolved. It is during this state of singleness, sometimes called singleblessedness, that a person is afforded the numerous opportunities to catch up on interests and activities which have had to go unattended while many energies were being directed towards the failing relationship.

The dissolution of a marriage then can be a time during which maturation and creative growth are enhanced and unique opportunities afforded by the rediscovered single state are used to advantage. It is most unfortunate when advantage is not taken of these opportunities, when someone moves from an unsatisfactory marriage all to quickly into another marriage to fill any void that might exist.

In my opinion, it is more important for a person to achieve a satisfactory independent state after an unsatisfactory marriage, and perhaps even never to remarry, than to quickly remarry and to possibly enter another unsatisfying relationship. How long a period of time this might take is difficult to say. Perhaps the absolute length of time is not as important as what the quality of psychic work that is done during this period has been. By work I mean a certain type of mourning that one must go through in acknowledging the death of a relationship, and the death of whatever fantasies may have existed about the satisfactory outcome of this relationship. In addition, this time should allow the single person to experience a variety of new relationships which could not comfortably have been achieved before. It is only after the successful experience of several relationships, that a person can truly feel that the choice of several people is theirs to make. At this time they know that they have a choice. They may want to commit themselves to A, B, C, or D, or perhaps to hold off, because E looks more interesting at the present time. At some point then, they are ready to commit themselves more fully and give up certain of the advantages and freedoms of the single state. I think it extremely important that a person is aware of his options and elects to do this because he feels that it is worth his while. I think it extremely unfortunate when a person remarries because he feels that a complete home is needed for the children. Though some or all of these reasons may be germain, it is still of paramount importance for the person to know that he doesn't *have* to get married, but that he *wants* to get married; that he is ready to forsake his independent state and its attendant freedoms for an interdependent relationship with the new advantages of sharing, partnership, home life, and the other joys.

One area that is frequently overlooked, when considering the various reparative procedures one goes through after the divorce, is the shape in which one puts his own body. As the marital relationship fails, the participants seem to care less about themselves, almost as a way of saying, "Oh, what's the use." Increasing use of alcohol and drugs, particularly tranquilizers, weight gain, and less attention to personal grooming frequently is a part of the tremendous personal and financial stresses of that period of time. Again, the single state affords an opportunity to "get back into shape." And, talking now specifically about the body and not about the emotional aspects, it allows a person to get into shape who perhaps has never before been in shape. The middle age male must be particularly cautioned in his eagerness to not over do it and run the risk of compromising his coronary circulation. However, the deep satisfactions and pride that one achieves directly from being able to put his own body in a state in which he can take pride, and the positive reinforcement that comes from others as a result of this, can be one of the simplest yet most valuable experiences after a divorce. To repeat, this has a twofold benefit in terms of allowing one to experience a direct personal sense of pride in having worked hard for something where success is so evident and meaningful, and also to be able to experience the rewards that come from being more attractive to others.

I would like to mention two other social phenomena which pertain to our present discussion.

I believe the preceding discussion applies with equal validity to varieties of homosexual relationships. It appears to me, and I realize this is a vast generalization, but nevertheless, it appears that more of these relationships involve a degree of dependence that all too soon seems to stifle the growth of both partners and rapidly becomes unsatisfactory to both. This appears related to the tumultuous disruptions of these relationships and the hectic events, particularly suicide attempts, which are part of the dependence and the attempts at manipulation. I also do acknowledge that there are many satisfactory homosexual relationships with the mutual respect and trust that make for a happy marital state.

Another relationship, about which much less is known, though it is becoming an increasingly important social phenomena, is the communal existence. Within this small complex society, the individual sense of identity is diluted vastly more than in the more usual marriage, but possibly the added values of positive identification with the many other members makes the rewards much more worthwhile. Possibly it might actually help a diffuse and unsure person to compare himself with the others, to incorporate the desirable qualities, to assimilate any negative feedback, and to grow within this experience. Certainly the complexities of a dyadic relationship seem to be vastly simpler than in this complicated sort of arrangement.

To briefly recapitulate, it is important for the initially dependent person to achieve a degree and sense of identity and independence before being able to commit himself anew to an interdependent relationship. Unfortunately, all too frequently, for various conscious and unconscious reasons, a new dependent relationship is established which may initially satisfy the individual needs of both partners. It is possible within the context of this relationship and with the cooperation of both individuals to allow for compromise and growth and change to take place. If this doesn't satisfactorily occur, and if the relationship eventuates in a dissolution, then the opportunity for a new period of the single state is afforded. During this time, even though there are frequently many additional responsibilities, a sense of independence can be achieved. The nature of man seems to be such that he voluntarily sooner or later again gives up this independent state for the additional advantages of an interdependent relationship.

Until the divorce, the marriage had seemed better than most. It had lasted seventeen years; there were nice kids, common interests, even mutual respect and affection. What went wrong? The startling truth, says a noted behavioral scientist, is that a good marriage is more fragile than a bad one.

WHY GOOD MARRIAGES FAIL

by Richard Farson

As impossible as it may sound, good marriages probably fail more often than bad ones. What's more, they fail precisely because they are good.

Richard Farson, "Why Good Marriages Fail," McCalls, October, 1971.

Human experience is full of such paradoxes. People often do just the opposite of what one would expect. For example, researchers have found that revolutions do not break out when conditions are at their worst, but when the situation has begun to get better. Once reforms have started, people gain strength and, more importantly, a vision of what their lives might be like—both of which are necessary to energize a revolution. Historians call this the problem of rising expectations.

The same kind of analysis can help us understand why so many good marriages fail. Perhaps if couples could incorporate such paradoxical thinking into their lives, their chances of maintaining a good marriage might improve. At least they might eliminate some of the ugliness of divorce by not deprecating what was, all things considered, a good relationship.

How can a good marriage fail? The easy explanation is that it wasn't basically good. It may have looked good on the outside, but it must have been flawed on the inside. That's the way we usually try to rationalize divorce. But what about marriages that by every conceivable criterion compare favorably with most other marriages? They can fail, too. And because of the heightened expectations present in good marriages, they are often in greater jeopardy than bad ones.

It is not easy to find support for this point of view, because we tend to look at divorces for things that went wrong, not for things that went right. In fact, the best evidence for this argument will have to come from marriages and divorces you know about, perhaps even from your own marriage.

Take, for example, the most recent divorce among your friends. Try to remember what the marriage was like. Chances are you thought of it as being as good as most. You knew of nothing seriously wrong. On the contrary, the couple seemed to enjoy family life, had adequate finances, physical attractiveness, common interests. Even more, they may have had a good deal of respect for each other, perhaps even deep affection.

Yet, they decided to separate. You try to imagine what could have happened. You look for some basic incompatibility, some distinct flaw, some terrible incident. But when you ask them why they are divorcing, they are apt to say something like, "Well, we've simply grown apart," or "I feel trapped in this relationship," or "We just can't communicate," or "He won't let me be me," or "We just felt that surely there must be more to life than we are getting from this marriage."

In all probability, there is no awful hidden truth. Probably there is nothing in their marriage that makes it different from, or worse than, most others.

The common element in all their answers is that they are expressing high-order discontent. Their complaints have nothing to do with the rather low-order justifications for divorce recognized by law—brutality, desertion, adultery, etc. Instead, their complaints reflect an awareness of what the good life should be. Their discontent comes from the difference between what they are actually experiencing in their marriage and what they have come to believe is possible.

The couples who get in the most trouble are those who know enough to see the things that are wrong with their marriage. And, ironically, it takes quite a bit of success in a marriage to make that understanding possible.

So good marriages fail because, by the very fact of being good, they generate discontent. The discontent may come from many sources, some rather unexpected. Here are eight of them.   DISCONTENT

1. Discontent arises because the basic needs of the marriage have been satisfied. Yet, people are never entirely satisfied. Once they have met one set of needs, they simply move on to develop higher-order needs, in an ever-accelerating pattern of demand.

Marriage, after all, was never meant to be as good as it is. It was instituted in the beginning to insure survival, then security, then convenience. Now we take for granted that it will not only meet all those basic needs but much higher needs as well. Marriage is now burdened with the expectations that husbands and wives should enjoy intellectual companionship, warm intimate moments, shared values, deep romantic love, great sexual pleasures. Couples expect to assist and enhance each other in ways never thought of as being part of the marriage contract.

The trouble is that these higher-order needs are more complex, and therefore less easy to satisfy on a continuing basis, than are, say, financial needs. For that reason, they give rise to more frustration and discontent when they are not met.   leading to frustration and discontent.

2. Discontent arises because mass education and mass media have taught people to expect too much from marriage. Today almost no one is ignorant of the marvelous possibilities of human relationships. Time was when people modeled their own marriage after their parents' marriage; it was the only model they knew. Now, with much of our population college-educated, saturated with books, recordings, films, and television, just about everyone has some new ideals for his marriage to live up to—and has, consequently, some new sources of dissatisfaction.

The problem is made even worse by the mass media: The romantic vision has been oversimplified, translated into a smoothly functioning, syrupy sweet "nuclear" family and sold to the American public. The perpetuation of this stereotype (two married adults and their own minor children) as the only acceptable marriage model, and the implication that a constant state of affection and unity in family life is actually achievable, give cause to rising dissatisfaction in one's own marriage.

Television is totally devoted to the nuclear family; the only variation ever shown is when one parent is widowed (rarely divorced) and is seeking a return to "normal" family life. Not only is the nuclear family a relatively new invention (never before in history were families formed along these lines), but many authorities now regard this arrangement as entirely too burdensome and difficult to remain workable. Two parents having to serve as all-purpose adults, accomplishing everything by themselves, is anything but easy. TV just makes it look easy.

The simple fact is that more than 60 percent of Americans now do not live in nuclear-family arrangements. They live in some other form of domestic unit—as single adults, for example, or divorced adults with children. But their constant instructions from the mass media are that to be genuinely fulfilled, they must be part of a nuclear family.

3. Discontent arises because couples succeed in filling their masculine and feminine roles. One would think that success in meeting society's expectations as men and women should make marriage work better. Shouldn't the woman who is feminine, gentle, tender, aesthetic, childlike, emotional, understanding, and yielding be a perfect companion for a man who is masculine, firm, strong, aggressive, rugged, decisive, rational, and dominant?

The odds are that it works just the other way. These roles are so limiting, and at the same time so demanding, that the result can be truly monstrous. As we are now beginning to see, the oppressive concept of "woman's role" and "woman's place" has led to great rage on the part of many women, rage that has only recently been openly expressed. Similarly, the man's role leads to such strong feelings of pressure, guilt, impotence, and artificiality that he, too, is now demanding relief.

One would think that the strain of such role demands could be alleviated in the intimacy and protection of the family unit, but for the most part, it is not. Unfortunately, the marriage relationship is not usually a place one can let down. Too often it serves not as a buffer against the impositions of society, but as a reinforcer. Husbands and wives are notorious in forcing these stereotyped roles on one another. The frustration that comes from an inability to deliver on such expectations only makes matters worse, and instead of blaming society for demanding that they perform these roles, they blame themselves and each other.

The various liberation efforts for men and women that are currently under way may eventually offer relief, but in the short run they simply deepen the problem. The stress on marriage that has resulted from women's liberation, for example, has already taken its toll in separation and divorce. No one can say why. It could be because the husband and wife are not being liberated at the same rate, or because they have come to see their marriage as symbolizing their slavery to these oppressive roles, or because their new understandings show their marriage to be so limiting that they can no longer live with the incongruity between what they have and what they feel they must have.

4. Discontent arises because marriage now embraces a new concept of sexual fulfillment. The deluge of words and images giving us a totally new idea of what human sexuality could be has become inescapable. We are no longer willing to settle for the sexuality of past generations. Married couples now expect sex to be playful, experimental, and greatly permissive. They expect a wide range of sexual performance and are seriously disappointed when the experiments don't succeed. Not only is there a desperate search for orgasm, but more—superorgasm, ecstasy, peak experiences. Not sometimes, but every time; so here again, while the sexual relationship in a marriage may have been quite adequate, it is now expected to be a good deal more than adequate. The better it is, the better it must become.

No one wants to turn back the clock, to deny the new understandings of human sexual potential and return to Victorian prudery. We should be pleased that individuals now demand the right to full sexuality. But we can't ignore the fact that in previous generations these high expectations were not a recognized source of discontent.

5. Discontent arises because marriage counseling, psychotherapy, and other efforts to improve marriage actually make it more difficult. It may be that marriage counseling and psychotherapy with married couples tend to create more discontent than they cure. Not because counseling isn't any good, but partly because it is good; by helping, it has made the problem worse.

First of all, any effort to improve life—whether by education or religion or philosophy or therapy—seldom makes life simpler. In fact, it makes it more complex. Just as labor-saving devices have caused us more labor and complicated our lives, so counseling has further burdened our marriages by asking us to live up to what we know to be our best. That always turns out to be difficult and painful.

Secondly, counseling provides an example of an intimate relationship that is achievable only under the special circumstances of the psychotherapeutic hour; nevertheless, it makes the client wonder why that level of intimacy and understanding can't exist at home. In comparison to an expert counselor, most marriage partners must seem obtuse indeed.

(handwritten annotation: "few spaces / or were / his up to / their intimates / at home.")

Third, most psychotherapists continue to endorse, even promote, narrow and outdated ideas, based largely on Freudian concepts of sexuality, male-female roles, and family relationships. They describe a model of marriage that is all but impossible to live up to, and is, in the light of newer understanding, not very desirable anyway. In this area, the psychotherapist is, for the most part, the unwitting enemy of the liberation movements for both men and women. This is especially tragic when you realize that human liberation, the chance to live up to one's potential, is what counseling and psychotherapy are all about.

Fourth, and perhaps most serious, counseling gives a person the feeling—much more than is probably true—that he is in charge of his own life, that his problems are basically of his own making, and that their solutions are within his control. People constantly live with the idea that they are beset with unique and *personal* problems—problems that stem from their own neurotic disorders or from mistakes they have made, conditions that are solvable and correctable by individual action. But more likely, for most people, it is the *situation* in which they find themselves that is the problem. And it is not always a situation that individual initiative can do much about.

Constant attention to our problems as personal rather than as universal (which happens in counseling) has given us a highly distorted picture of what we can do about the problems we find in marriage. We actually have very little control over the major conditions that affect our marriages, and, consequently, marriages change very little as a result of counseling.

Finally, it is rather well known that psychotherapists and marriage counselors themselves have a high incidence of separation and divorce. This is not cited to suggest that, as a way of justifying their own actions, they subconsciously welcome their clients' decisions to separate. Rather, it points out yet another example of how constant attention to marriage, and the consequent high-order expectations about the marriage relationship, can produce casualties in those one would think best able to avoid them.

6. *Discontent arises because marriages suffer from the gains made in the consciousness revolution.* This revolution, thought by some to be the only revolution that is actually changing behavior, stems from the hippie movement—drug culture, new-left politics, rock music, Eastern philosophy, occult phenomena, encounter groups, etc.—all combining to paint pictures of what life might be if we were to reach the human potential.

The alternate life-styles that have grown out of this revolution are now affecting the values of all of us, and, most certainly, they have reshaped our concepts of married life. Consider, for example, the impact of the encounter group and other group efforts to develop awareness and sensitivity to one's self and others. More than 6 million Americans have now participated in encounter groups of one form or another. As is the case with psychotherapy, the encounter group has given its participants moments with other people that are remarkably beautiful, intimate, and fulfilling. These experiences can't help making a person think that he is going to be able to bring this new awareness and strength into his own marriage. But it seldom works that way. More likely, it has furnished him with a reference point indicating what a relationship *might* be, but which his marriage can never achieve. Not because his marriage isn't good, but because it can't match the freedom of a temporary relationship.

The consciousness revolution works in other ways to make marriage more difficult. For example, the value placed on honest relationships, on complete truthfulness in dealing with others, puts such an excessive strain on marriages that some cannot survive. The idea is, the more honesty the better. Following the teachings of the new-consciousness gurus, husbands and wives have regaled each other with all manner of honest statements in what appear to be efforts to enrich marriage, but in fact make it almost impossible to endure. Most marriages can't take such honesty as sharing fantasies about other people during sexual intercourse, detailing extramarital affairs, etc. Jean Kerr wrote a good line for a wife who has just been told by her husband that he has been cheating, "If you had the decency of a truck driver, you'd keep your lousy affair secret!"

The values of the new consciousness emphasize honesty over loyalty and kindness. Honesty is rarely unadulterated, however, and all too often is used to alleviate guilt and transfer responsibility. It may help to remember that marriage, like any other important institution, needs some myth and mystique to keep it vital.

Above all, the new consciousness has created the expectation of high-level intimacy in marriage, something that is very rare indeed. There is little question that the intimacy of shared feelings that occurs between teen-age friends, for example, far and away transcends that which is possible in most marriages. Perhaps marriage is too important to be burdened with such intimacies. People simply cannot take such risks with a relationship that matters to them.

7. *Discontent arises because of fantasies about what other marriages are like.* Just as individuals find it necessary to present a façade in life, married people feel that they must create an image of their marriage that shows only its best side. The truth is that we live in almost total

ignorance of what other people's marriages are like. Everyone recognizes that no marriage is perfect, that everyone has fights and difficulties and disillusionments. Yet, many times we undermine our marriages by assuming that other marriages must somehow be better. This fantasy, like a casual flirtation, doesn't have to pass any real tests of real life. And, if we really could know more about other people's marriages, we would see that they are much more similar than different—painfully, hilariously, reassuringly alike.

8. *Discontent arises from comparing the marriage relationship with itself in its better moments.* The memories couples carry of their pre-marital or early marriage experiences inevitably make their current situation seem less romantic and exciting.

This is particularly true for couples with children. For most people the major change in life comes not with marriage, but with the birth of the first child. It is at that point that real commitment is required, that major limitations set in, and it is then that the affection and attention of the wife moves from husband to child. A decrease in sexual activity, and an increase in the complications of family life, as treasured and as beautiful as they may be, are sources of discontent when compared with what went before.

But probably the most important source of discontent is the comparison of the marriage with its own good moments in the present. Not too many marriages have great moments, but the best ones do. These peaks, however, are inevitably followed by valleys. Couples lucky enough to have these moments find themselves unable to sustain them, and, at the same time, unable to settle for ordinary moments. They want life to be a constantly satisfying state. But to be a constant state, to avoid the valleys, it is necessary to eliminate the peaks, which puts the marriage on a narrow band of emotionality and involvement. Good marriages are not like that, but the price they exact in depression and pain is high.

The constant talk today about marriage, whether it's positive or negative, has only led to greater hopes for it, making it more popular and desirable than ever. As someone once remarked, "Marriage is like a beseiged city. Everybody that's out wants in, and everybody that's in wants out."

What's difficult to remember is that marriages of all kinds, bad and good, are very fragile, easily wrecked. They can withstand some kinds of trauma, but they cannot stand the abuse of unmet expectations. They particularly can't stand comparisons between what they are and what they might be. It is that kind of comparison that leads to separation and divorce. That is why maintaining a good marriage is more difficult than maintaining a bad one.

The calamity of divorce is not in the failure of the relationship; the relationship has probably succeeded fairly well, right to the end. Instead, the calamity comes from the problems of child custody, property, finances, social stigma, unsolved feelings of dependency, responsibility, guilt, and failure—the feelings of having let everyone down.

It's a pity that we must regard the end of a marriage as proof of its failure. In order to justify a separation, we must somehow put down the marriage, negate it, make it less worthy than it has been.

Society won't allow us to celebrate separations, but perhaps that's not such a bad idea. There is some reason to believe that people leave one rich relationship to find a richer one. Sociologist Jessie Bernard's classic study of divorce and remarriage suggests that couples move on to seek and find high-order marriages, sometimes several in a series. Clearly a new concept of evaluating marriage must be brought into being, one that assesses not longevity or satisfaction but the quality and level of the discontent it engenders.

Somehow we have the idea that we can only leave a marriage if it's bad. We simply can't bring ourselves to see that the reason for leaving a marriage may be because of the new vision it permitted us to have of what life could be like. Too bad we can't live with this paradox— that it is because of the *success* of our marriages that we have developed this high-level discontent.

If we could realize that the better the marriage is, the worse we will sometimes feel, then we might prevent the incidents that occur in any marriage from leading to separation and divorce. Such an understanding could give us the insight we need to make one good marriage last a lifetime.

———————————

Everything is "even"—the husband has a
job; the wife has the children. He makes
decisions; she makes dinner. Here is
one man's challenging answer to young
women who do not want marriage to
mean what it meant to their mothers.

MUST MARRIAGE CHEAT
TODAY'S YOUNG WOMEN?

by Philip E. Slater

A year or two ago I gave a course on the generation gap to a group composed primarily of middle-class women who had college-age children. Since I also was teaching a group of undergraduates concerned with the same issues, I thought it might be interesting to bring the two groups together.

The students could have been the women's daughters, so similar were their backgrounds—ethnically, socially, educationally. Both groups were equally intelligent and sophisticated. Yet their fundamental assumptions were so different that they could scarcely communicate with each other.

The mothers were concerned with young people's attitudes toward sex, drugs and appearance; the students, with interpersonal relationships and self-development. (It was a somewhat apolitical group.) If one of the girls discussed her doubts concerning the future of her relationship with a boyfriend, the mothers were completely distracted by the fact that the two lived together.

In one session a few women launched a rather vicious attack on some of the students who were discussing their personal lives. The other women made little attempt to stop the attack, although several of them later expressed distress over it. The more the women attacked, the more open and self-revealing the students became; and the more the students opened up, the more they were attacked.

The girls were very depressed by this encounter. Even though they assumed that the attacks were motivated mostly by jealousy (in particular, envy of their sexual freedom), the girls were afraid that their own radically different life-styles would not protect them from falling into the same pattern at the same age. Most of the students seemed to fear marriage, but they felt they and their friends were drifting helplessly into it—either out of some vague insecurity or for convenience (our society is, after all, structured around marriage).

They saw little in marriage that was appealing. Most of the girls felt that their parents were trapped in unhappy and destructive relationships, and they wanted to avoid this experience at all costs. They also feared life-style changes. They told stories of friends who, after marriage, had begun to wear more conservative clothing and had become engrossed in acquiring possessions. They imagined themselves 20 years hence, bored and isolated, preoccupied with material things, hating and envying young people as they were hated and envied now.

I felt that these young women's fears were well-founded. Men coming out of college can carve new living patterns for themselves that preserve their existing values and their way of life. New occupations are emerging that do not reflect the old self-aggrandizing, the junk-amassing system that we used to call the American Way of Life. And even traditional careers are being redefined within many professions.

But women participate only marginally in this process. A woman who does not maintain a fierce and dogged foothold in the job market will find herself slipping helplessly into old cultural patterns. Isolated, deprived of social and personal stimulation, she will be under intense pressure to make a career out of child rearing. And at that point it is difficult to escape the clutches of the culture that encourages living beyond one's means and "sacrificing" for the children.

I felt concern for the young women who wished to escape this way of life, but I also felt concern for those who already had accepted it. I thought they deserved more than life had given them. What sort of society is this if even its most advantaged women are so unfulfilled?

The ladies themselves (and what a hideously condescending phrase that is—"the ladies"—and with what snide chuckles it is usually delivered!) would probably object to my characterization of their lives in this way. Indeed, they competed in asserting their contentment—and it cannot be denied that their lives *were* richer than those of many women their age. They had great resources, personal as well as material, and they had made adaptations that were difficult to fault. But a well-appointed prison is still a prison, and a healthy prisoner who uses his time to good advantage is still a prisoner.

The hollowness of their position was revealed by their self-contempt. When their expectation that I would simply lecture to them collided with my efforts to engage them in a more personal way by getting them to talk with me and the others in the group, they expressed distaste at the idea of sharing ideas and feelings with one another. "Who wants to talk to a bunch of women?" they asked.

A central point of this article will be that women can transcend their present condition only by affirming their own worth and their unique power to reclaim our ailing society. But such affirmation will depend upon development of feminine solidarity; I will say more about that later.

What follows is addressed primarily to young women. Although I can show women who are enmeshed in society's web; how they got there, they pretty well know that already. To tell them what to do now would be irresponsible, for I do not know what matters most to each of them. For young women, however, I can describe the pitfalls that lie ahead and I can suggest alternate routes to follow; ultimately, of course, everyone chooses her own pathway.

Graduation speakers have always been fond of telling students they are beginning a life "on their own." But these speakers are pointing merely to the most conspicuous highway leading from school to adult life. Being "on your own" in our society is not just a matter of assuming adult responsibilities or leaving the bosom of one's family. For most college women, graduation means abandoning the very real community life that school provides.

By "community" I mean something very simple: a group of people spending most of their waking hours in the same place and engaging in a common enterprise. A community life exists when one can go daily to a given location at a given time and see many of the people one knows.

This effortlessness is central to my definition of community life. A large high school or university or corporation is not of itself a community, but it may contain a number of small communities—"the crowd," "the group," "the gang." These groups assemble automatically; no one has to bring them together. The nearest approximation to this in a suburban setting would be a group of mothers who go daily to a community swimming pool. But such groups are involuntarily monosexual and aimless, and any sense of community usually is dilated by the necessity of watching individually over small children.

Before industrialization most people lived a community life. To be deprived of it was punishment, an exile. For a woman today, graduation itself can be an exile, a permanent end to community life. If she is married and not working, her community will not extend beyond her own home.

Of course, she will have friends, neighbors and family. She may participate in local activities; she may join clubs and work for causes. But these relationships and activities are separate and fragmented; her various friends may not be part of the same group and may not even know one another.

Furthermore there is no outside structure supporting these relationships; they must be maintained. There is no spot where everyone "hangs out"; people must be called and invited over, usually with due regard to such irrelevant considerations as whose turn it is to be hostess or which people have been owed an invitation the longest. Many women become involved in the escalating competition of dinner parties. This system of formal entertaining minimizes the sense of shared activity upon which good times so often depend and maximizes anxiety over achievement and the mechanical dreariness of obligatory social occasions so that even close friendships can seem hardly worth the effort.

I'm overstating the case a bit—dinner parties *can* be fun, especially for men. My point is that by and large, pregraduation social life is effortless whereas postgraduation social life tends to be effortful.

Most men retain some community life in their jobs; so do working women—within the limits of the inferior jobs available to most of them. But a woman who accepts only the domestic role loses all remnants of community life and finds it virtually impossible to re-create one within the confines of conventional living arrangements.

The kind of clutter a woman creates to fill this vacuum depends on the kind of person she is. If she is gregarious and extroverted, she will suffer less, because she will be able to surround herself with people and thus seem to belong to something.

Some women will try to create a community *within* the household by raising a large family; but this works only for the children, not for her. Most women just look around, see that they are in a little prison and try to improve the cell by making it larger or better appointed.

Throughout the ages women have played the role of a domestic in their own home without protest. But isolation was rarely a part of the picture. (Pioneer women often are cited as models, but they are poor examples because they had a tendency to die a lot.) Wherever domesticity seems to have worked well for women there have been considerable community life, a variety of group activities, a reasonable amount of mobility and a sharing of household and child-rearing responsibilities with other adults. The idea of expecting the average mother to spend most of her time alone with her children in a small house or apartment is a relatively modern invention, and a rather fiendish one at that. A few men may engage in work that is as stultifying and tedious as domestic work, but usually they do not have to do it alone.

The process through which a woman drifts into her prison is gradual and subtle. She and her husband may begin by sharing household chores, especially if they have lived together before marrying. But if the wife does not work, as time goes by she finds usually that his job and his need for mobility begin to take precedence while she assumes most of the domestic tasks. As she becomes increasingly isolated in her home she begins to demand more from the house itself. This heightens financial pressures and pushes her husband into a more aggressive career role, which in turn permits him to demand even more mobility and freedom from domestic responsibility. And the pattern is established.

The clincher, of course, comes when children are born. The wife may welcome them (she is supposed to, in any case). But after all, a child is not a full-time toy; and by the time a woman becomes aware of the futility of trying to build a whole existence around baby tending she finds that she has made decisions that push her deeper into her prison. Perhaps she thinks that a backyard would save her pushing a stroller to the park or perhaps she worries about good schools. As a result the family ensconces itself in a house in a suburb. Her husband has to drive to work, but he at least can get out. She cannot.

The husband has to make more money, of course, to finance the house, and if his wife is not to be physically as well as emotionally imprisoned, they may need a second car. The house now becomes enormously important to her and must be improved endlessly. The husband must make still more money. And so it goes: husband driven and wife trapped.

I suspect that if this way of life is to be changed, only women can do it. Most men are too enmeshed in the system to understand how it works. But if women were to stop colluding in the division of labor that now exists, men would be forced to begin to work *with* them in changing the process that creates this division. If women were to stop suppressing their curiosity and ambition, men would stop suppressing their own emotionality and humanity.

At this point I wish to emphasize that the temperamental traits assigned to men and women in a given society are completely arbitrary. In some societies men are supposed to be emotional and flighty and women stoical and down-to-earth; in others the reverse is supposed to be true. In some societies men are supposed to be more sexual; in others, women. In some societies men are supposed to be the vainer of the sexes; in others, women.

But no matter how these traits are assigned in a given society, it is always assumed that male and female attitudes are biologically based. In raising children, however, we always are very careful to see that these supposedly inherent biological characteristics are drummed into them. We say that a man or a woman instinctively acts in such-and-such a way. But our behavior indicates merely that we feel he or she *should* act that way.

By reinforcing certain behavior we effectively "keep women in their place." If a woman does not act according to our cultural stereotype, she may be accused of being "unfeminine." Male logic, for example, gives us the following syllogism: Women are not logical; this woman is logical; therefore this woman is not really a woman.

In recent years blacks have learned how important it is not to let whites define who they are; women obviously can profit a great deal from this lesson. Most of the Women's Liberation groups, in fact, *have* profited from it, and their movement has been able to leapfrog some of the early trial-and-error phases that most such enterprises undergo.

Feminine unity is, in fact, at the crux of the matter. Most women are shamed out of it—shamed into isolation and powerlessness and forced to accept a male definition of their essential nature. To the question "How can I avoid the pitfalls that women of my parents' generation fell into?" the most general answer I can give is: "Don't let them hang you separately."

Many women will be unable to apply this suggestion to their own lives. "Why should I view the man I love as an enemy?" they will ask. Is any relationship more important than the one between a man and a woman? Don't both the man and the woman subordinate all other relationships to it?

Yes, they do. But the man hedges. With the best intentions, he winds up having it both ways—he has a marriage affiliation and a male affiliation—while the woman abandons her loyalty to other females to a far greater extent. However many friends a nonworking wife may have, she does not have a community life. Her husband has. Furthermore, if her husband changes his affiliations—leaves his job or is transferred to another city—she must change hers whether she wants to or not.

It is important to realize that this imbalance occurs not because men are malevolent or unjust but because the culture prescribes it. The most loving and devoted husband must leave each morning for work; he must invest a lot of energy in a community system from which his wife is excluded. If he is sensitive to her needs, he feels guilty, but he doesn't know quite how to help.

The wife, on the other hand, particularly one who has not yet had a child, sees that her husband's role of breadwinner gives him satisfaction. She may feel guilty that her domestic role isn't fulfilling her the way books say it is supposed to. And so she decides that perhaps she should make an even bigger commitment by having children. Her husband is likely to support the idea with some relief ("Kids will give her something to do, be company for her").

Now everything is "even"—he has his job; she has the children. He has a community life; she has someone to take care of. She is not only committed; she is in over her head, completely dependent upon the marriage for everything in her life.

Marriage, in other words, can be a very unequal bargain. But as long as men and women are assigned markedly different roles in our society, every marriage will be a contract between Romeo and Juliet—between a Montague and a Capulet. Women considering marriage don't like to think this way—nor do men, for that matter. But men can afford to have a more romantic view because it is Juliet who gives up her family name, who ceases to be a Capulet, while Romeo continues to be a Montague.

In advising women to unite, then, I am urging each woman to afford herself the same group protection her husband has. What do I mean when I suggest that women unite? Certainly I do not mean more bridge clubs or casserole exchanges. I *do* mean that little girls must not be taught that their role in life should be auxiliary and subordinate no matter how gifted they are. It is shocking and painful to see a brilliant little girl believe that she can aspire only to becoming a nurse, while her dull playmate can confidently imagine himself a doctor. But most immediately I mean that women should have the same solidarity that men have.

Women are taught to compete with each other for men, even at the risk of sacrificing friendship. Men are more likely to preserve a close friendship even at some cost to their marriage. Men also are more apt to discuss their marriage with a friend. But for women—especially middle-class women—the need to confide is hampered by a competitive need to prove that "my marriage is happier than yours." There is a very simple reason for this. A man talking to another man thinks of himself as an individual; a woman talking to another woman is more likely to think of herself as a member of a marriage.

These attitudes are changing somewhat. College women seem to care more about their friendships than they used to; they seem less willing to sacrifice a friendship to "get a man." And even though Women's Liberation groups have been subjected to considerable ridicule and accused of being "unfeminine" (a male term for "uppity"), through participation in such groups an increasing number of women are rediscovering themselves as individuals.

Women have many problems in common, problems they endure in needless isolation. Because they cannot share these problems and experiences they feel uncertain, confused, lethargic. The discovery of common problems and aspirations often produces intense feelings of relief, bursts of energy and a sense of purpose.

If today's young women wish to change the patterns that have produced half-lives for so many of them, they must organize. Without some explicit organization to bring about change, their struggle will encounter insuperable odds. For women not only must change men; they also must rid *themselves* of their own doubts, confusions, brainwashed attitudes and automatically self-defeating responses. They can do this only with the support of other women.

As a man I cannot presume to tell women in any specific way how they can or should work to change our society, because it is in the *deciding* that women will find their solidarity and their will to succeed. I do want to point out here, however, that it is of the utmost importance for women to re-evaluate the division of labor by sex that now exists in our society.

There is nothing inherently wrong with a division of labor as such. But a division that forces people into emotionally crippling sex roles can have only unfortunate social consequences in the long run. Some of these consequences are highly visible today; the mechanical, inhumane and dehumanizing society we live in could have been created only by beings who had delegated the expression of feelings to others.

Female solidarity, then, has social as well as individual significance. If this were not so, I could simply tell a young woman: Don't get married, for marriage is a trap for women; or, Don't have children; or, Insist on living in a commune. Or at the very least I would say: Change the basic nature of the typical bargain made between a man and a woman who intend to commit themselves to each other. A reasonable bargain would necessitate guarantees against isolation and immobility, refusal to accept the role of domestic servant and insistence upon equal job priorities.

But even these changes would not be enough. If women imitated men, we all would be worse off. The superiority of women rests in the fact that unlike men, they have not learned to deaden their feelings. They have not become mere machines but have remained feeling human beings. Job equality should not simply be a matter of women's moving in a "male" direction, but also should force men to stop using work as a justification for life-destroying activities.

People always have said jokingly that if women ran the world, they could hardly do a worse job than men have done—that there would be fewer wars, less ecological destruction. This is a joke no longer. The homes people live in and the planet people live on should be the equal concern of everyone. When women are responsible for the home alone and men for the planet alone, both do a terrible job.

Our planet suffers from being run by people who ignore their own needs for intimacy and hence the needs of everyone else. Our homes suffer from being run by those who are ignorant of their interdependence on all other homes. This division of labor by sex helps people forget the connection between the fumes they create and the fumes they inhale. If this kind of connection is re-established, we will inhabit a more humane environment, one in which both men and women can live richer lives.

---

*Are there some cultural marital traditions
that seem designed more to destroy marriage than sustain it? In what sense can
being taken for granted be good or bad in
a marital relationship? Do change and
variation in marital patterns need to upset
the marital configuration? What are
some signs of marital rigidity? What steps
can married couples take if they wish
to enliven their relationship? Are we wise
to expect perfection and uninterrupted
harmony in our marital relationships?
Is it dangerous to give up one's defense
mechanisms? What is left to build a marriage on? At what price do we exact marital
fulfillment?*

MAKING IT TOGETHER: GROWTH FROM WITHIN

by John F. Crosby

The difference between a "rut" and a "groove" seems to be the difference between losing variety and making constructive use of routine.
A rut is negative in that variety and spontaneity have been choked to
death; a groove is positive as long as the routine and the ordinary are
continually used as springboards into experiences involving variety and
spontaneity. People who wish to deny the need of "routine" and the
"ordinary" may find fulfillment in one of the emerging marital patterns,
but they probably will not find it within traditional monogamy. Two
people cannot live together over a long period of time without coming
to terms with the routine and the ordinary. The only option (but a most
important one) available to couples who commit themselves to a monog-

amous, sexually exclusive union is the option between the rut and the groove.

To Kill a Marriage

If someone were to appoint a presidential commission on "how to destroy marriage" we could offer some cogent suggestions on strategy. The first maneuver should be to use the mass media to condition people to believe that change and variety are wrong—and to be resisted at all costs. Such a step would allow cultural traditions and patterns, myths, and taboos to be absorbed into a rigidity of form and function within marriage. Isn't it true that we often oblige the commission by commiting "maricide" and "familicide" the very instant we say "I do"? Oh, not intentionally, but in a rather subtle, sneaky way don't we conclude that since he or she is now mine there is no need to continue to score points— no need to be creative, imaginative, spontaneous, or interesting? Many promising relationships begin to die when the relationship becomes legalized—not because a legal bond works some sort of deadly witchcraft but because legalization becomes an open invitation to take the partner *too much* for granted. Our second suggestion on how to kill a marriage is therefore, Take each other for granted—always!

There is no doubt that marriage should provide a couple with a haven in which they can bask in the luxury of not having to put on facades or false pretenses for anyone. This freedom to be oneself provides the joy of being taken for granted, of being loved (agape) "in spite of" one's faults, idiosyncrasies, and hang-ups. Yet there is something in us that doesn't like to be taken for granted, even though we may persist in defending our right to take the other for granted. To be taken for granted is both a relief and a threat; it is both a security and an insecurity; it is both a joy and a peril. Thus, a delicate balance must be maintained in a marital relationship; agape must never be too much out of balance with philos and eros. (In-spite-of love must be balanced with friendship love and physical, passion-filled love.) Whenever equilibrium is upset, it is probably because one or both partners are demanding the right to take the other for granted while claiming that it is not the other's prerogative to take him for granted.

Case Study

Frank and Sarah have been married for two years. They have one child, a daughter, age 8 months. Sarah and Frank have come to a marriage counselor because they feel they are at an impasse in their relationship.

Sarah: He just doesn't pay any attention to me. No matter what I do or how hard I try to carry on a conversation he ignores me. He comes home from work and hardly even says "hello." I tried getting dressed up in the late afternoon but he never noticed. When we eat he is silent. When we go out in the car he's silent. Even when we are angry about something he remains uninvolved and unemotional. It's like I'm married to a machine. If only he would acknowledge that I'm alive!

Frank: Sarah makes it sound as though I'm a criminal. Look, I need peace and quiet when I get home from work. All day long I've been selling—sell, sell, sell—and it feels damn good to just turn it off. If I can't relax in my own home where am I ever going to be able to be me? I never did talk much—socially I mean—and if you ask me, Sarah is just making a lot of fuss about nothing. I love her, but that doesn't mean I have to keep on courting her—like I was still trying to impress her.

Sarah: If you love me why don't you ever show me?

Frank: Show you! I work hard for us. What do you call working five days a week going from customer to customer? Of course I love you, but that doesn't mean I have to go around proving it by saying nice things all the time. If you only knew how much I have to sell myself in order to get an order you wouldn't be talking that way.

Sarah: Well it's no joyride taking care of Judy all day long either. All day I care for her, do laundry, cook meals, clean house; and you act like it's too much work to talk to me.

This is a classic situation, portrayed in women's magazines, cartoons, and TV shows. The situation will be accentuated if either partner is especially dependent, because the dependent personality relies on affirmation from others, especially the spouse, for his self-esteem. Even without personality problems, this situation can be destructive if either partner has special legitimate ego needs which only the spouse can fill. For example, Frank's job requires him to be outgoing, aggressive, alert, and "a nice guy." Frank may normally be some of these things some of the time, but he finds it fatiguing to be all of these things all of the time. Consequently, it is natural that he would relish the idea of coming home to peace and solitude. However, Sarah's situation is the reverse, and it is one shared with unknown thousands of young mothers. Sarah has been living in a child's world all day, and she anticipates an exchange of conversation with her husband—even if the exchange is small talk or an abbreviated account of the day's events. Sarah yearns for this verbal sharing; Frank can't abide it.

Thus, we have two normal people who both need to be taken for granted in some ways; but Frank is taking Sarah for granted in a way that fails to take into account her basic need for human warmth and adult companionship. Sarah, on the other hand, has failed to understand Frank's needs after a long day at work. Experiences in role reversal, or in a modified role reversal, could probably help Frank and Sarah develop increased empathy into the situation of the other. Role taking, in which husband and wife practice adopting the other's point of view, can often serve to temper the excessive or unrealistic expectations a couple has of each other. A child can often upset the balance of a relationship also, and Frank's and Sarah's daughter may have made them more sensitive to being taken for granted. They are probably going through a reorientation stage since their child has necessitated a new daily life style for Sarah and perhaps an ego threat to Frank. We have all heard that new fathers are threatened by their children because father is no longer number one. While most men negotiate this adjustment quite well, it is unusual for new fathers to admit that they feel displaced and taken for granted when a child appears.

The rut that Frank and Sarah find themselves in brings us to the third suggestion we will make to the presidential commission: create a cultural milieu in which no one is rewarded for creativity and imagination. Once we convince people that deviation from the traditional role assumptions and marital expectations is wrong, risky, and unnecessary, we can then quickly proceed to the marriage funeral. The rut will become unbearable. I suspect that such a commission would suggest that "imagination" be checked permanently at the door of the (church) (courthouse) (J.P.) (Synagogue)—check one!

Answers to the following questions would indicate that the presidential commission had been highly successful. Answers implying "seldom," "a long time ago," or "we never would" indicate a rigidity in marital roles and a successful campaign to destroy marriage.

When was the last time the couple was separated for at least several days? When was the last time the husband stayed home with the children while the wife went away? When was the last time the couple went away together, leaving the children with a sitter, alone if older, or with friends? Where did the couple go? A nearby motel for overnight? Away with another couple?

How often are the traditional roles of male and female reversed? When did "he" last cook dinner? Does he even know how? Or clean house? Or go to his child's teacher's evaluation conference instead of his wife? When was the last time sexual intercourse was engaged in other than in the bed the couple ordinarily sleeps in? Outside? In the living room? On the floor? Indeed, the sexual technologists have a good point when he is bound to have an increase in understanding and empathy. Further, they lash out at our sexual rigidities and suggest positions in intercourse, changes in technique, and exploration of intimacies beyond coitus.

When has the couple varied the time of sexual intimacy? Must it always be evening, or morning, or on certain night of the week? When has the couple last reversed the so-called traditional sex-role which assumes that the male is always active and the female passive? A passive male and an active female may be a welcome relief and change for both.

How many couples have ever seriously attempted to learn transactional analysis? How many married couples and/or families use transactional analysis as a means of learning to cope with the conflicts, changing moods, and everyday situations that are common fare in family life?

All of the foregoing questions and statements presuppose a motivation to change, to grow, to explore, and to enrich and enliven. Once a couple agrees to give up, however slowly and gradually, the defense mechanisms and safety devices that they have used to avoid intimacy there is no limit to what can change, with or without outside help. People may protest that centers for development of human potential are out of the question for ordinary people with limited means. Perhaps, although even a growth workshop can be given priority over more traditional vacations or a new car.

Church groups have been increasingly concerned about marital and familial interaction and some have become involved in sensitivity training. It is becoming more and more common for clergy in the more liberal religious traditions to receive training in group marital enrichment. Thus, couples who complain of a lack of understanding friends who might share such group training might not need to look further than their own church, or the YMCA, YWCA, or community educational program.

Many larger cities have pastoral counseling centers where clergymen with specialized training are available for individual counseling, for group therapy, and for marital enrichment groups. Many county and city mental health clinics and Community Chest family agencies also have special groups and classes pertaining to marital growth and family interaction.

But a couple can also work together, separate from an organized counseling group, to improve their marriage. Indeed, transactional analysis is emphasized in this book because anybody can learn it, as has been shown with children, older people, and the mentally retarded.

Two married people can also learn role taking in a matter of minutes —that is, he plays the wife and she plays the husband. Using this format, many conflicts can be dealt with and many feelings explored, for when any one person tries to think and feel himself into the role of another when another assumes my role (plays me) I am bound to get insight and find myself reacting in interesting ways. Others who know us deeply and intimately can give us a glimpse of how we come across to others—can give us feedback. Feedback in human relations can be either divergent or convergent. Divergent feedback is a communication (whether verbal, written, or symbolic) we usually don't want to hear; convergent feedback is welcome because it agrees with or confirms our self-image. Role taking can drastically reduce the divergent feedback and increase the convergent feedback because it can help one "feel into" the other person and learn to change one's attitude and behavior. More positive feelings (positive feedback) are bound to result from such new insight. Role taking can also help us cut through idealized images of the self and the other by forcing us to see ourselves the way we come across to others. Since idealization militates against a realistic acceptance of oneself and of others, role playing may serve as a tremendous aid in learning authentic self-acceptance and acceptance of others.

Role playing can also help a husband and wife uncover some of their traditional expectations. Thus, a fourth suggestion that the presidential commission should implement is to mount an attack on those who would test traditional male-female and husband-wife roles. The commission should demand role rigidity and a strict sex division of labor, duty, and responsibility to guard against honest self-examination of role expectation, which can often change a conflict-ridden, rut-oriented marriage into a growth relationship. A husband may relate to his wife for ten years on the mistaken assumption that because his mother starched his shirts and cheerfully made a career of housekeeping and mothering, his wife should also be contented to stay at home as sole housekeeper. Similarly, a wife may expect her husband to be domineering and sole breadwinner like her father was, even though she may consciously dislike her father or bear animosity or resentment toward him. Such role expectations, which are deeply embedded in cultural and religious traditions, often provide fertile ground for manipulation of the mate.

A government thrust to "freeze" traditional husband-wife, male-female, father-mother, and parent-offspring roles would go a long way toward killing the potential of monogamous unions. Whenever either partner fails to measure up to the sacred institutionalized expectations of the other, feelings of hurt, anger, resentment, and hostility are likely to run rampant. Thus, a fifth suggestion might be, "Create a national climate that encourages perfection and harmony." A careful manipulation of the mass media could be used to create the illusion that happy successful marriages are those in which there is no conflict, and everybody is improving day by day in their quest for perfect relationships.

Analysis of so-called happy, vital marriages often reveals a total absence of perfectionism and a total acceptance of each other despite character defects, personality flaws, and hang-ups. *Perfection* and *lack of conflict* may yet prove to be the most reliable predictors of *unsatisfactory* marriage—perfection because it is blatantly nonhuman and stupid; lack of conflict because it signals a fundamental dishonesty through denial of feelings.

A final suggestion for our commission (the reader can carry on from here) is to create a marriage ritual law which prescribes phrases of the wedding ceremony that define the marriage contract once and forever as nonnegotiable and nonamendable. Such a nuptial requirement would prevent the constructive orientation that Sidney Jourard describes as "serial polygamy with the same spouse." By serial polygamy Jourard means the reinvention of marriage by the same husband and the same wife. Impasse is struggled with; the old union dies, and a new union is born—between the same two people. The fallacy in traditional marital relationships has been the assumption that people do not really change. While a case may be made for a person's "core" personality as relatively consistent over time, it is also true that we are always changing, growing, reverting, regressing, progressing, or discovering. Hence, it is totally unrealistic to think that two adults should be confined to the (implicit) contract they both agreed upon at the time of marriage. What Jourard calls reinventing marriage is perhaps better described as "redefining," "recreating," or "revitalizing" the present relationship. Redefinition (by that name or by any other name) needs to take place if the marriage is to be a self-actualizing contract for both spouses. Redefinition is an ongoing occurrence; the two partners are committed to the fulfillment of each other and to the fulfillment of their relationship.

Perhaps redefinition springs from a certain set of values. If the highest values held by a couple are aliveness, creativity, authenticity, vitality, health, lovingness, intimacy (sexual and spiritual), and productivity, then redefinition will come as naturally as day and night. On the other hand, if the most basic values are loyalty to past traditions, conformity to societal expectations, ancestral beliefs and mores, and the authoritarian triad of obedience, respect, and duty to one's parents, then redefinition will be difficult at best.

The Residual

What remains after we have torn down our defenses in a marital relationship? What is left upon which to build? The residual remains after the tearing-down process has taken from us our defense mechanisms and our safety devices. The residual is the foundation beneath the taboos and myths in which we took refuge; it is the sperm and ovum which united to conceive the marriage in the first place. Many marriages have far more going for them than the partners permit themselves to see. People seem to celebrate failure and divorce by pointing out the things that went wrong—the incompatibilities, the impasses, the drudgery, the disillusionment. Yet at the conception of each union there are legitimate hopes, dreams, and possibilities; there are trust and love, commitment and spontaneity.

What is love's legacy? What is the residual we seek to uncover and recreate? What is it to which we seek to give vitality and fulfillment? The question may be approached in several ways but the underlying assumptions are much the same. Monogamy as it has evolved in our society has tended to work against the development of individual potential; it has tended to create rigidity, joylessness, frustration, monotony, boredom, hostility, anger, and a pleasureless sexuality.

Perhaps the initial step in the direction of change is to opt for a continuing revision and updating of the marital contract. Herbert Otto has spoken of the "New Marriage," which is a framework for developing personal potential. In another article Otto asks, "Has Monogamy Failed?" Both articles are variations on the theme of monogomous marital enrichment:

> Has monogamy failed? My answer is "no." Monogamy is no longer a rigid institution, but instead an evolving one. There is a multiplicity of models and dimensions that we have not even begun to explore. It takes a certain amount of openness to become aware on not only an intellectual level but a feeling level that these possibilities face us with a choice. Then it takes courage to recognize that this choice in a measure represents our faith in monogamy. Finally, there is the fact that every marriage has a potential for greater commitment, enjoyment, and communication, for more love, understanding and warmth. Actualizing this potential can offer new dimensions in living and new opportunities for personal growth, and can add new strength and affirmation to a marriage.

Virginia Satir has also spoken to the issue of "marriage as a Human-Actualizing Contract." Another way of presenting this view would be to advocate the ongoing process of defining the relationship. There are times when marriages peak; there are times when these same marriages are void of vitality and joy. We have noted that the actual wedding ceremony can be an open invitation to decay and stagnation, simply because the two people now legally possess and are possessed by each other. Duty, responsibility, and obligation, however important and necessary, have a repressive intonation and may be cited as the reason for loss of spontaneity in marriage.

Growth centers and organizations for actualizing human potential have sprung up all over the United States. The basic purpose of these centers is to help individuals and couples break out of the binds which constrict the full expression of oneself. In order to do this there must be a willingness to experience some discomfort as one permits the breaking down of barriers and defenses against intimacy. Reawakening of the senses, openness to others, spontaneity in self-expression and honesty in interpersonal relationships are encouraged, usually in a group context.

The history and background of such centers is a story within itself. Our concern here, however, is to suggest that traditional monogamy is still the overwhelming marital pattern within our society and that much can be attempted to revitalize and to actualize the marital relationship.

Yet in defining marriage as a "human actualizing contract" it is all too easy to fall back into the same trap as before—the trap of excessive and unrealistic expectations. Just as romantic and societal expectations often lead one to post-honeymoon disillusionment, so also expectations regarding marriage as the heart-bed of psychic intimacy may lead a couple to discontent and disillusionment. Is it possible for a couple to have peak intimacy experiences day-in/day-out? If the answer to this question is "no," why do we conclude that something is wrong with the marriage? Richard Farson has pointed out that discontent in "good" marriages arises from several sources, including heightened expectations about sexual and psychic intimacy, comparison with other marriages, and comparison of the marriage with itself in its better moments. Farson says: ". . . probably the most important source of discontent is the comparison of the marriage with its own good moments in the present. . . . These peaks, however, are inevitably followed by valleys. Couples lucky enough to have these moments find themselves unable to sustain them and, at the same time, unable to settle for ordinary moments. They want life to be a constantly satisfying state. But to be a constant state, to avoid the valleys, it is necessary to eliminate the peaks. . . . Good marriages are not like that, but the price they exact in depression and pain is high."

If the residual, the core of the marriage, is to be secured and cultivated it must be tempered with realistic expectations, "realistic" meaning what is considered real in line with what we know about human life through experiences and the testimony of others, including historical and literary confirmation. For example, when Farson speaks of "peaks" and "valleys," he is giving witness to a basic human experience. An idealistic person might say, "Why? Why can't life be filled with peaks?" A pessimistic person may claim in the name of "realism" that Farson is wrong because "life is basically valley after valley with no peaks."

We cannot secure our residual, let alone cultivate it, until we are able to see through the self-destructive tendencies born of unrealistic expectations. As illustration consider the rather common occurrence of a meeting between two strangers on a bus or plane. In a matter of an hour or two, such relationships often yield deep-felt emotions and problems from one or both of the travelers. A common reaction to such an experience is the wish that one could attain and remain in such an intimate level with one's own spouse. But is this a realistic expectation? Can a married couple live day-in and day-out in such an emotionally charged manner? In the majority of bus-airplane instances, the two people involved will never see each other again . . . and they know it! And if, perchance, they do meet again, the odds are that any effort to re-create a semblance of the intimate moment of the past will end in frustration and disappointment.

Thus, the residual has great potential only if it is intellectually and emotionally placed in a context of balance and perspective. If, as we discussed earlier, variety is a desirable quality in human experience, then it follows that we would do well to welcome variety in the range and type of marital relationships as well as in any particular relationship. A couple may achieve a great deal of variety in their sexual relationship, but even this desirable quality will not fill the need for variety in meeting other basic needs.

The residual is, in short, more than enough to sustain the great majority of monogamous and sexually exclusive marriages providing the residual is placed within a congruency of life values and goals which form a configuration. Once the romantic expectations stemming from the media and the conditioning process of socialization are seen through and placed in perspective, there follows the challenge of seeing through the double-bind created by unrealistically expecting our mate to fill all our basic human needs. Let us hope for meaningful peak experiences between husband and wife, yet without either feeling guilty or apologetic about the transitoriness of such experiences. In a very real sense they are meaningful *because* they are transitory.

There are those who will claim that the residual can survive only if the marriage includes the standard of sexual permissiveness. The argument is advanced that if we embrace the value of psychic intimacy with people other than the spouse, we therefore should also embrace sexual intimacy with people other than the spouse. O K for those who so define it. I do not think it is either necessary or logical. What is often desired in sex is an affirmation of the self by the other. It is no more logical to conclude that psychic intimacy must culminate in sexual intimacy than it is to conclude that sexual intimacy must culminate in psychic intimacy. A fair statement about the relationship of psychic and sexual intimacy seems to be this: sometimes and in some situations psychic intimacy progresses into sexual intimacy and in other situations psychic intimacy is destroyed by sexual intimacy. Sexual intimacy often creates only an illusory facsimile of psychic intimacy; that is, when one fails to experience psychic intimacy he deludes himself into believing that sexual intimacy will be an effective substitute. Significantly, a common manner of seduction depends on the manipulation of desires for psychic intimacy as a means of achieving sexual intimacy.

What Price Fulfillment?

The quest for fulfillment comes at a price, both for the individual and the marital relationship. The price is paid in the form of pain and discomfort, the slow process of learning new patterns, the break with security mechanisms, or the parting with games and strategies calculated to manipulate or dominate the other.

The growth toward maturity, toward self-acceptance, toward learning to deal with conflict and unlearning standards of perfection are four specific areas of growth which exact a toll upon those who would build on the residual in their quest for marital fulfillment within a monogamous relationship.

The maturity required to make it together reveals itself most forcefully in the ability to see through the illusions of romantic, societal, and parental expectations of marriage. Further, maturity is manifested in the ability of a person to make viable assessments of the expectations posited for a "human actualizing contract." The more we thirst for the peak experiences the greater will be our discontent with the "down" experiences. This discontent is predictable and inescapable to the extent that we fail to see through the dynamics that we allow to play through us.

Marital fulfillment requires, probably above all other qualities, the grace of self-acceptance. The self-accepting person is the one who is best able to recognize his own foibles and hang-ups without becoming defensive or unnecessarily compulsive in compensating for them. Consequently, he is most free to analyze societal and cultural data and to consciously decide his own level of content and/or discontent. There is little doubt, either experimentally or clinically, that the self-accepting person is best qualified to accept others, most especially his mate.

The myth of conflict-free interpersonal relationships has been treated in an earlier chapter. Suffice it to reiterate that acceptance and confrontation of conflict are essential requirements for human growth and development. Once we accept conflict as an amoral fact of life, we are in a position to be done with old patterns and voices that told us we would not be loved if we expressed our deepest and innermost feelings. In dispelling one myth, we run the risk of falling prey to another myth— the myth that all conflict is resolvable. It is not! To believe otherwise is to add to one's own level of discontent.

Perhaps the greatest price to be paid in building on the residual is the death of perfection. I can hear murmurs and protests to the effect that this villain had been put to death years ago (or at least several pages or chapters back). Maybe so. Likely not! The perfectionist tendency has been reinforced by one's family, competition with siblings, the educational establishment (nursery through postdoctoral), the mass media, and the ecclesiastical establishment. Perfectionism may have been conquered in one or several areas of one's life without having been recognized in one's marital expectations. The purists will maintain that to settle for anything less than perfection is a cop-out or a compromise, yet perfection and the perfectionist fallacy have, in my opinion, been among the greatest curses with which mankind has been historically enslaved. The fallacy of perfectionism is its tacit promise that we will one day be satisfied, when at last we reach the coveted goal. Even if the perfectionist claims he is realistic and that he knows the goal is unattainable but that the meaning is in the striving, he deceives himself precisely because he is unable to live in the present. How can he? He doesn't accept the present without superimposing his own qualifications and improvements. He is then thrust into the future—where all perfectionists dwell—and hence, happiness itself becomes part and parcel of the future illusion.

Perhaps the price of fulfillment can best be described by people who are endeavoring to pay it.

Case Study

Gene and Dorothy have been married for five years. They have two daughters, ages 2½ and 4. Gene is self-employed as a proprietor of a sporting goods store. Dorothy is not gainfully employed. Gene and Dorothy record their own story a year after the conclusion of a marital enrichment therapy group in which they participated for twelve weeks.

Gene: I find it hard to think on paper. The past two years have been a whirlwind. First, I was convinced our marriage was a big mistake. I was positive another woman would be much better for me than Dorothy. I have no idea of which "other woman"—I just had the constant thought that there must be a better match available somewhere and somehow. Then I reluctantly joined the enrichment group. I hated it at first. I went more out of appeasement and curiosity than for insight and enrichment. The first couple of meetings left me cold. I know I had a chip on my shoulder. I was critical of everyone in the group, which made me feel quite superior. At the fourth meeting Dorothy put herself in the center ring. I thought, "Oh boy, here she goes in her 'Let's get Gene' game. She didn't. Instead she talked only of her own problems she had been struggling with and how when she was starved for intimacy she would shut people out. I don't recall much else except that whatever she said changed my attitude toward the whole enrichment group. I no longer felt defensive or superior. Slowly I began to participate in the discussions and exchanges. It was very uncomfortable at times, especially when the group members moved in on me and pinned me up against the wall. I guess one thing led to another and I began to get introspective. Then for a while I withdrew into myself. I felt scared and tense. A few more weeks and I began to look forward to the weekly session. My feelings about Dorothy were different now. It wasn't any great turnabout or electrifying romantic episode, just a warm feeling within myself toward both me and her. Somehow I knew that I had been kidding myself about making it with someone else. Sure others might attract me, but now I began to feel that if I couldn't make it with Dot I probably could not make it with anyone. I also began to feel happier within myself, sort of like "a welcome home to me by me."

The year since has not been easy. Many times I have felt despair. It used to be I never felt despair—I guess because I ran away from it. My feelings toward Dorothy have been deeper than ever although, and I can't make much sense of this, we seem to fight a lot more. I express my feelings and so does Dot. This isn't very comfortable. Sometimes things get worked out. Sometimes they don't. I can only say that even though we fight more there is something better between us than ever before.

Dorothy: It is a strange feeling to put something down on paper that you have carried around within yourself for so long. I don't know where to start. I was becoming more and more dissatisfied with my marriage. Everything seemed to be turning in on me. I felt Gene no longer loved me or even cared. The two girls seemed to occupy most of my time and for a while I guess I escaped unpleasant feelings by concerning myself exclusively with them. The more I allowed the girls to possess me the more I felt resentful toward them. I became depressed and irritable to such an extent that I started to look for help. That's how we eventually ended up in the enrichment group. Gene was against it from the start, but I sensed that unless we did something it would all break up anyway.

The group and I got along fine for a while. I really ate it up. It was obvious that Gene didn't share my enthusiasm. About the fifth or sixth week I started to sour on the group. I felt they were merciless toward me; I felt attacked and I wanted to get out. About the same time Gene started to show signs of interest in the whole thing. So there we were, me against and him for! One night I really opened myself up only to be criticized instead of pitied. It took awhile, about three weeks, for me to look at some of the things people had said to me. More than anything I was wanting group support for my self-pity. They would sooner crucify you than give you pity. My resentment grew worse until one night I told the group how I resented their not giving me pity. Someone in the group looked me straight in the eyes and said: "Pity! Why do you insist that we feel sorry for you?" I started to cry and, of course, I had no answer. When the group ended, I felt about half. It was Gene who benefited most from the group. Since that time things have been better. I seem to be able to live with myself now without being so uptight and depressed. I can't say that the situation has changed any: Gene still works long hours and the girls are still very demanding. Yet there is a difference. I no longer resent the situation, you know what I mean— Gene, his job, the kids, the routine. I don't like lots of things, but I no longer hide my frustration or pretend to myself that some day everything will be different. It's easier for me to express myself to Gene, and when the girls expect too much of me I no longer feel guilty about drawing a line. I have learned to ignore some of the housework that used to bug me, and I've become interested in antiquing furniture of all things. I believe in our marriage more than ever, but it's not a blind belief. I guess what I'm trying to say is that life is better for all of us even though we have the usual stresses and strains. I guess I grew up a little and now I don't need to escape into my "self-pity chamber" as I've come to call it."

This case study illustrates the necessity for the death of perfection. The perfectionist fallacy leads couples to expect the impossible of each other and thus to deny each other's humanity and personhood. As reflected in their forthright honesty with each other in conflictual situations and in their efforts to cut through some of their divisive tactics, Gene and Dorothy are beginning to mature in their relationship. The price of fulfillment does not seem to be cheap; the way is sometimes quite painful and usually uncomfortable. Yet those who travel the road seem to return a unanimous verdict that the price is well worth it.

---

*Men and women share many of the same
crisis periods, but they don't react to
them in the same way. The woman who
understands the differences can help her
husband to cope—and strengthen her
marriage in the process.*

UNDERSTANDING THE CRISES
IN MEN'S LIVES

by Fredelle Maynard

Last year I went to a wedding that turned into a situation comedy: the
groom didn't show up; neither did the bride. Some weeks later, after
the couple had been quietly married by a justice of the peace, we talked
about their eleventh-hour panic. "I guess the same thought hit each
of us at the last minute," the bride said, *"Maybe I've chosen the wrong
person."*

Her husband registered astonishment and dismay. "Was *that* what
scared you? I never had any doubts about *you*. For me the question was,
Do I really want to get married at all?"

This sort of basic difference—and misunderstanding—is common. Because women share most major life crises with men, they tend to assume
that pressures (and resolutions) are the same for both sexes. Nothing
could be further from the truth. Even sexual intercourse, the most intimately shared of human experiences, has a different meaning for men
than for women. So have marriage, parenthood, the choice of a career
and retirement. If a woman is to cope effectively with the problems of
men who are important to her—husband, father, son, lover—she needs
to understand what precipitates crisis in a man's life and how to react
to it.

For a man, crisis usually occurs within a competitive framework.
Whether the situation involves making money or making love, a man's
apt to ask himself, "How do I look? Am I measuring up?" Getting the
girl, winning the promotion, fathering a successful family—all these be-

Reprinted by permission of *Women's Day Magazine* and Curtis Brown, Ltd. Copyright © 1972 by
Fawcett Publications, Inc.

come ways of proving masculinity. Why men feel driven to prove their masculinity is a complicated question. Some psychologists insist that anatomy is destiny—that male competitiveness is rooted in physiology. Others explain it as the result of cultural pressures from a society that says, "Push harder, you're a man."

Both arguments contain a measure of truth. American society has always glorified a rugged frontier image of maleness (rough, tough, striving) and pushed boys to perform. Although the unisex drift of youth and the consciousness-raising of women's liberation in recent years have modified the old male-female stereotypes, the facts of biology still force men into a special sort of competition. A girl doesn't have to *prove* she's a woman; menstruation, childbirth and menopause do that. A boy's biological processes provide no such dramatic and absolute evidence of sexual identity. He must demonstrate capacity, show—by doing, achieving, winning—that he's a real man. No wonder the rate of suicides and mental breakdowns is far higher for men than for women. From the cradle to the grave, males are involved in what social critic Paul Goodman calls "an endless compulsion to prove potency and demand esteem."

The Marriage Crisis

One of the most severe crises—if not the first—occurs when a man gets married. Marriage is a crisis for women, too, but the shock is generally greater, the apprehensions more profound, for men. In part, this is because boys aren't groomed for marriage the way girls are. More important is the fact that the traditional role of provider weighs heavily on a man. "I feel tied down," or "Being suddenly responsible—that's scary" are typical comments.

"After we got back from our honeymoon," one young husband told me, "I sat with my head in my hands. I wanted Janet. I still do. But I felt like the walls were closing in. Already we owe thousands—on a car, furniture, the whole bit. I see myself in ten years with a mortgage, a power lawn mower and kids that need braces. It's like *my* life is over."

Not having thought much about marriage before it happens, men are peculiarly vulnerable to shock. This seems to be true even if a couple has lived together before making it official. A permanent arrangement introduces a whole new game. A man can't live for the moment anymore; he has to think about the future. He needs insurance. His old friendships are threatened. Relationships with the bride's parents (or his own, for that matter) suffer new strains.

Studies show that men are more likely than women to be disappointed with their spouses. This is due, in part, to what one researcher calls "the sheer naiveté with which men enter marriage." Maybe his bride doesn't, as in the ancient joke, take out her dentures and remove her wooden leg at night, but he may be amazed to discover how much art goes into the "natural" look. (Rollers to *straighten* hair?) Losses tend to be particularly great in the area of shared activities. Once she loved football games. She wasn't faking, exactly; she just wanted to be with him. Now that she can be with him most of the time, she admits she never cared much for football . . . or bowling. Or rock climbing. In a study of marriage adjustment problems, sociologist Charles Hobart concludes that post-marital disillusionment is significantly stronger for males. This is especially true in matters involving neatness, money and savings, attitudes towards husband-wife roles, having children—and the acceptance of limitations on personal freedom.

Obviously no single all-purpose formula will solve all these problems. It takes many years, many kinds of adjustments, to make a marriage. But if a man suffers a post-wedding sense of confinement, a woman can ease tensions by resisting any temptation to fence him in socially, sexually or financially. Sulking if a husband wants to go hunting with his pals, ostentatiously taking possession when attractive women sidle up to him at parties, persuading him into a car or a stereo or a vacation he can't afford—all these make a man wonder why he gave up the bachelor life. So does the sudden metamorphosis of a capable, self-supporting girl into a delicate flower who must be supported for the rest of her days. "Penny's a first-rate teacher," a disgruntled husband told me. "She had tenure, a secure future. I have this lousy job in a bookstore—and what I really want to do is write. I've got a novel I would finish in six months if I could work at it full-time. But right after we got married, Penny resigned. She want's to have a child. My God! I hardly make enough to support myself."

The Career Crisis

Many intelligent women fail to understand the crisis a man faces when he commits himself to a lifework. "I don't see why Jeff agonizes so," a young friend said of her fiancé's indecision. "He's got his degree and an offer from a good law firm. To me, that's as simple as nuts and bolts." What is not simple, from a man's point of view, is finding a career that will satisfy two very different goals: the need to make a good living and the desire to find a good life.

"If I don't pull down a five-figure income I'm not much of a man," a business school graduate told me. "So maybe I take this job as a catalog copywriter. It pays ten thousand. But then I spend my days writing blurbs for gag cocktail napkins and dog deodorants. What kind of man does *that* make me?"

The dilemma is genuine. Money carries special significance in our society as a symbol of manliness and power. A woman can lessen the pressures on her husband by letting him know that *she* doesn't judge a man by his earning power, but it's not easy to overcome accepted middle-class values. And even if a man does *not* feel the need to earn a lot of money, he's still faced with the problem of finding meaningful work. Where does a man look for significant, satisfying work in the modern world?

Many of the traditionally manly occupations have been wiped out by complicated machines that not only eliminate the need for muscular strength, but may also require little or no supervision. Business is no longer a proving ground for heroes. Instead of making all the major decisions for his own small shop or company, today's businessmen may be limited to action taken by committee. Even executives with six-figure incomes have to clear their decisions with someone higher up. The professions, too, have been fragmented in a way that reduces the sense of real achievement. Where the old-time general practitioner pulled teeth, performed appendectomies and delivered babies, a specialist in 1972 may "do" nothing but noses. Many lawyers never set foot in court, and an architect, if he's part of a team, may never see the building site.

When work is devalued—made impersonal, automatic—men suffer in a very special way. As anthropologist Margaret Mead reminds us, women can acquire a sense of "irreversible achievement" simply by bearing children, but men have no alternative; they must realize themselves through the work they do. If that work, whatever it is, has no meaning to the man himself, other things lose their value, too. I am reminded of a marriage that survived the strains of a wife's supporting her husband through college and graduate school, then broke up when he graduated. The reason? Having trained for a career in engineering, the young man decided to become a carpenter. He derived more satisfaction from working with his hands than from working with plans and specifications.

"It doesn't make any sense," the wife told me. "All these years I've lived in crummy apartments and worked at menial jobs. I haven't complained because I always thought that when Rob graduated we could begin to live—have a baby, make a real home. Now he wants to throw away everything we've worked for." To this young woman, work is a secondary pursuit—something you do in order to make other things possible. To Rob, as to most men, it's an expression and test of personal capacity, a major condition of self-esteem. If Rob's wife had just understood her husband's need to find work—and a life—that made sense to him, she might have saved her marriage.

The Parenthood Crisis

In a comprehensive study of fatherhood, sociologist Leonard Benson concludes that men derive relatively less satisfaction from parenthood than women. This is not surprising. Males are neither biologically nor socially prepared for the experience as females are. Men do not generally long for progeny in the abstract (an exception being during wartime, when children promise some form of survival). Sex researcher Albert Kinsey found, among his subjects, that though most women thought marriage without children would be incomplete, many men had no such feeling. A woman's hormonal cycle, from menarche to menopause, is a continuous readying for motherhood. A man experiences no comparable rhythm. And where a woman from the moment of impregnation is caught up in an absorbing physical process, the father-to-be remains a spectator to the drama he initiated. Fatherhood is simply a less dramatic, less intensely cultivated role than motherhood. There is also far greater discontinuity between the husband-father roles than between the wife-mother roles. After the first surge of phallic pride—"I did it!"—an expectant father may feel like a man who started a corporation and ended up as stock boy.

"First pregnancy," says psychiatrist Stanley Eldred, "is a nine-month crisis. Thank God it takes nine months, because a child's coming requires enormous changes in a couple's ways of relating to each other." Even before the child arrives, a man faces difficult adjustments. While his wife dreams happily of an infant to feed and cuddle, he envisions new financial burdens. She looks forward to being part of a family, he dreads the loss of freedom and privacy. Sometimes a pregnant wife loses interest in sex, or fears, unreasonably, that "it might hurt the baby." Or the husband may be put off by milky breasts and a protuberant stomach. If a man has not worked through his ambivalent feelings toward his own mother he may be uncomfortable about a mother-figure as a sex partner.

The actual process of childbirth is traumatic for many men, evoking feelings of anxiety, helplessness and guilt. Then the baby comes home, and no man is ever prepared for that. Where there were two, now there are three—and relationships of three tend to break down two against one. However careful a wife tries to be about her husband's sensitivities, she can't escape the infant's urgent needs. Her day is now planned around a stranger's eating and sleeping habits. The once-gay companion to her husband may appear to be an exhausted, preoccupied caretaker.

In a study of male attitudes towards impending fatherhood, R. J. McCorkel found essentially three different reactions. Romantic men approached fatherhood in a spirit of self-absorption and awe; they saw it in terms of putting aside their carefree youth, accepting adult responsibility. Career-oriented men reacted to fatherhood as a burden interfering with professional advancement. (One, speaking of a projected trip, said, "It's our last chance to be human beings. After this we're going to be parents.") Family-oriented husbands welcomed their responsibilities as conferring a new and valued status. Such men identified closely with all stages of the pregnancy, were excited by growing evidence of the child's realness ("it moved!"), and had completed some of the necessary adjustments before the actual birth.

For all first-time fathers, though, the period following a child's birth constitutes a prolonged period of strain. Sociologist E. H. Dyer found that the most frequent crisis involved lack of sleep: 50 percent of the new fathers he questioned reported sheer physical weariness. An equal number spoke of difficulty in accepting new responsibilities and adjusting to infant routines. The amount of work required and getting used to being tied down were subsidiary complaints. As one would expect, Dyer found the degree of crisis closely related to marriage stability. Where the parents were educated, not too young, married at least three years and reasonably close in age and background, the male crisis was notably less severe.

Fathers who have taken a prenatal training course, like Lamaze, usually adjust more speedily to the realities of life with baby, but any man can be helped through those first difficult months by an understanding wife. If a new father is given an active role in infant care, he's less likely to feel left out. (Helping with laundry does not count as infant care, but holding a restless baby before feeding and burping him afterwards can create a bond.) Above all, a man needs to be reassured that he has not been supplanted in his wife's affections. When the question, "If you were on a sinking ship and could save your spouse or your child, which would you choose?" was raised at a party recently, most of the guests insisted the child came first. Then a new young mother, still at the stage where she telephoned the baby-sitter every hour, spoke up, "Maybe I'm selfish," she said, "I'd save John. We could always have another child, but what would my life be without him?" Whether this young woman really knew how she would behave in an emergency is irrelevant. Looking at her husband, visibly haggard from all those night feedings, I knew she had said exactly what he needed to hear at that moment.

The Mid-life Crisis

A definitive turning point for men occurs in mid-life—somewhere between thirty-five and forty-five. Although males experience no physiological change as dramatic as the female menopause, changes in hormones secreted by the endocrine glands do produce distressing effects. When he reaches his forties, even an athletic man may have trouble keeping his weight down and his stomach flat. He doesn't sleep as well as he used to. His hair may begin to thin. He hasn't the old get-up-and-go, and—more than likely—he worries about his virility. Is he really as good in bed as he used to be? Do worldliness and distinguished gray hair make up for a loss in sheer physical magnetism? In older patriarchal societies, age could be welcomed as a badge of status; in present-day America, the cult of youth and physical beauty makes signs of aging an occasion for fear, if not downright panic. The loss of youthful attractiveness can be even more painful for a woman, of course, but it's a mistake to discount the effect it has on a man. Each can be a great source of reassurance to the other in this area.

Any marked physical decline is often accompanied by a new, sharper awareness of death. "This sounds childish," a man in his forties told me, "but up until recently I used to think *If I die* . . . Now I say, *When I die.* It's real." Reading the obituary of a colleague—"Forty-six! Good God, younger than I!"—produces chill premonitions. The death of parents, especially a father, has powerful reverberations. It suggests, says Douglas Derrer formerly of Yale's mid-life research group, "that there is no longer any generational barrier between a man and the grave." Although women also suffer from the awareness of death, by middle age a woman may have done the things most crucial to her fulfillment. She has married and borne children, for instance. But a man at the same period has an acute sense of life going swiftly by with so much still to do, or left undone.

By the forties, says psychologist Kenneth Keniston, "the thrust of early adulthood is effectively spent. Whether and how well a man is going to 'make it' is usually clear. A kind of summing up may take place, and it is perhaps not an accident that depression is common among men in middle life." The man who chose his high school sweetheart and a career in dentistry twenty years earlier examines both those commitments with a different eye. Fundamental questions arise. What has he accomplished so far? It is what he really wanted? Is he resigned to continuing with the same job, the same marriage, for the rest of his life? What doors are still open? Suddenly the most stable man may be seized with a sense of last chances. John Cassavetes' film *Husbands* vividly portrays one such crisis when three ordinary guys who have "made it" attend the funeral of a friend and acquire a shocking new perspective. "I hate that house," says one. "The only reason I live there is a woman. You know—the legs, the breasts, the mouth." Between them they have three wives, seven kids, six garages, four cars. *And that's all there is; there isn't any more.* The realization sends them off on a frenetic orgy.

The departure of grown children, according to Dr. Gerald Klerman of Harvard Medical School, often necessitates a major renegotiation of the marriage contract. Suddenly a man and wife are thrown together with no one else to talk to or watch television with. A familiar topic of discussion or argument ("We've got to do something about Jill and the car!") has disappeared. Though the "empty nest" syndrome is described as a maternal problem, it's often Father who suffers most when the last teen-ager cleans out his closet and takes down the posters. The child who was Mommy's little girl at six has become Daddy's special pal, and when she goes, he is devastated.

Understandably, sexual proving takes on a new importance. The marital relationship may have dwindled to a Saturday night routine; the once nubile partner is, as one husband put it, "not exactly centerfold material." A standard joke among middle-aged men is, "It's all very well being a grandfather, but who wants to make love to a grandmother?" Plagued with fears of impotence or prostate trouble (the classic midlife complaint), many men turn to extramarital affairs for reassurance.

This is not suprising when you consider how common it is for a man to learn, early in life, to identify with his sex organ and rate himself by its efficiency. And whenever maleness is equated with sexual performance, inability to perform becomes a devastating blow to the self-image. Though women sometimes think of men as perpetually eager for sex, the truth is that ability to sustain an erection is an uncertain gift. One drink too many, a partner's ill-timed remark, the wrong setting, and the most confident Don Juan may suffer humiliating failure. It's a failure that has no real counterpart in women.

Although total impotence is rare, occasional impotence is normal and —judging from novels, movies, sex guides—more common than it used to be. Sometimes the trouble is overearnestness, sex entered into as a competitive sport. (How much? How often? How good?) In that case, all that's needed to solve the problem is an affectionately relaxed attitude, a communicated pleasure in, say, just being *held*. The man who feels truly appreciated at home is less apt to look elsewhere for sexual satisfaction.

Sexual adventuring may, of course, have nonsexual origins. Psychiatrist Herbert Klemme suggests that many middle-aged men who chase girls are really expressing disenchantment with their whole life-style. Unable to accept the fact that they're no longer young, they revert to earlier behavior patterns—much as a four-year-old, unable to accept his babysister, regresses to infant behavior like bed-wetting. "A man in his late thirties," says Dr. Klemme, "may resume behavior more characteristic of his early twenties and enjoy the relative comfort of behavior already learned—perhaps to avoid the pain of advancing to another developmental level." Risk-taking activity—whether the risk involves sex, drinking or business speculation—at least gives the feeling, "I'm a real man."

The mid-life crisis need not end in depression or breakout behavior. Special studies have revealed that reassessment often leads to regeneration, new energies and new commitments—a happy resolution most likely to occur in the context of a live marriage. (Unfortunately, just when a man needs special support, a woman in mid-life, freed from the household ties, may embark on a round of independent activities leaving her husband starved for intimacy, alone.)

The Retirement Crisis

Retirement can be a serious crisis for men. Working women, accustomed to two work roles, generally retire to one of them, but when a man retires, he loses almost all the routine that formerly organized his day. Even in a good marriage, he may find it a strain to be home most of the time—and available for domestic chores. Some degree of social diminishment is inevitable. Few job friendships outlive the job, and membership in a Senior Citizens Club can't replace associations based on shared work experience.

Women, surveys show, generally like the idea of retirement. But though a man of fifty may look forward to it as welcome leisure, he's likely to see it as a sign of declining powers fifteen years later. In one study of job attitudes, employed men were asked whether, if they inherited a considerable fortune, they would continue to work or quit. Sixty-one percent of those between fifty-five and sixty-four said they would continue to work—and 82 percent of those sixty-five and over. The reasons are revealing: "to keep occupied," "gives you a feeling of self-respect," "enjoy the kind of work," *"justifies my existence."* Obviously, work means much more than livelihood for most men. "It is through the producing role," conclude the authors of this study, "that most men tie into society . . . and most men find the producing role important for maintaining their sense of well-being."

For approximately forty-five years in American society, a man defines himself through his work. He is what he does. Except in very special circumstances he doesn't identify himself as "Larry's father" or "Susan's husband." He says, "I'm a computer programmer," or "I'm a plumber." Throughout this period he's expected to compete, to overcome obstacles and move steadily forward. Suddenly he's sent home with an engraved punch bowl and told to take it easy. No wonder so many men suffer "retirement shock." It isn't that the retiree has nothing to do. Most men, released from a nine-to-five routine, find ways to fill their time. But paneling the family room—when the family has gone—is not real work to a surgeon. The salesman who's been negotiating big deals finds no similar challenge on the golf course. Whatever a man's former job, he misses the distinction it conferred (and, often, suffers at the thought that someone else now performs *his* work).

For both sexes, certain moments in the life cycle bring conflict and anxiety. Nothing will change that. But men and women can help each other to cope—and grow through coping successfully—by an understanding and sensitive response to need. "Freedom to choose what and how to be, as male or female . . . this is what each sex should make possible *for* the other sex," writes Dr. Mary Calderone, director of the U.S. Sex Information and Education Council. "Women will have to make the first gestures on behalf of men's liberation, for at this moment men are still entrapped in their own centuries-old power play. But women can afford such generosity, for women have forged ahead of men at other, deeper levels. The obligation is on us, as women, to ease the way for men to those deeper levels of relationships where power is powerless and the truest satisfactions as human beings are to be found.

"Then the power questions won't matter at all, nor even exist anymore."

part
Parent-Child FOUR
Relationships

Parenthood has been described in a variety of ways throughout the centuries. Many myths abound about the joys of being a parent. Nevertheless some social and behavioral scientists have described parenthood as a crisis experience. Many couples discover that their relationship changes drastically when the first child enters the picture. As children grow they take on their own unique personalities and develop their own identity. This process can be very difficult for parents, especially when few people have any truly relevant training for parenthood. How does a child learn self-responsibility? How does a child learn a sense of autonomy? To what extent should children be permitted to question, rebutt, and perhaps even contradict their parents' statements, edicts, and judgements? In our culture, parenting receives a great deal of attention, especially in the middle class, and yet this is precisely where we find the greatest amount of guilt in parents. Perhaps parents are guilt ridden about the wrong things, for example, instead of guilt over children who seem difficult, stubborn, and recalcitrant, the parents might be better off coming to terms with their own modeling behavior in these same areas.

Articles in this section are concerned with some of the realities of parenthood and attempt to dispel some of the myths. In "Let 'Em Fight: How to Rear Kids and Stay Sane," Mark R. Arnold helps parents realize the potential children have for resolving their own conflict and struggles. When parents realize that the goals of parenthood are to work themselves out of a job as parents, they will relinquish power used to control their children. In the process the children will learn what is involved in growing from dependent to independent to later interdependent relationships as adults.

Behavior modification is the basic theme in the article by Alice Lake, "How To Teach Your Child Good Habits." Persons continue unrewarding and destructive behavior because there is a payoff. When the payoff is no longer present, frequently the behavior will greatly diminish. Critics of behavior modification, according to the author, point out that the technique is superficial; that behavior therapy fails when problems are complex; and that there is something distasteful about the emphasis on material rewards for children and other patients: it smacks of bribery.

Barbara Wyden in "The Difficult Baby is Born That Way" helps parents develop a perspective on the realities of why some children are difficult. The reason is not that something is wrong with parents or baby. Their child is a unique individual, and blaming their child or themselves for this fact is self-defeating for parents and children.

Parents frequently blame themselves for their child's disposition and choose to feel quite guilty. Some children are born difficult. The baby will eventually adapt if the parents are consistent, firm, and loving.

"What's A Mother To Do?" describes the dilemma in which mothers find themselves today as they attempt to sort out the vast material relating to child rearing practices. The question most frequently raised by mothers is, "Which way is right?" In this article the author briefly reviews the history of child rearing practices in our own country. As one moves from the United States to other countries of the world, the diversity in child rearing practices becomes even more widespread.

LET 'EM FIGHT: HOW TO
REAR KIDS AND STAY SANE

by Mark R. Arnold

Stan and Joanne Kaplan are suburbanites in their late 20s whose three small children fight continually. Danny, 5, is "an absolute tyrant," complains his despairing mother, and Michael and David, 3-year-old twins, meekly submit to his thrashings. Punishing Danny prevents fights for only a few minutes, and intervening only provokes a shouting match that upsets everyone.

A familiar problem? Yes indeed. So the Kaplans brought their problem to an unusual family-education center here, and they took home some unconventional advice:

If the children want to fight, let them. Leave the room if it bothers you. Don't mix in. Make them settle their spats themselves. And stick to your guns.

Behind the advice lies this provocative theory: Parents reward misbehavior by entering their children's conflicts. Withhold attention, and the misbehavior may diminish.

That reasoning may mystify many, but it makes perfect sense to the growing legion of parents who have become child-rearing disciples of 74-year-old Chicago psychiatrist Rudolf Dreikurs. A Viennese immigrant with a thick accent and "little old wine maker" looks, Dreikurs believes that the facade of harmony in most American families masks a bitter struggle for power. As he sees it, this dreary scenario is acted out daily in millions of American homes:

Parents seek to impose their will on their children.

The children resist.

The result is stalemate, leaving all involved angry, guilt-ridden, and frustrated.

A student of the late Alfred Adler, Dreikurs offers parents "a democratic alternative" method of child-rearing, one that increasing numbers

Mark R. Arnold, "Let 'em Fight: How to Rear Kids and Stay Sane," *The National Observer*, January 1, 1972. Reprinted by permission from *The National Observer*. © 1972, Dow Jones and Co., Inc.

of Americans are practicing. In the past five years, Dreikurs-oriented "parent study groups," each enrolling from a few dozen to several hundred parents, have sprung up in two dozen cities. They use Dreikurs' primer, *Children: The Challenge,* as a text.

Dreikurs' views are controversial, for he argues that family harmony can stem only from parent-child relationships based on equality and mutual respect. Freely translated, that means adults must voluntarily relinquish power over their children's lives. "In a democracy," asserts Dreikurs, "you can no longer 'make' a child do anything for very long. Force simply does not work. What you must do is win his cooperation."

His techniques for winning cooperation are ingenious, and families psychologically able to practice them insist that they work. Dreikurs calls for adults to extricate themselves from power conflicts, let children accept the consequences of their own acts, and—most difficult of all—keep cool amid stress.

This Is a Movement

Here in Minneapolis 5,000 parents have taken the basic 10-week Dreikurs child rearing course since a local enthusiast began promoting the doctor's doctrine in 1966. Almost every night 40 or more parents and professionals (social workers, psychologists, teachers, clergymen, counselors) attend group counseling sessions at one of eight nonprofit family-education centers run by the four-year-old Alfred Adler Institute of Minnesota here. In addition, Dr. Dreikurs' videotaped child-rearing lectures have been televised here and in 17 other cities.

"We estimate there are 20,000 people engaged in Dreikurs study groups at any one time," says Dr. Walter O'Connell of Houston, president of the American Society of Adlerian Psychologists. "This is a movement that has grown like Topsy, with almost no attention from the media, largely out of a feeling of parental failure."

No one knows precisely how many Americans consider themselves failures as parents, but more than 2,000,000 annually consult local family service agencies. The phenomenal sales of such books as Dr. Benjamin Spock's *Baby and Child Care* (over 22,000,000 copies since 1946) and Haim Ginott's *Between Parent and Child* (over 2,000,000 since 1965) suggest that millions are groping for guideposts to avoid serious mistakes with their kids.

"Parenthood," says Miami psychologist Stephen E. Beltz, author of a new book on child-rearing, "is the one profession entered into by most people with no training at all. It's no wonder so many feel inadequate to the job."

Rousseau's Noble Savages

For those who seek help, there is no end of willing advisers.

At one end of the spectrum, the permissivists believe that creative energies can flower only if young people are allowed to grow up, somewhat like Rousseau's noble savages, free and unfettered.

Few authorities today still counsel letting children do precisely as they please, but some preach an almost-equivalent brand of easygoing parental tolerance. A. S. Neill, founder of Britain's experimental Summerhill school, teaches that "childhood is playhood." He argues in a recent book that, "A wise society would not ask anyone under 20 to do a stitch of work."

At the spectrum's other end, the neoauthoritarians—stern disciplinarians—argue for a return to traditional rewards and punishments. "The Dr. No of child-care authorities," a magazine article recently called Bruno Bettelheim, director of Chicago's Orthogenic School for severely disturbed children and a Vienna-trained Freudian psychoanalyst. The leading neoauthoritarian, Bettelheim argues that children cannot develop self-control and become responsible adults unless they conform to strict rules of conduct and behavior.

"What was wrong with old-fashioned authoritarian education," Bettelheim writes, "was not that it rested on fear. On the contrary, that was what was right with it. What was wrong was that it disregarded the need to modify the fear in a continuous process so that irrational anxiety would steadily give way to more rational motivation."

The behaviorists offer a currently fashionable variation of authoritarian discipline. The foremost behaviorist is Harvard professor B. F. Skinner, author of the Utopian novel *Walden Two* and the newly published *Beyond Freedom and Dignity*. Unlike the Freudians, the behaviorists' concern is not inner feelings, but outward conduct; they advocate conditioning men's reactions to achieve predetermined results.

Two new books apply behavioral technology to child-rearing. They are Stephen E. Beltz's *How to Make Johnny Want to Obey* and John and Helen Krumboltz's *Changing Children's Behavior*. Both books advocate a sophisicated system of bribes and favors, from warm praise to cold cash, to achieve socially desirable conduct in children.

DREIKURS: IN THE MIDDLE

Critics say behavior modification manipulates human beings like animals, and that many young people today are rebelling precisely because they reject the rewards society holds out as the price for their conformity.

Resting somewhere between Summerhill and *Walden Two* is Dreikurs, chief exponent of "democratic" child-rearing. A professor emeritus in psychiatry at the Chicago Medical School and director of the Alfred Adler Institute of Chicago, Dreikurs has preached for more than 30 years that democracy is more than a political arrangement. It is, he says, a value system that profoundly transforms all human relationships.

Most of the nation's conflict—racial, sexual, generational—begins because people cling to traditional authoritarianisms when democracy necessitates shared power, Dreikurs wrote in 1954. "Trying to impose one's will on the child violates respect for him and makes him more rebellious," Dreikurs has written, "while permissiveness and indulgence violates respect for one's self and produces tyrannical children and anarchy in the home."

To the uninitiated, Dreikurs' doctrine is a compendium of puzzling do's and don'ts. *Don't* spank, yell, preach, lecture, command, order, reward or punish, threaten or bribe, or call attention to mistakes. "When something goes wrong, all mothers do the same thing," says Dreikurs. "They talk. Only the kids don't listen; they're mother-deaf. So the mothers yell; the kids are still mother-deaf. That's why we say, before you can do anything, you must learn to keep your mouth shut. Don't talk, act."

And how should parents act?

Dreikurs' first rule is: *Stifle the initial impulse* in dealing with misbehavior. It's usually an emotional reaction, certain to make the situation worse.

Rule No. 2: *Ignore the undue demands of the child.* Misbehavior staged for the parents' benefit is only rewarded when they acknowledge it. Temper tantrums often disappear without an audience.

Rule No. 3: *Withdraw from power struggles.* Children are usually less interested in winning an argument than in provoking one. If parents refuse the bait, they won't be caught. Parents unable to restrain themselves should leave the room. Many Dreikurs parents take refuge in the bathroom.

Choice Is the Key

Rule No. 4: *Use natural and logical consequences,* not punishment. Punishment, says Dreikurs, is "retaliatory, not corrective." Discovering the consequences of their acts teaches youngsters more effectively while also teaching them to exercise responsibility.

A child who won't put his dirty clothes in the hamper needn't be chastised or picked up after, Dreikurs says. Let him go without clean clothes and he will get the message. Clothes not put in the hamper don't get washed. Toys not put away—after one reminder—should disappear. A child who forgets his lunch should go hungry. A mother interrupted by bickering while making supper should patiently explain that she can't function in such an atmosphere. "It's up to you whether you want to fight," she might say, "but if you do, supper will be delayed."

Applying natural and logical consequences makes inevitable Rule No. 5 of "practicing Dreikurs": *Each family member is responsible for his own actions; no one has a right to impose his will on anyone else.* Nor has anyone a right to interfere with another's liberty.

Thus a parent can physically remove a child who disrupts the family's TV watching. The child should be calmly told, however, that he may return when he can conduct himself without interfering with others' rights.

Some footnotes: Dreikurs says parents may intervene if the child is actually or potentially in danger; the parent may remove a toddler playing in the street or permit the toddler to remove himself. Sticks or other dangerous objects may be taken away from children fighting with them. A child who wants to play outside without a coat in cold weather should be allowed to (unless, for example, he has a cold); he'll come in for the coat if he gets cold. But a child who jumps in puddles and comes in with wet feet should not be allowed to go out again; the consequence of being wet is that one needs to dry off.

Dreikurs' critics argue that his "consequences" are little more than punishments in disguise. His followers contend that there are important differences between the two concepts. For one thing, his teachings involve choice: The child can choose to wear the dirty clothes. Too, the consequences are driven home without the rancor or humiliation inherent in punishment.

Traditional Authority Outdated?

"Logical consequences," says Dreikurs, "express the reality of the social order; punishment, the power of a personal authority."

The idea that adults have no right to impose their will on children galls many parents; it undermines the traditional authoritarian family structure. Dreikurs argues, however, that authoritarian relationships can no longer work. In an age when polltakers and style makers court the young, children will not meekly submit. More important, parents relieve themselves of a needless burden by relinquishing authority, Dreikurs says.

Consider Fay Moog, a 38-year-old Minneapolis housewife. She begins a phone conversation by asking if you can hold for a second. Returning, she explains she was busy with her youngest, Donald, a third grader, when the phone rang. She wanted to explain to him why it was important that she take time out for a lengthy phone call. "He's been home from school sick for a week and is getting awfully restless," she adds.

Mrs. Moog, an accountant's wife, says frankly that her three children used to run her ragged. A relative introduced her to Dreikurs' *Children: The Challenge* five years ago, at a time when she felt she needed help. She explains:

"I was having a difficult time with our oldest child, Dana. I was 27 when he was born, and I'm afraid I made him overprotected, spoiled. When the second child came, a girl, I felt, 'That poor first kid,' and I poured it on all the more. By the time he started school he was in trouble. I knew I was the cause of it. I was trying to control everyone's life, but I couldn't do anything about it.

"Dana wouldn't get ready for school, so I would have to dress him. He wouldn't do his work, or play with the other children; he just did whatever he pleased. I asked for a conference with the principal and asked him what I should do. All he could say was I should love [Dana] more. 'For gosh sakes,' I said, 'how can I love him more? I love him so much now.' I was crying all the time, I was so upset. I knew I was ruining the child. I even turned on my husband. He said, 'Quit doing so much for him and let him make his own mistakes.' I'd say, 'Well, you just don't care as much as I care'."

'I Kept My Mouth Shut'

Mrs. Moog began practicing Dreikurs a step at a time.

"The first thing I tried was telling Dana he would have to get himself ready for school. I'd wake him once and get his breakfast. 'The rest,' I said, 'is up to you.' It took all my willpower to stay out of it. I would wash my hair before breakfast and do laundry, anything to keep myself from going to see how he was coming. "The first day he barely made it out the door in time. But I kept my mouth shut."

Now, says Mrs. Moog, the children take care of themselves in the morning. "I never even mention the time. They decide what they're going to wear. If it doesn't look clean or it's a poor match, I might say, 'Why don't you see what it looks like in the mirror?' But if they're satisfied, it's okay with me. The problem before was that I wasn't really doing all those things for the children. I was doing them for myself. It wasn't fair to any of us."

Dreikurs estimates that 75 percent of American families begin the day by fighting. Most fights, he insists, can be avoided by letting children shoulder their own responsibilities.

Dreikurs' child-responsibility theory goes back to his days in pre-Hitler Vienna, where he and Alfred Adler operated a string of child-guidance clinics. Adler broke with Freud in 1911 over Adler's belief—tested in these clinics—that misbehavior stems not from natural instincts, as Freud believed, but from mistaken goals.

In seeking to identify those goals and design therapy to correct them, Dreikurs developed a sympathy for children that sometimes shocked others. Once, substituting for Adler at a lecture, he was asked if he believed in spanking. Yes, he replied: Parents who abuse children should be spanked.

In 1937 Dreikurs fled Hitlerism. Settling in Chicago, he opened his first child-guidance center in 1939; today there are dozens, now called family-education centers, across the nation. There parents, teen-agers, and professionals learn Adlerian techniques of child guidance by observing psychologists counsel families with problems.

At one recent Minneapolis session, Stan and Joanne Kaplan—the young couple with the three warring boys—frankly discussed their problem. About 40 other parents listened intently as they described specific fights and their reactions of frustration and anger. They also noted that the boys rarely hurt one another. The boys were with other youngsters in a playroom nearby, supervised by Barbara Hertzke, 17, a long-haired high-school student whose parents are confirmed Dreikurs followers.

After describing the problem the Kaplans were sent out of the room. Their three boys were brought in. They shifted uncomfortably on folding chairs while group leader Don Crannel, a psychologist and Methodist minister, asked them why they fight.

"Could it be you feel discouraged?" he asked. No response. "Could it be you want to show Mommy she can't boss you around?" A momentary grin crossed the face of Danny, the 5½-year-old "troublemaker."

Crannel later explained that he believes the three boys cooperate to upset their mother. Accordingly, the Kaplans were given some of the hardest advice in the Dreikurs' manifesto: Profess unconcern at fighting.

Family Councils Make Decisions

They also were given advice easier to follow: Encourage the children when they are good. Show them they needn't misbehave to get your undivided attention. Before sending the Kaplans on their way, Crannel reminded them of one of Dreikurs' favorite aphorisms: "Encouragement is to a child as water is to a plant."

Some Dreikurs families also hold weekly family councils, with rotating chairmanships, at which problems are calmly discussed—and resolved either by consensus or not at all. If conflicts develop at these sessions, any family member is free to leave.

Baby-sitter Barbara Hertzke, whose parents began practicing Dreikurs on their four children when she was 12, says her family has a stack of ring binders containing the minutes of five years of family councils. "It's a kind of family history," says her father, Karl Hertzke, a civil engineer. "You can even see how the children have developed handwriting skills over the years."

Few would disagree with Dreikurs' dictum that quiet actions speak louder than angry words. But other elements of his teachings do draw criticism. Some psychologists accuse him of dispensing cookbook recipes for instant action. Behaviorists contend the world is organized around a system of rewards and punishments to which children should learn to adjust.

A Minneapolis mother says she began wondering about the utility of taking refuge in the bathroom—as Dreikurs suggests—when she heard her children discussing *her* behavior. "Don't worry about Mommy," she remembers one child telling another. "She always goes in there when she's mad. But in a few minutes, she'll come out and make us lunch."

Equality Concept Controversial

Most of the fire, though, is directed at Dreikurs' concept of family equality and all that it implies. Traditionalist Bruno Bettelheim, for one, rejects the concept out of hand. A Freudian, Bettelheim thinks that "being pushed back when you push" is essential to developing self-control.

Children require discipline, even desire it, Bettelheim argues. Furthermore, "the idea of democracy within a family simply doesn't apply. Some people—the parents—know more than others—the children; they should therefore be more equal."

"Dreikurs," Bettelheim adds, "would have our kids watching TV eight hours a day if they want, because we couldn't interfere with their freedom to choose."

Dreikurs' followers reply that their children don't watch TV eight hours a day. "Kids given responsibility in a nonthreatening way will not abuse it, as a general rule," says Harold McAbee, an Adlerian psychologist at Bowie, Md., State College and former program director of a Job Corps center.

Emily Geckler, a young Minneapolis mother who practices Dreikurs with her children, says: "I can't say the problems are ever completely solved. But we do have a way of handling them that works for many people."

Behavior therapists have learned that the difference between a well-behaved child and a poorly behaved one may be a parent who knows the difference between a bribe and a reward, a punishment and a penalty.

HOW TO TEACH YOUR CHILD GOOD HABITS

by Alice Lake

Have you ever given your crying child a lollipop? There's probably not a mother who hasn't. The youngster starts to wail over some real or fancied hurt, and you say, "Don't cry. Here's a lollipop." It works. He sucks the candy and stops crying.

But does it really work? Not according to psychologist Ogden R. Lindsley. The next time the child wants a lollipop (or your attention) he knows exactly how to get it—by wailing. You have made the mistake of rewarding the wrong behavior.

Dr. Lindsley belongs to a new group of doctors called behavior therapists. These psychiatrists and psychologists use principles of learning developed in laboratory experiments with animals to help human beings overcome persistent neurotic fears and habits. Once derided as "rat psychology," behavior therapy is now recognized as a promising new approach to many emotional ills.

Behavior therapists do not aim to change human personality, but only to alter neurotic behavior. Within this limited goal they claim these credits:

curing adults of fears that made a burden of daily living; developing self-control in wildly aggressive children; curbing bizarre behavior in schizophrenics; quickening learning in retarded youngsters. Behavioral techniques also show promise of luring autistic children out of a self-imposed silent retreat. Hitherto considered hopelessly resistant to treatment, many of these children had been doomed to life in institutions.

In addition, behavioral methods are being used to curb such minor but irritating childhood habits as tantrums, bed-wetting, thumb-sucking; to help adults stop compulsive eating; to encourage husbands and wives to communicate more honestly with each other. Finally, behavior therapists are examining traditional schoolroom tactics for maintaining order and motivating children to learn, and they are coming up with some surprising conclusions: Scoldings and punishment are largely ineffective, but rewards—a modern version of the old-fashioned gold star—can spur a class to achievement. Some experimental teaching programs are using a point system, allowing pupils eventually to earn perhaps a telescope or a transistor radio.

Working in the laboratory with rats and cats and birds, these scientists have observed how animals learn and how they acquire, maintain and get rid of habits. Briefly, the conclusions of the researchers are these: All habits, good and bad, are learned behavior, and can be unlearned or extinguished. Learning, or habit formation, occurs whenever random behavior is reinforced or rewarded. Undesirable behavior in a child persists only because in his eyes it pays off. If it is ignored, it will not become habitual.

Using these learning principles in the laboratory, behavior therapists can consistently teach a pigeon—any pigeon—to execute a graceful figure eight, train a rat to play the piano and a myna bird to sing a tune. When, for example, a psychologist wants his pigeon to crane its neck, he watches for a random upward movement and rewards it with a food pellet. Soon the pigeon gets the idea and starts stretching higher and higher for its reward.

Adapted to human beings, the technique sounds merely like common sense. This is the way a mother toilet-trains her child. She places the toddler on the potty, and if by chance he happens to urinate, she praises him inordinately. Babies are as smart as pigeons, and soon he too gets the idea. Toilet, urination and pleasing his mother are firmly linked, and a habit has been formed.

But because human beings are more complex than animals, parents and teachers often inadvertently strengthen exactly the behavior they want to weaken, and vice versa. Children crave attention, and in some circumstances even a scolding can be welcome. They perceive it—like the pigeon's food pellet—as a reward. When a mother, perhaps preoccupied with a new baby, takes her toddler's toileting for granted but scolds him for wetting his pants, she is likely to have a damp youngster. For she has turned a learning principle backward; she has ignored the desired behavior and made a fuss over the undesired. "Whenever a child persists in behaving badly," a group of sociologists at Washington University, in St. Louis, recently wrote, "some adult, perhaps inadvertently, has been rewarding him for it."

Unlike most psychotherapists, behaviorists are not concerned with the origins of unsocial behavior. It may be true that Johnny has temper tantrums because his baby brother stole his mother's affections, but their practical goal is how to get rid of the tantrums. According to the behaviorist, the symptom is not a manifestation of neurosis; it is the neurosis. Cure the symptom—tantrum, fear of heights, stuttering, gluttony—and you will have cured the patient. This is where they part company with traditional psychiatry, which claims that only when a patient develops insight into why he behaves in a certain way can he free himself from neurotic behavior.

Behavior therapists claim two advantages for their method of treatment. It is quick, effecting a change in weeks or months; and it does not always require the expensive attention of a psychiatrist. Particularly in work with disturbed or retarded children and with patients in mental hospitals, behavior therapists train parents, teachers, and nurses to act as their substitutes.

Since only the wealthy can afford years of psychiatry, since there are just not enough psychiatrists to go around, these are important advantages. If a brain-damaged child, so disruptive that he has been expelled from school, can be taught within weeks to function in a normal classroom, it is obviously better for him, his parents, and society than dulling him with tranquilizers or maintaining him in an expensive private school.

Dr. Lindsley, who worked at the Harvard Medical School for 15 years with psychotic adults, moved five years ago to the University of Kansas, in Kansas City, where he has been training parents and teachers to help troubled children. There he has treated over 1,000 youngsters—children who are retarded, brain-damaged, handicapped by cerebral palsy or epilepsy—without ever seeing one of them. "My goal is to improve children's behavior," he says, "but I can't afford the luxury of working directly with them."

Lindsley has developed a four-step program to eliminate undesirable behavior in these problem children. He does not claim that his system is new except for its precision. By measuring, recording, graphing, he knows whether a technique works or whether it should be discarded.

Essentially he uses a judicious mixture of rewards and penalties to break disagreeable habits and to motivate a child to study more effectively. Lindsley has taught his four steps to hundreds of parents, teachers, and nurses, and claims they can be applied to specific behavior problems in the home. They are:

1. Pinpoint the behavior you want to alter. When Lindsley asked a group of fathers what bugged them most about their children, one said, "When my boy goes to the bathroom, he leaves his stuff around. You'd think it was a secondhand clothing store after he's been in there." Others complained about sloppy rooms, dawdling at bedtime, monopolizing the telephone. His advice: Pick a single target, whether it's a habit you want to strengthen, such as neatness, or one you want to disappear, such as thumb-sucking.

2. Record how frequently the behavior occurs. How often does Jimmy pick a fight with his brother? How many temper tantrums does Sarah throw each week? Recording should be exact. Dr. Lindsley suggests that a parent purchase a small counter, the type that golfers use to keep tabs on the number of strokes. Transfer each day's record to graph paper, and keep the graph for at least a week before starting treatment.

In about one case in a dozen, merely recording the behavior motivates a child to change it and further treatment is unnecessary. A spectacular example of this occurred with an 11-year-old retarded boy who habitually sat with his mouth open and his tongue hanging out.

One day the father explained to him that he was going to count the number of times the youngster's tongue fell loose from his mouth. As he sat, counter in hand, the little boy made a mighty effort. The father told Dr. Lindsley later. "I just couldn't record the behavior. It never happened again."

3. Pick a consequence for the behavior and enforce it, continuing to record frequency of occurrence. The consequence may be pleasant. For dressing fast in the morning, one child was allowed to choose his favorite breakfast. Or it may be a penalty. Eager to cure herself of thumb-sucking, a little girl agreed to wear a glove for a half hour every time her thumb went in her mouth. It took her just a month to break the habit.

Cooperation from the child is necessary, of course, and the more responsibility the youngster assumes for his own treatment, the speedier its success. One boy, a morning dawdler, agreed to try to dress in 40 minutes instead of the hour it usually took him. Significantly, he set the timer himself. "He dressed so fast," his father reported later, "there never was a time he didn't beat the bell."

4. Try, try again. This step is necessary only if the first consequence fails to alter the behavior. One teacher promised a preschool boy a chocolate candy every time he placed all the pegs in a pegboard, but the reward didn't work. For some unknown reason, his pegboard rate slowed instead of quickening. So the teacher tried a new reward. She put a mark on the back of the boy's hand with a watercolor marking pencil, and the delighted child doubled his pegboard rate.

Even when a serious behavior problem requires long and complex treatment, a parent can sometimes handle it under a therapist's guidance. One couple, desperate over his habit of setting fires in the home, took their seven-year-old to the psychiatric clinic at the University of Windsor, in Ontario, Canada. The waiting list at the clinic was so long and the need so urgent that Dr. Cornelius Holland agreed to steer the parents through a self-help treatment program.

Following his suggestion, the father stopped spanking, pleading, and punishing and set one consequence. The next time the boy started a fire, he would lose his most cherished possession, a baseball glove. And to break his habit of striking matches, the child was promised a nickel every time he found a matchbook and brought it to his father. He was allowed to strike matches in his father's presence, but received a penny for every match left in the book.

The first time, he struck ten matches. For the ten matches left in the book he got ten cents. Then he struck three matches and got 17 pennies, and finally no matches for 20 cents. The father tapered off the monetary reward (but not his praise) by giving pennies only occasionally, and did not tell the boy in advance when he would win them. The child has not set another fire.

The behavior therapists say it is not necessary to keep rewarding a child indefinitely. Reward each act of good behavior while the behavior is being established; then reward it intermittently until it becomes stable. Eventually inner satisfaction becomes its own reward. For when a disturbing habit is licked, a child's ego swells. His parents like him better; he no longer feels like a social outcast.

Symbolic rewards—attention or approbation—are also important in motivating a child, but too often parents and teachers forget this simple fact. Unconsciously they choose words to spur a child that succeed only in discouraging him. One behavior therapist, training teachers in remedial reading, frequently had to remind them to stop saying, "Try harder" or, "You can do better." Teachers typically scold a class when their attention wanders, but fail to praise them or plan a treat for attentive behavior.

Whether to punish—and how and when—are questions on which behavior therapists do not always agree. Some say punishment is unnecessary and even ineffective, that merely ignoring unwanted behavior will cause it to vanish. Dr. Lindsley believes that penalties must be invoked occasionally, but that spanking or severe punishment is self-defeating. "In my home deprivation is the most effective penalty," he says.

No matter which is involved, reward or penalty, it must be swift. For if a consequence is deferred, a child is likely to fail to make a connection between the penalty and the behavior. A mother who warns her youngsters, "Wait till your father gets home" accomplishes little besides making him fearful of his father.

A similar error is often made at school, according to Harvard's Dr. B. F. Skinner, the psychologist who developed the teaching machine and many of the principles on which behavior therapy is based. If a test is given on Monday and the child gets his paper back on Tuesday, says Dr. Skinner, he is less likely to learn from his errors or to be motivated by his correct answers. (A teaching machine that tells a child instantly whether he is right or wrong avoids this mistake, Skinner says.)

Since delay between behavior and its consequence is often unavoidable, behavior therapists have hit on a method of bridging the gap—the use of a token system. A token is essentially play money that may be won and accumulated, to be cashed in later for a trinket, a snack, an outing. With it a child gains something he values, and also gains proof of the donor's approval. It is a system, say behavior therapists, that can easily be used in the home.

The group of sociologists at Washington University reported using a token system in a variety of school problems—to control a class of highly aggressive boys, to encourage timid ghetto preschoolers to speak up, to curb disruptive behavior among autistic youngsters. They even found that with tokens as a spur, two-year-olds learned to read just as fast as five-year-olds.

Studying the progress of the aggressive boys—four-year-olds who were the despair of their psychiatrists—the group made these observations. No traditional methods—sternness, kindness, being "fair"—worked. The boys enjoyed battling their teacher; and the more she reacted, the better they liked it. But once she started to ignore aggression and reward cooperation behavior with tokens, aggressive behavior decreased from 150 to 60 sequences a day, and the incidence of cooperative acts more than doubled. Punishment—charging tokens for aggression—was a failure. Drawing attention to the unsocial behavior increased its level.

A system of rewards and punishments is not a technique merely for children. Behavior therapists claim it can also work for adults who want to get rid of compulsive habits such as overeating or nail biting, or to curb antisocial behavior—gambling, shoplifting.

When an adult is strongly motivated, he often is willing to inflict painful punishment on himself. A secretary who was a compulsive eater agreed to her therapist's suggestion that she briefly remove a false front tooth every time she broke her diet. She ate one doughnut at an office coffee break, and was so desperately embarrassed by the consequence that she never strayed again. An alcoholic who decided to burn a five-dollar bill every time he took a drink became permanently dry.

These penalties are designed to break a habitual link between stimulus and response. Such a link is also present in a phobia, an unreasoning fear of an object or a situation that is not intrinsically fearful. One housewife was so terrified of cats that she refused to leave the house. A businessman kept losing promotions because he became tongue-tied with anxiety when he was required to give a report at a meeting.

Phobias are serious neurotic problems that usually require long-term professional treatment. Often, however, a victim merely wants to rid himself of a phobia without years of psychoanalytic investigation into its origin. A technique for desensitizing a victim of his phobic fears in a few months, or even weeks, is one of the important contributions of behavior therapy. Developed by Dr. Joseph Wolpe, a founder of the new discipline, it is based on two principles. First, fear cannot exist in the presence of an opposite sensation. Second, fear can be brought under control step-by-step.

Suppose, for example, a person is afraid of heights. He may become hysterical at the thought of climbing to the top of a ladder but is only mildly anxious on the bottom rung. Once this mild anxiety is overcome, the second rung is no more frightening than the first used to be. If he can conquer his mild fear of the second, he can step on the third rung and then the fourth, until eventually he can climb to the top of the ladder.

Dr. Wolpe, a South African psychiatrist who is now at Temple University, in Philadelphia, found that deep relaxation is incompatible with anxiety. When a person is completely relaxed, his pulse rate slows, blood pressure sinks and muscles go slack. Fear arouses opposite reactions— a quickened pulse, heightened blood pressure and contracted muscles. Dr. Wolpe reasoned that if he could teach a phobic patient how to relax and remain relaxed when confronted with his phobia, the anxiety reaction would be conquered.

Within the confines of a psychiatrist's office it is impossible to present the actual phobic stimulus—a crowded elevator, the roof of a skyscraper, a slithering snake. Dr. Wolpe learned, however, that when he could evoke in his patient a vivid mental image of the thing that frightened him, he could help the patient to conquer the fear.

With fearful children Dr. Arnold Lazarus, a South African psychologist now at Yale University, modifies the technique by drawing on a youngster's proclivity for imagining himself the hero of a drama. A ten-year-old was so afraid of the dark that he tried to keep his parents from going out in the evening. Dr. Lazarus learned that the child was an ardent admirer of the "Superman" television serial, and suggested that he imagine himself an agent of his idol. After only three sessions, the little boy was able to picture himself waiting in a dark room for instructions from Superman, who was sending him on a secret mission. Once the phobia was gone, the boy's schoolwork also improved. "He's a completely different child," his mother said.

When a child suffers acute anxiety, professional help is needed. But a sensible parent can use the principles of desensitization to overcome the fears normal children experience. If your toddler is timid at the seashore, for example, avoid the rough surf. Carry him to a shallow cove and, holding him close, dabble his foot in the water. Then splash a few drops on his chest, never pressing him to the point where fear becomes strong. Slowly, still holding him, immerse his body inch by inch until he is ready to laugh and splash by himself.

Piecemeal introduction to new situations also can help overcome the anxiety most small children feel in the face of the unknown. Holding his hand, you can take your five-year-old to school for a preview a short time before he is to be enrolled. Or on his first trip to the dentist you can encourage him to play in the chair and touch the instruments.

A school phobia is a particularly sticky problem. If you allow the child to remain home, you're reinforcing his fear. Make sure he doesn't have a concrete cause, such as a school bully or a sadistic teacher, the behavior therapists advise. Then take him back to school and choose among a variety of techniques to help overcome the fear. Sit in the classroom with him or ask the teacher if he can sit beside his best friend. Assure him that you're waiting outside in the corridor or in the parking lot. Promise that he may leave whenever he becomes anxious, but challenge him to try increasing his time in the classroom each day.

Behavior therapists have found that a technique called behavior rehearsal will aid timid adults in learning to assert themselves. The best assertive response is a direct and frank expression of a person's feelings, but some people just can't imagine this. A woman may break into a cold sweat at the thought of standing up to her husband. A man may become speechless at unwarranted criticism from his boss.

Dr. Lazarus says of behavior rehearsal, "Although I'm not quite sure why, empirically it works. Once a patient can speak up in a situation she has rehearsed in advance, she finds it much easier to assert herself next time, even when she's unprepared."

He cites the case of a woman who wanted to get a job, a step her husband opposed. He and the patient went through several sessions of play acting. First she acted herself. Listening to a playback on the tape recorder, she became vividly aware of how ineptly she had presented her case. Then the therapist played her role, showing her how to marshal her arguments without becoming belligerent. Then she again acted herself. Gradually she gained the confidence to broach the subject effectively to her husband.

Successful assertive therapy subtly changes a person's relations with those around him. "I've seen marriages on the verge of crack-up that were saved once the wife learned to assert herself," says Dr. Herbert Fensterheim, a New York psychologist. "It places a tremendous burden on a man to live with a person who automatically answers, 'Well, all right,' to every plan he proposes. He tries to guess what she really wants. She resents being masterminded, sulks and eventually explodes with anger, which takes him completely by surprise. For years neither has really known what the other was thinking. Once she learns to assert herself in little ways, she becomes more honest about all aspects of the marriage."

Most psychiatrists believe that one must change what a person is in order to change what he does, but conscious of the far-reaching effects of small behavioral changes, the behavior therapists suggest that this dictum may sometimes work backward. Once a person acts differently, he can become different inside.

Behavior therapy is still in its infancy, its future unclear. Whether it will become *the* method of psychiatric treatment, as its proponents claim, is doubtful. That it will become a useful additional method is certain. Within its own goals—changing behavior rather than reconstructing personality—it has proved effective in treating phobias and compulsive behavior in adults and in changing unsocial and destructive behavior in children. Yet the charge of its critics that it is limited in application also has validity.

Critics of behavior therapy make these points:

1. *The technique is superficial*, altering behavior without touching its well-springs. One example is that of a young housewife who chewed her nails to the quick, particularly on nights when her husband worked late. Using the technique developed by Dr. Lindsley, she broke herself of the nail-biting habit. Yet its apparent cause, her nervousness in her husband's absence, remained untouched.

2. Behavior therapy fails when problems are complex—deep-seated depressions, generalized anxiety, character disorders. Some behaviorists claim that even these neuroses can be broken down into specific bits of behavior to be changed; but Dr. Lazarus, a pioneer in the technique admits: "Those who try to reduce complex neurotic disorders to phobic clusters and then apply specific counterconditioning techniques will seldom achieve profound or durable change."

3. There is something distasteful about the emphasis on material rewards for children and other patients; it smacks of bribery. Furthermore, some critics object on philosophic grounds. Allen Wheelis, a San Francisco psychoanalyst, has agreed that as far as he knows, behavior therapy "works in principle." But, he has written, "If one's destiny is shaped by manipulation one has become more of an object, less of a subject, has lost freedom. If, however, one's destiny is shaped from within . . . this is self-transcendence, a process of change that originates in one's heart and expands outward, always within the purview and direction of a knowing consciousness."

To this the behavior therapists answer that all human achievement is motivated by the promise of reward, whether it be the inner satisfaction of doing one's best, the joy in pleasing a person one respects or recompense in the form of a lollipop or a paycheck.

Some children, the behaviorists point out, function effectively with only the lightest touch; they need no more than a smile and a pleased nod from a parent. Others require motivational first aid to get them moving. The reasons may lie deep in their personalities, but to the behaviorists this is not the point. They choose a material over a symbolic reward simply because experience teaches them it is usually more effective.

Today most psychiatrists no longer cling rigidly to a particular "school" of treatment but have become eclectic, adapting the method to the patient instead of trying to fit the patient to the method. Although insight-oriented psychiatrists are still suspicious that behavior therapy only skims the surface, leaving the neurotic core untouched; although behavior therapists are unconvinced that probing deeper into the psyche gets any better results; advocates of both groups are now borrowing from what is best in the other's technique. Both admit that treatment of troubled human beings is still far from an exact science.

One behavioral psychologist puts it candidly: "Behavior therapy doesn't necessarily help everyone, but neither does psychoanalysis. We still have much to learn about what kinds of people respond to what kinds of treatment."

"Eventually. That's the word parents of difficult babies must remember. The baby will eventually adapt if the parents are consistent, firm and loving."

THE DIFFICULT BABY
IS BORN THAT WAY

by Barbara W. Wyden

One out of 10 babies is born difficult. The difficult babies are the red-faced infants whose howling wakes the other newborns in the hospital nursery. They're the babies who twist and scream when their faces are washed. Who spit out new foods. Who'd rather cry than sleep—or so it seems to their harassed parents, who are often not only bewildered by these cantankerous infants but deeply anxious, even guilty. What are they doing wrong? Could there be something wrong with the child?

The answer is nothing is wrong with them or with the baby. But if they don't come to understand their baby's temperament, they will almost inevitably start handling him wrong, and their difficult baby will grow up to be a difficult adult who may bully his wife and children or be angrily dismayed that the world does not revolve around him, or simply be an irritable, uncooperative person.

Fortunately, researchers have discovered how to bring up these rambunctious babies happily and healthily.

Early in the course of their long-term study on personality, known as the New York Longitudinal Study (now in its fifteenth year), Dr. Stella Chess, professor of child psychiatry at New York University School of Medicine; Dr. Alexander Thomas, professor of psychiatry at the same institution, and Dr. Herbert G. Birch, professor of pediatrics at Albert Einstein College of Medicine, found that most babies fall into three temperamental categories. (Many, of course, cannot be neatly pigeon-holed; they are a little this and a little that.) These temperamental categories are simply a description of the child's style of reacting to the stresses and strains—and joys—of life. They have nothing to do with intelligence, ability, character or even charm.

The majority of infants are born with positive, sunny dispositions. They are "easy babies."

"Slow-to-warm-up babies" form the second largest group. Wary of new situations and people, they tend to withdraw. Once parents understand this rather cautious temperament, they usually find it easy to allow the child to adapt to change at his own rate while gently encouraging him to try new experiences.

Then there are the "difficult babies." Difficult babies manage to get mother and father on the run very early. In extreme cases, baby becomes a ruthless household tyrant whose whims cannot be anticipated soon enough and whose rages are so violent that his parents will do anything for a little peace.

"These children are often irregular in feeding and sleeping," report Drs. Chess, Thomas and Birch. "They are slow to accept new foods, take a long time to adjust to new routines or activities and tend to cry a great deal. Their crying and their laughter are characteristically loud. Frustration usually sends them into a violent tantrum.

"They are a trial to their parents," the researchers sympathize, "and require a high degree of consistency and tolerance in their upbringing."

The authoritarian versus permissive argument has gone on for generations now, but in the case of the difficult baby, there can be no argument. The findings of the New York Longitudinal Study indicate that he will thrive and become easier under a kindly consistent and firm regime (and turn into a holy terror if his parents try to use the permissive methods that work so well with some children).

Since the beginning, the N.Y.L.S. team has been helping the parents of the difficult children among the 231 youngsters in the study to understand their offspring and bring them up happily and effectively. Dr. Thomas, whom I interviewed in his roomy, old-fashioned corner office at Bellevue, pulled out a sampling of case histories from his files and reviewed some of the advice the research team had given parents.

"Here's a boy we've followed since 1956," he said. "We'll call him Bob. Bob was very difficult. When he was eight weeks old, he would not sleep more than half an hour at a time. He would wake up and shriek and scream for long periods.

"His mother could not stand the screaming for long. She would give in, give him a bottle. He would take it. Afterwards he would vomit. She really struggled to keep some kind of feeding schedule, but she just couldn't take the screaming. And she was distressed because he seldom smiled.

Both parents feared he might be abnormal. We were able to reassure them. The physical and neurological exams showed that he was normal—simply very difficult.

"We advised them to handle Bob very gently and smoothly when he had to be fed and changed. This would help minimize his intense reactions. And to leave him alone the rest of the time. This was hard for them. But we told the mother that she just could not continue the pattern she was establishing, in just two weeks—of course, that's a long time in baby's short life—she told us that Bob had become much easier to handle. And he had started to smile more often, which delighted her."

Difficult babies are often thought to be colicky and vice versa. "It is easy enough to distinguish between them," Dr. Thomas says. "The colicky baby has intense negative reactions about food and feeding times. His troubles are centered around the gastrointestinal tract, and we simply have to wait for him to outgrow them. The difficult baby, on the other hand, has intense negative reactions to almost everything. And he will not outgrow them. He has to be taught to control them."

Intensity is the key characteristic of the difficult baby. His every reaction is intense. Fortunately, not all are negative. And when he responds positively, this intensity is delightful.

"Annette is a good example," Dr. Thomas said, picking up another folder. "She had an intensely negative response to her paternal grandmother. So negative that her mother was embarrassed when her mother-in-law visited. Annette would scream when her grandmother picked her up. Wouldn't smile. Refused to be cuddled.

"But she had an immediate spontaneous positive reaction to children. When she saw another baby, she would laugh. And she loved it when her mother held her up in front of a mirror. Annette would smile at herself and hold out her arms."

This intensity throws many parents off. The N.Y.L.S. team stresses that parents must simply accept it. It's there. It can't be changed. And there's nothing "wrong" about it.

"Here's a case," Dr. Thomas said. "Lewis fought every new experience. He screamed during his first bath. It took days before his mother was able to complete a face washing. When she started him on Pablum, he screamed and twisted and spat it out. When she first gave him strained squash, he got so upset it took 10 minutes to quiet him. 'It was absolute chaos,' his mother reported. 'It took two of us to calm him and hold him after that first spoonful of squash.'

"We advised Lewis's parents to handle him as calmly as possible, to be consistent, to keep introducing and reintroducing foods until he accepted them.

"They managed very well after that. By the time Lewis was 18 months old, his parents took great delight in him and his exploits. They enjoyed his intense reactions. The father told us he was proud of having 'such a lusty kid.'

"When Lewis went to nursery school, things got rough again. He screamed and acted up and refused to stay. But, his mother told us, he eventually adapted and got to like it.

"Eventually," he repeated. "Eventually. That's the word parents of difficult babies must remember. The baby will eventually adapt if the parents are consistent, firm and loving.

"They must learn to grit their teeth and sweat it out. They must learn it is wrong to do something, anything, to stop the crying. This only teaches baby he can get anything he wants by howling.

"Parents must also learn," he continued earnestly, "to stop feeling guilty. They are not to blame for the child's difficult temperament. It's just the way he was born."

Nobody knows the origin of temperament, be it easy or difficult. It has nothing to do with birth order. Difficult babies can be first-, last- or middle-born. It has nothing to do with sex. Girls and boys are about equally represented in the three temperamental categories. It seems to be unconnected with emotional stress during pregnancy. It may be hereditary. And again it may not. It will take time and study to determine whether or not the difficult child is the offspring of difficult parents.

"It is more difficult to determine temperamental character in an adult than in a child," Dr. Thomas points out. "The adult has been formed by his inborn temperament and by his environment. It is hard to distinguish which characteristics he was born with and which he acquired through the impact of people and events.

"I hope that if we can keep this study going until our present children get married, we can learn about the role of the parent's temperament by observing the babies of this group that we have come to know so well."

It may be more important—and more helpful—for mothers of difficult babies to understand the origin of mother love than the origin of temperament. Many women feel no love for their newborn infants—especially the mothers of difficult babies. This overwhelms the mother with guilt. She feels there must be something wrong with her. Otherwise, why doesn't she love the baby she so eagerly awaited?

It turns out that mother love is not an instant emotion. A pioneering study on the beginnings of mother love carried out by Dr. Kenneth S. Robson, assistant professor of psychiatry at Tufts Medical School, and Dr. Howard A. Moss, a psychologist at the National Institute of Mental Health, destroyed the cliché fantasy that normal women love their babies at first sight. Not so. No more than most women fell in love with their husbands at first sight.

The two researchers studied 54 bright young women and their first babies and discovered that 34 percent of the mothers had no feelings at all for their babies when they first set eyes on them. Seven percent reported negative feelings—"I couldn't look at her." "I wanted them to take him away." About half said they had positive feelings, but only seven women described these feelings as love.

It took most of them from six to nine weeks to feel love, and the emotion was triggered by very specific happenings. Mother after mother reported that when baby began smiling at them, looking into their eyes and watching them as they cared for him, that they felt more and more deeply attached and loving.

These findings are particularly meaningful for the mothers of difficult babies. The researchers tell of one young mother "whose baby had cried and fussed inconsolably for the first ten weeks. She became angry and exhausted and felt unable to love or care for a baby who gave little cause for pleasure." And of another woman who told them, "I felt she was completely unconnected to me in any way. She was just a little thing that had come into my life and brought all this trouble." Both mothers eventually came to love their babies very much. It just took them a little longer than the mothers of easy babies—probably because it took a little longer for their difficult babies to respond positively to them.

It may be possible to cut down this response time. The New York Longitudinal Study has inspired other researchers to examine temperament with an eye to pinpointing it as early as possible. The sooner parents can recognize their baby's temperament, the sooner they can apply the most appropriate child-rearing method. And the sooner baby feels comfortable in his world, the sooner he will respond positively.

In Philadelphia, Dr. William B. Carey, a pediatrician with the Children's Hospital, recently completed a project with the cooperation of 210 mothers and their infants that showed it was possible to establish a baby's temperament as early as four to eight months. He designed a simple 70-point questionnaire that can be filled out by the mother in about 20 minutes and analyzed by the doctor in ten. Even the most harried pediatrician can use it to give a mother an objective view of the type of baby she has, the kinds of problems she may face and how to handle them.

Another researcher, Dr. Arnold J. Sameroff, a psychologist at the University of Rochester, thinks it may be possible to spot clues to a baby's temperament even earlier—between the first and third day of life. In a pilot project with 30 newborns that will be completed this spring, he is trying to measure such characteristics as intensity, activity, and adaptability. He then hopes to go on to apply these measures to a larger sample of some 100 infants.

Dr. Sameroff has already succeeded in determining learning ability. By means of a special feeder, he has discovered that a baby, not even 24 hours old, can learn to suck at a certain pressure to get the maximum amount of formula. By varying the degree of pressure necessary to get the most food, the researcher can find out how quickly an infant learns to adapt to the new situation. The difficult baby, of course, is slower to adapt.

It may be that in a few years, when a mother goes home from the hospital with her baby, she will have some indication of his temperament, just as she knows his sex and weight. And with this awareness, the battle is half won.

The N.Y.L.S. team has found that "most middle-class parents, once they have been exposed to the idea of temperament, are sophisticated enough so that they can work patiently and persistently to help their child adapt."

"If the difficult child is handled correctly," says Dr. Thomas, "he finally adapts to the routines of living." After all, as you get older, there aren't so many new things that happen in life. Most situations, even if they are new, tend to have some familiar element about them. The child also develops self-awareness. He knows how he reacts to things.

"We'll know in a very few years whether the difficult children in our study have developed in a healthy way," he said. "We do know that more of the difficult children have behavioral disorders than other children. This is understandable. It's simply because their adaptation is harder and more of a demand on parents. What also seems to be true is that they respond to treatment as well as other children. There is no difference here."

Dr. Thomas has great admiration for the positive qualities and potential of these difficult children. He refuses, quite correctly, to speculate about the final conclusions of the study, but he says, "I'll tell you what we will know. In six years or so, we'll know whether this will be the kind of kid who can battle harder and be a leader. We'll be able to forecast how he will react to serious adult stress—flunking out of college, losing a job, divorce." It is evident that he thinks they will be able to handle future stresses competently.

There's one thing he is positive of, even now. "By helping parents understand and handle their difficult child," he concludes in gentle triumph, "we're taking a lot of business away from child psychiatrists."

WHAT'S A MOTHER TO DO?

by Matt Clark

On the most superficial level, they wear their hair too long and their skirts too short and play their transistors too loud. Worse, some smoke pot and use obscene language. But of all the insults that the young inflict upon adult society, perhaps the most galling is that they systematically thumb their noses at authority—at the values of their parents, the precepts of their teachers and the actions of their governments.

In their outrage, many adults have looked for simple explanations for all this unsettling behavior. Chicago's Mayor Richard J. Daley, for one, sees Communists behind the riot, romanticism and rebellion of the young. But other critics discern a villain closer at hand, and recently much in the public prints for his anti-draft, anti-Vietnam positions. He happens to be a baby doctor and his name is Benjamin Spock. Dr. Norman Vincent Peale says Spock's doctrines add up to: "Feed 'em whatever they want, don't let them cry, instant gratification of needs." The result, he said, is "a student generation that thinks it can get what it yells for." After the Chicago convention, Mrs. Lyndon Johnson's press secretary, Liz Carpenter, called the troublemakers a "charming group of little children who never made it through the toilet-training chapter of Dr. Spock."

There are adults, of course, who admire the younger generation. Dr. Spock is one. Another is Dr. Halbert Robinson, a professor of psychology at the University of North Carolina, who notes that "the youth of today is much more thoughtful, responsive, idealistic and concerned than they were in our day. If Spock is responsible for this, he should be happy."

Is Spock to blame—or to praise?

There is no doubt that Spock's words have reached a wide audience. Among many middle-class families in the U.S., a well-thumbed copy of the "Spock book" has replaced the Holy Bible on the night table. With more than 21 million copies of Spock's "Baby and Child Care" sold in the U.S. alone since the first edition appeared in 1946, it is safe to assume that few modern parents have missed the Spockian message.

Triumph: In essence, Spock argued that young children should be treated with kindness in a relaxed atmosphere and taught to love rather than fear their parents. And there is some new evidence that his strictures have indeed helped produce a more socially conscious generation of young people. Psychologists M. Brewster Smith, Norma Haan and Jeanne H. Block conducted a three-year study of 1,000 students at Berkeley and San Francisco State—including some who had been jailed for taking part in the 1964 Free Speech Movement—to see if this involvement in protest was related to the way their parents reared them. The FSM participants, they found, described their parents as being more permissive and less authoritarian than did the other, uninvolved students. These parents had a close relationship with their children and avoided imposing flat prohibitions and arbitrary punishment on them. As a result, the FSM students tended to challenge their parents' beliefs and values—in politics, religion and the choice of careers.

The California psychologists concluded—quite approvingly—"that the emergence of a dedicated spontaneous generation concerned with humanitarian values and personal authenticity is a triumph of Spockian philosophy."

A similar study of students in Chicago-area colleges by sociologist Richard Flacks of the University of Chicago showed that activist students considered their parents "mild" or "lenient" while their less-involved classmates remembered their parents as being "stern" or "hard." Flacks, however, puts more emphasis on the shaping influence of parental values than on the specific techniques of child rearing. Spock, Flacks concludes, is not so much a cause of the new attitudes of youth as a reflection of the general move away from Victorian morality. In a way, Flacks is right, for if Dr. Spock didn't exist, it would have been necessary to invent him.

The era of the child-care expert in the U.S. is a relatively recent development. Traditionally, the hortatory advice of ministers and grandmothers determined how a child was raised. Jonathan Edwards told Puritan parents their child was a "young viper in God's sight."

Advice: In the Victorian age, mothers told their daughters to raise their children by example—showing off the virtues of courtesy, honesty, orderliness and generosity. But as such institutions as religion and mother declined in authority, other forces rose to take their places. In the 1890s, the women's magazines gradually took over some of the advice-giving role. Mothers were told that "petting and indulgence" would do no harm as long as the child was taught to be unselfish and obedient. By 1910, discipline was being stressed again; it was the era of Theodore Roosevelt and muscular Christianity. Parents were discouraged from handling babies on the theory that it would deprive them of their strength.

With the demonstrable successes of science and technology in so many other fields, a drive began to make child rearing "objective." Around the time of World War I, the behavioral psychologists, led by Dr. John B. Watson, decided to turn their backs on such unmeasurable qualities as motives, emotions and aspirations. To the behaviorists, the development of the child was shaped entirely by the habits he acquired through contact with his environment. It was up to the parents to see that the child learned the right habits. Watson instructed them to avoid coddling and treat their babies like miniature adults. "If you must," he wrote, "kiss them on the forehead when they say good night, shake hands with them in the morning." Such "objectivity," Watson taught, insured that the child would be independent.

Defects: During the 1930s, however, Watsonian objectivity came up against the growing influence of Freud and progressive educators such as John Dewey. The Freudians taught that the child's emotional development could be harmed by unfavorable experiences during the first years of life, resulting in neurotic personality defects. Severe toilet training, the Freudians' theory held, encouraged the development of a compulsively fastidious personality. The progressive educators thought that infants were naturally inquisitive and needed to be able to explore their surroundings more or less at will.

The importance of nature over nurture in child development was introduced at this time by Yale's Arnold Gesell, who watched thousands of infants and young children through a one-way mirror in his laboratory. Gesell concluded that a child's potential for intelligence and personality are inborn. Within these inherited limits, Gesell argued, a child passes through predictable stages of development at predictable times. Training and the child's environment "modulate" but do not determine development. At odds with both the Freudians and the Watsonians, Gesell helped push a more relaxed style of child rearing by discouraging forced attempts to wean and to toilet train. Gesell also helped allay parental concern over thumb-sucking or sudden changes from good to bad behavior by showing that such habits come and go as a natural part of development.

The 50-year trend in what the experts thought should be done to and for young American children is neatly graphed in the eleven editions of "Infant Care," a booklet first published by the U.S. Children's Bureau in 1914. In accordance with Watson's theories, readers of the first edition were told never to rock their babies, even when they cried; by 1942, the book carried a picture of a mother rocking her child with the caption: "Sometimes the baby needs a little extra attention." In 1914, toilet training was recommended by the third month or earlier; the latest edition suggests starting around fourteen months by placing the child on the potty at the first facial hint of incontinence and, if the venture is successful, showering praise on him when he's finished. The first edition advised parents to prevent thumb-sucking by pinning the child's sleeve over his fingers; by 1963, "Infant Care" was telling mothers that the habit is one of the baby's "fascinating little tricks." In 1914, mothers were told to breast-feed, since mother's milk was considered more nutritious and safer than nonpasteurized cow's milk. Today, like most pediatricians, "Infant Care" regards breast-feeding as a matter of preference. On two questions, "Infant Care" has never wavered; each edition has expressed disapproval of harsh punishment and has noted that "all babies need mothering, and should have plenty of it."

Guidance: "Infant Care" has gone into eleven editions; 50 million copies have been printed (most distributed free); like Spock's book, it offers guidance for young parents who have rejected the notion that a thing is worth doing again because it was done in the past—or in any case for young parents who are cut off from that past in a mobile society.

By and large, American parents have tended to favor these more relaxed ways to raise a child. As in much of the Western world, breast-feeding has declined steadily in the U.S. New affluence, the greater independence of modern women, the early separation of mothers from their infants—and improved bottle-feeding formulas—are among the factors responsible for the decline. Some studies show that women with college educations are more likely to breast-feed than those who have not gone through high school. Many women are convinced that breast-feeding is psychologically better than bottle feeding—and some researchers believe breast-feeding may increase in the future.

A 'Typical' Baby: After studying families in a New England town, Harvard anthropologists John and Ann Fischer drew this picture of "typical" child-rearing practices in the U.S.: most infants were on "demand" feeding and, on the average, were drinking from a cup by the age of 1. Most mothers studied had read the strictures against severe toilet training. However, the "difficult" child was occasionally spanked and often shamed by disapproving looks and words for failing to respond. Interestingly, mothers who were determined to toilet-train their children early were usually successful; ambivalent mothers, wavering between leniency and harshness, had the most trouble. Most boys and all of the girls in the study had been toilet-trained by the time they were 2½. Most parents regarded crying as a sign of good health in their infants; when a mother feels that her child's crying is an attention-getting device, she will ignore him. The severest spankings were provoked by temper tantrums, talking back or physical aggression directed against the parent.

The women of Orchard Town (the fictional name of the New England town), like mothers throughout America, tend to regard their babies as bundles of largely inherited traits and abilities. The goal of child rearing is to help the child achieve the most from his potential. Mothers differed on the most effective way to achieve this goal. "While some mothers still adhere to the old ideas of rigid scheduling in such things as feeding and sleeping times," Ann Fischer notes, "the most permissive ideas of Spock are the ones most women follow."

The same social factors that loosened the rigid grip of Victorian practices on U.S. children—liberal philosophies, psychiatric insights, mobile, highly atomized family life—have been at work in other nations around the world as well. A NEWSWEEK survey shows that Spock speaks to young parents in a score of languages—and that many nations have their own liberating child-care advocates as well:

ENGLAND: Good-by, Nanny. Naturally enough, the Victorian tradition died hardest in Great Britain. "Allow no sweets or scraps between meals," cautioned Miss Mabel Liddiard in her Mothercraft Manual, first published in 1928. "A mother who gives in because she has not the time, or because she cannot bear to see the little one cry, is starting on the downhill path."

Much of this has been supplanted by the liberal teachings of Spock and Britain's Dr. John Bowlby of London's Tavistock Clinic. More than 200,000 copies of "Baby and Child Care" have been sold since 1955, and a new edition is coming out in November. "Spock is very much a middle-class cult," says Dr. Leo Stimmler, a pediatrician at Guy's Hospital in London. "He's taught British parents to enjoy their kids."

The British nanny has all but disappeared—fewer than 3 percent of households employ governesses today—and that has produced a further relaxation in child-raising practices. Symbolically enough, in many homes the nanny has been replaced by a miniskirted *au pair* girl, a part-time helper for the busy mother. "More likely than not," says one pediatrician, "the au pair girl is busy listening to pop music and the child goes to the toilet only when he asks to."

Breast-feeding, although more prevalent than in the U.S., is declining steadily in Britain. Some middle-class mothers feel guilty if they don't try—another vestige of Victorian times. Closer contact between parent and child has encouraged permissiveness and fewer restrictions on children. But rudeness is not tolerated—especially in public. British parents insist on retaining some control," says Stimmler. "In the American pattern, the kids seem to turn out intolerable to everyoi.e but their parents.

FRANCE: Petits Singes Savants. French mothers have less to learn from Dr. Spock, says Dr. Cyril Koupernik of Paris, because in Latin countries there is "the greater feeling of warmth toward the child." In general, French mothers still obtain much of their advice about child rearing from their own mothers. Spanking is the rule rather than the exception. "There's still a housing shortage," Koupernik explains, "and babies can't be allowed to disturb the neighbors." Also, infant masturbation is still considered harmful. Yet Spock's book has had wide sale in France and his ideas find an audience in women's magazines and in training courses for nurses.

Two centuries ago the philosopher Rousseau spoke of the child as a "noble savage" who had to grow like a flower shielded from the corrupting influences of society. The ideal is noble but the practice is something else again. "French children," says Christine Lambert, an author and the daughter of a pediatrician, "are drilled like clever little monkeys in a circus [des petits singes savants]." They are slapped and reprimanded for the slightest missteps. And parental insistence on academic excellence has been known to wreck a child's health. "You have no idea what the life of a French child of 5 can be," Lambert says. (Lambert has done her part toward liberating the French baby by writing "Three Stars for Babies and Juniors," a child-care book that combines Freudian psychology with recipes from some of France's finest restaurants adjusted to the age of the child.) "One of the primary early sensations of the child is through digestion of food," Lambert observes. "So from a psychological point of view, adjusting a child's menu to his tastes is giving more freedom to the infant to express himself."

GERMANY: All in Order. After World War II the wife of a U.S. occupation official in Germany once observed a group of American Army youngsters playing chaotically in a sandbox, scrambling about, one boy making a sand cake, another digging with a toy shovel. Then the American children left and a group of German boys and girls took over the sandbox: immediately the oldest child shaped up all the others into one organized game.

Today German parents are valiantly trying to adopt a middle ground between those two forms of play: the traditional authoritarianism of German culture and the more democratic methods imported largely from the U.S. Child-care articles stress the need for German parents to give explanations to their children rather than steady commands.

In a comparative study of traits most valued by German and American parents, two U.S. investigators found that German mothers ranked obedience first, followed by honesty, good grades and orderliness. American mothers, on the other hand, ranked social compatibility first, followed by respect for others' rights, loving conduct and self-confidence. The virtue of obedience came dead last on their ranking list.

The authoritarianism of the home, according to Dr. Carmen Doer-Eller of the Cologne Clinic, tends to prolong the child's dependence on his family. "German preschool children lack the self-confidence of American children," she explains. "The German parents tend to over-rear their children, cutting off the child's impulse, initiative and curiosity."

The authoritarian atmosphere of the family is carried on by kindergarten instructors. Dr. Anne Marie Tausch, a Hamburg psychologist, studied thirteen typical kindergartens and found that 82 percent of the teachers' words to the children—even in play—were actually commands. "Now lay the dolly in the bed," Dr. Tausch heard one teacher say, "Good, and now lay the Teddy next to the dolly . . . so, now stroke the dolly."

Japan: Understanding. Superficially at least, Japan should produce the world's most spoiled children. From the moment he is born until he goes to school, the Japanese child is a guest in his own home. He gets what he wants when he cries, is seldom punished, and is allowed to sit on a train while his mother stands. Yet he is also taught to bow to guests and to understand his responsibilities to his family.

Increasing Westernization of the country since the war has complicated the problem of raising children for the average Japanese mother. There is now a large number of *kyoiku mama* (education mothers) who try to drill their children early in order to get them into the best schools and, later, the best business firms. With the mass movement to the cities, the Japanese family—which typically included several generations—has been broken up. Without advice from their elders, mothers have had to depend on advice, much of it contradictory, appearing in books and magazines. Many mothers abandoned breast-feeding, once universal in Japan, because their reading taught them that bottle-feeding was "the smart thing" to do.

Japanese mothers are renowned for their patience, and one reason why they are able to train their children with little discipline is that they wait until the child is in a cooperative mood. The Japanese mother tries to get her child to understand rather than obey. Since they believe striking a child is "low class," the typical Japanese mother seldom inflicts greater bodily punishment than an occasional pinch, and that never in public. The father plays little part in taking care of his children. "The image persists," says Mrs. Isoku Hatano, a child-care authority, "that the most important aspect of a man's life is his job. A good Japanese father is one who is kind and considers his children as his toys."

U.S.S.R.: No Child Is Alone. The standard for Soviet child rearing was set by the late Dr. A. S. Makarenko with the publication of "A Book for Parents" in the Stalin years before the war. "The Soviet State," he wrote, "demands from you correct upbringing of future citizens." Children reared without parental love, Makarenko said, often become "deformed" members of society.

Parents are warned against forcing their children to eat. But toilet training is begun early, usually at three or four months. Soviet pediatricians stress the importance of breast-feeding on the ground that "there is no real substitute for mother's milk." One special target of Soviet pediatricians has been the once-common practice of swaddling—wrapping the infant in tight baby clothes. The doctors hold that the practice impairs physical development. (The British anthropologist Geoffrey Gorer once suggested that swaddling did much more harm, constricting the Russian character into a phlegmatic, stolid personality. Certainly, old swaddling bonds have been broken with a vengeance.) In fact, some pediatricians advise simple gymnastics for infants only 45 days old as a means of developing the child's nervous system.

Collective training in the nursery school, Soviet experts insist, favors individual development so long as it fits usefully into society. "The child does not live in a desert," says Dr. Tatyana Markova of the Soviet Academy of Pedagogic Sciences, "and is not alone in the world. It must be integrated into society." Extreme permissivism, obviously, doesn't fit into this scheme of training. "There are two approaches to freedom," Mrs. Markova points out, "the freedom to break windows and the freedom to install them. We try to encourage the latter."

Many countries, of course, remain untouched by the newer ideas of raising children. Spain is one example of a pre-Spock culture. Spanish mothers learn how to raise their children from their own mothers, not from books, and, according to a Madrid pediatrician, "no doctor can tell the *abuela* [grandmother] how to raise children."

There are also some signs of post-Spock cultures. Some specialists believe a child may be better off reared in a communal society away from his family. Children on some Israeli kibbutzim see their parents only in the evening; in theory, life in the kibbutz protects the child from sibling rivalry and other tensions of life in the family and at the same time produces a child better able to function for the good of society.

Too Complex? U.S. experiments with group care are based on the belief that today's parents are unable to equip their children to survive in an increasingly technocentric culture. With the decline of unskilled labor, note the University of North Carolina's Halbert Robinson, the child of poor parents faces a bleak future. And at best, he adds, the better-educated parents can do little more than act as independent contractors for services for their children—going one place for health care, another for preschool, another for music lessons.

At the Frank Porter Graham Child Development Center, Robinson is trying to bring all the essential services for raising a child together under one roof. In his experimental program, some 40 youngsters from infancy up to age 4 spend the day at the center receiving medical and dental care as well as intensive early-learning training. The youngsters are surrounded by "learning stimuli," from the sound of Moussorgsky piped into the nursery to the sight of goldfish dangling in a plastic bag on the crib. The early-learning program includes fine motor skills, art, languages—every 3-year-old can read—and even toddlers are shown simple scientific experiments. "What we're trying to do," says Robinson, "is find the best possible mix between the family as a child-rearing institution and society as a child-rearing institution."

Whether group care will supplant the role of the family seems doubtful, particularly in the U.S., where a premium is placed on independence. "I hope," says Spock, "these experiments are done carefully so nothing precious is lost between parent and child." Spock, of course, is on the sidelines; these are problems for tomorrow's parents. How will Spock's "children" raise their children?

part
FIVE Conflict
Resolution

The selections in this section center around one of the most important concepts in all interpersonal relationships. The way an individual faces and handles his feelings of anger is a crucial factor in predicting his ability to enjoy reasonable degrees of success in primary relationships. In western tradition conflict has been considered as something to be avoided because it was a sign of evil, wrong, or sinfulness. Consequently our culture has helped us learn to avoid conflict by denial and repression. What is conflict? Why is denied or repressed anger a dangerous thing? Is power admissible as a means of solving interpersonal conflict? How does positive conflict resolution come about? To what extent is marital "fighting" a sign of a healthy relationship? To what extent is marital "fighting" a sign of marital discord? Is it wrong to appease? Is it detrimental to "give in" to the wishes of the mate in order to please the mate? How can the learning of means for conflict resolution stimulate growth and vitality in a marriage? What are the results of "dirty" fighting and "sick" fighting? In what way is conflict resolution ability necessary for keeping alive feelings of love and the desire for intimacy? What is the effect of marital "fight styles" upon the children? How do we teach children to face conflict?

The first selection, "Conflict: The Key to Sustained Reality by George Bach and Ronald Deutsch, is an example of how dealing with conflict can change the nature and tone of an intimate relationship. Bach and

Deutsch claim that the attitude toward and the approach to conflictual situations form the groundwork for intimacy and genuineness in interpersonal relationships. A case study with two possible scenarios provides the reader with a first hand illustration of how Bach and Deutsch teach intimate pairs to handle conflict.

The second selection, "The Politics of Marriage: A Delicate Balance" by Vivian Cadden, deals with the questions of power within the marital relationship. Politics in marriage has to do with the exercise of power. While Cadden feels that probably no marriage is entirely free of the politics of coercion she holds that the politics of love are the exact reverse of the politics of power; that is, while power politics applies pressure, withholds resources, and threatens withdrawal, love politics releases pressure and gives freely of itself.

The third selection, "Money and Sex: Two Marital Problems or One" by Morton Hunt, is subject specific in that Hunt takes the two most frequently listed marital complaints and attempts to show their dynamic interrelatedness. Hunt feels that people often choose either money or sex in order to express their negative feelings toward each other. Hunt feels that sex and money continue to be the most effective ways of exerting power over one's mate and that in spite of female liberation and equalitarian emphases the "quid pro quo" is financial support in exchange for sexual favors. Hunt's article serves as a practical consideration of the dynamics which lead people to attempt to handle conflict by withholding of resources.

The final selection, "Conflict: Modeling or Taking Flight" by Carl Williams, points up the negative effects of a socialization process wherein conflict is considered to be evil and morally wrong. Williams shows that the parent model is the single most important influence in the child's attitude toward conflict and upon his future ability to deal with conflict. Often under the pretense of good intentions the child is shielded from witnessing the actual conflict interchange, but the child can never be shielded from inevitable aftereffects of the conflictual situation. This article may help the student question the socialization process which moralizes and exhorts about "good examples" and yet is reluctant and afraid to act on its own precepts concerning the facing and handling of conflict.

CONFLICT: THE KEY
TO SUSTAINED REALITY

by George R. Bach and Ronald M. Deutsch

AGGRESSIVE assertion of one's real feelings can do much more than forestall harmful illusion. It can, for example, keep small hurts and annoyances, born of carelessness and misunderstanding, from becoming buried resentments that build up to block a pair from real intimacy.

Unless you say "ouch," your partners cannot know that they are stepping on your toes.

Inevitably, pairing partners do things that offend one another and reveal irritating habits or points of view. Caring about each other, most healthy lovers would be glad at least to try to modify whatever bothers a partner the most. But most people are peace-loving. They tend to overestimate how much one can swallow and forget. Nobody likes to "spoil" a nice day or evening. But, like DDT, these irritations are not eliminated; they accumulate. By constructive aggression, pairers can ask for change, promptly, before anger mounts.

By asserting your identity, you preserve it and continue to have impact on partners, so that they know and respect that identity. If you continually compromise identity, it becomes eroded and confused. You feel smothered. Then the usual reaction is to push the partner away in order to gain breathing space.

One of the important uses of pairing aggression is to set a comfortably compromised distance between the individual lives of the partners. Each needs breathing room, enough elbow room to move freely, time alone to refuel—otherwise a partner can change from a desired lover to a resented jailkeeper.

Aggression assertion is also the only effective way to win real inclusion in another person's life and to become central in his thoughts and feelings. (This does not mean exclusive. Only the neurotic demands to be an entire world for the one he supposedly loves.)

There are many other uses for aggression. Sometimes it is nothing more than what we call *leveling,* an impactful frankness. At other times it means demonstrating the open transparency that can be so powerfully attractive in the beginning of a pairing and generate an attractive force for a lifetime as well.

It is this frankness, this assertiveness, this expressed hunger for being recognized and respected and real, that the senior author has popularized for educational purposes as "intimate fighting." His widely used fight-training system is a way of controlling assertiveness so that it is fair and not hurtful and does not deteriorate into destructive nagging and squabbling.

Passionate assertion is useful only when both partners express their demands and needs. These expressions are bound to conflict. That conflict can be healthy as long as it takes place under control, and need not injure. The fight system slows down the collision between identities, puts it into slow motion, so that what could be hard blows become, instead, forceful appeals to reason and good will. Constructive fighting draws good pairers together. It reassures and builds trust, for it keeps the partners real and understandable to each other. Its intent is neither to wound nor to "win," by outdoing the other. In fact, the system equalizes the partners, so that one is not strong and the other weak. For intimate love can survive only when both partners respect one another as peers.

The fight system is detailed in the senior author's earlier popular work, *The Intimate Enemy.* We cannot outline the entire system here. But in making intimacy grow, in resolving problems and conficts, and in evaluating pairing relationships, we will frequently refer to the use of aggression. So we will highlight the basic principles of pairing conflict to allow the reader to put them to work.

Peter and Cathy came to the Institute to try and rescue a highly rewarding pairing that threatened to break down. They had recently had a terrible fight in the old no-holds-barred style of infuriated lovers. They were still angry and suspicious. They told Dr. Bach about the fight, and he then had them conduct the same fight in a systematic, noninjurious, growth-producing way.

Here is a reconstruction of the original battle, a painful Donnybrook. Cathy and Peter had been paired for some months in a close and supposedly exclusive way. But for more than a month both had been feeling uncomfortable, dissatisfied. They were upset about this decline from a very passionate beginning. Their lovemaking had begun to fail at times. Both sometimes were reluctant about seeing one another, but kept this secret. They were starting to feel tense at times when they were together.

Cathy was twenty-six and had never been married. Peter was thirty-four and divorced. Sexually ardent, Cathy had gone through a number of affairs. Peter had become rather promiscuous during the later phases of his breaking marriage and mistrusted himself because of this. He tended to be rather jealous, and with seeming tact, questioned Cathy closely about what she did during his occasional business absences that usually lasted several days. He had just returned from one of these engineering-sales expeditions when the explosion came. They had finished dinner at her apartment:

PETER (proudly):
I've been saving my good news for dessert. I closed the Comstock deal. Tyler called me in today and congratulated me himself. He said that one more like that and they'd just have to let me take over a department. Openings are coming up.

CATHY (genuinely pleased for him):
That's wonderful, dear. Do you get a big raise? You really deserve one.

PETER:
I'll get something; I don't know how much. But it isn't the money—though I know you're used to fancier dates than I can afford, with my alimony and child support.

CATHY:
I don't care about that, darling. I keep telling you. But I do wish you didn't have to be away on weekends. I get pretty restless sitting home on my days off.

PETER (knowingly):
Well, you didn't sit home last night, at least. I started trying to call you at four in the afternoon, and I tried up to one in the morning. (He studies her.)

CATHY:
Oh, for God's sake, not again! What do you expect me to do? Yes, I went out. Is that against the law?

PETER:
Probably shopped in the afternoon . . . (He tenses.)

CATHY:
Well, yes. (Impatiently.) And I got my hair done.

PETER:
And then you went to dinner, I guess.

CATHY (tightening; getting up to clear the dishes):
Yes.

PETER (trying to seem casually inquiring):
With your sister?

CATHY:
No. Do you want more coffee?

PETER:
No, thanks. With Joan?

CATHY:
How about an after-dinner drink? I've got some Grand Marnier.

PETER:
Okay. I see you're splurging. That's over your usual budget, isn't it? And you've already had some. Drinking alone?

CATHY:
Damn it, Peter, cut it out!

PETER (sounding injured):
Cut what out?

CATHY:
You know goddamn well what you're starting. No, I did not buy the cordial. Okay. It was a gift. Okay? So just stop playing detective. It drives me crazy.

PETER (he goes into the kitchen and turns her around, holding her arms):
What are you so defensive about? Where were you last night, while I was working in Cleveland?

CATHY:
Are you going to let go of me?

PETER:
Dammit, stop evading me!

CATHY:
All right, Mr. Prosecutor, the booze came from an old friend who took me to dinner and a play last night. Okay? I knew you'd get upset about it. Did you have to drag it out?

PETER (backing up just one step, his face darkening):
What old friend? Must have been a pretty good friend.

CATHY:
It's none of your business. (Coldly stares at him.)

PETER:
It *is* my business. Who was it?

CATHY:
I'm not married to you. Get off my back. I was bored to death yesterday.
I got a chance to have some fun for a change, and I took it. That's all.
It was harmless.

PETER:
You don't have fun with me?

CATHY:
Not when you're in Cleveland, I don't. Satisfied?

PETER (coldly):
Who was it?

CATHY:
No one you know.

PETER (tight with anger):
Cathy, I have a right.

CATHY:
Oh, no you don't. I'm the one who has the right. I have a right to have
friends besides you. I'm young. I have a right to go out on Saturday
night. I'll bet anything *you* were out boozing it up on your expense account.

PETER:
Dammit, you know the customers expect to be entertained.

CATHY:
And what do their wives do?

PETER:
Joe and Ted brought their wives along. I took them to dinner, and to a
bar with a combo. Hell, a lot of the time we talked shop and the three
girls talked—

CATHY (furious):
THREE girls? Why, you—Roasting me like that when you're out with
somebody else! I could *kill* you! That really tears it! You pompous, holier-
than-thou—

PETER (shouting):
For God's sake, shut up and listen! Joe's wife just brought her sister along, and I— Who were you with?

CATHY:
Cliff Richards! He was down from Chicago, and he called me. I don't care now. You can know, you hypocrite.

PETER:
One of those guys in Chicago you used to screw with, isn't he?

CATHY (shouting):
You bastard! At least I wasn't two-timing my wife the way you were. I loved Cliff, and—

PETER:
And every other man in Chicago. Do they *all* call you whenever they get into town and want to get laid?

CATHY:
Get out of here! Get out!

PETER:
Maybe that's why I turn you off in bed, lately. You're so tired from good old Cliff, and good old Tom, Dick, and—

CATHY:
I hate, you, you bastard! I trusted you. I told you everything—Get the hell out of here!

PETER:
You slut! And feeding me his booze, to make me feel like dirt. (He grabs the bottle and starts to pour it down the kitchen sink. She snaps it away from him, and throws it at him, missing, but splashing him.) Why you little bitch—(He raises his hand, then wheels and slams out of the apartment.)

This fight involves many of the most common problems of pairing, including the respective rights of the pairers, the abuse of trust, as well as the partners' distance, individuality, independence, and how central each is to the life of the other. This makes it informative but it also makes for bewildering confusion between the pairers. One can see that each is trying to express important feelings, that these are expressed in muddled terms, and that neither really is hearing the other.

Yet such "blow-ups" may signal not the end, but only a need for change and improvement in communications. The fighters say to one another: "That was too much, too painful. Let's cool off and sort things out. What do you want from me?"

The elements of a fight such as the one between Cathy and Peter can be sorted out and controlled. With coaching, this conflict became a fair, noninjurious experience for both and led the pairing to growth and progress, instead of destroying it. Peter and Cathy are now in Dr. Bach's office nervously stealing glances at one another.

DR. BACH:
Now, let's see. Which of you two would like to begin? Under our system, one of you would tell the other that he or she has a gripe.

CATHY:
He started it before, with his dirty mind.

PETER:
MY dirty mind! At least I don't—

DR. BACH:
Hold it. This is not a boxing contest; it is an attempt to have communication and reality. All right. You, Peter, begin by stating your gripe, and—

PETER (interrupting):
That will take at least an hour. But basically, this is all about Cathy's immature, irresponsible—

DR. BACH: (raising his hand for a halt):
No, no. Never like this. We do not label. We do not sit in judgment. We state a *specific* source of dissatisfaction. First we meditate for a minute, quietly, to find in ourselves what the specific thing is that really bothers us. Try that. Then tell her.

PETER (complies):
All right. Cathy, it really bugs me when you see other men. I love you, and you say you love me, but you won't be just mine.

DR. BACH:
Ah! A demand for exclusivity. Now, Cathy, when we hear the gripe, we feed it back, as exactly as we can. This slows things down. It also makes us listen, instead of just waiting for the other to stop so that it becomes *our* turn. Please do so.

CATHY:

That seems pretty silly. But okay. Peter, you are saying that it bugs you if I have any friends, and—

DR. BACH:

No, no. You must feed back exactly. What you have done in your minor change is to shift the meaning quite a bit.

CATHY:

It bugs you when I see other men. You love me, and I tell you I love you, but I won't be just yours.

DR. BACH:

Very good. Now, if this is what bothers you, Peter, some change should make you feel better. Tell her the change you would like.

PETER:

But that's obvious, isn't it?

DR. BACH:

Nothing is obvious in pairing. Tell her.

PETER:

Cathy, I want you to stop dating other men. Wait now. There must be something else.

CATHY:

You want me to stop dating other men.

PETER:

It's funny, I had this whole complicated thing in my mind when I came in, you know, about your attitudes and such, but this is all I can think of just now.

DR. BACH:

It's really not so funny. That is what tends to happen when we meditate on finding specific demands for change. Now, Cathy, you have heard and fed back Peter's demand for a change. Do you want to make the change?

CATHY:

No. I do not want to stop dating other men.

DR. BACH:

Feed it back, Peter. Then it will have impact on you.

PETER:

You do not want to stop dating other men.

DR. BACH:

We appear to have an impasse here. But maybe there is a way to compromise. Peter, is your demand negotiable? Are you willing to compromise in some way?

PETER:

How can I compromise?

DR. BACH:

Well, you could find out how much other dating she wants, and perhaps agree on some kind of limitations that would satisfy you both.

CATHY:

I don't want any limitations. I want to be free. I think this is really what it's all about. Peter wants to own me. It makes him angry when his property isn't safe.

PETER (protesting):

That's not true.

DR. BACH:

You hear, Cathy? He says you're wrong. You are making assumptions. Also, you are mind-reading him, really mind-*raping* him. This will only make him angry. We must state only what we know. If we have an assumption, a hypothesis about the other person, we must check it out by asking. It's all right to read minds, but only if we ask permission and get it. Otherwise, when we tell someone what they think or feel, we are engaging in the practice of what we call crazy-making. It is maddening.

CATHY:

All right, may I read your mind, Peter?

PETER:

I suppose so.

CATHY:

I think that you want to own me. You want to do whatever you feel like, without any commitment to me, but you want me safely on the string.

PETER:

That isn't true. I can be loyal to you. That business in Cleveland really was what I said it was. I admit I'm tempted a little by other girls. I'm human. But I'd rather give them up to keep you exclusive with me.

DR. BACH:
What about the commitment she says you don't want to make.

PETER:
Well, that's it. I'll be exclusive if she will.

DR. BACH:
We have a negotiating offer, Cathy. What do you think?

CATHY:
That's not a commitment, as far as I'm concerned.

PETER:
Well what would a commitment be?

CATHY:
There's only one kind of permanent commitment between a man and woman, even though I know that isn't always so very permanent.

PETER:
You mean marriage?

CATHY (dropping her eyes):
I guess so.

PETER:
You mean you want to marry me? Now I've told you that I have to—

DR. BACH:
Check it out, Peter. Is that what she means?

PETER:
Is it?

CATHY:
Yes.

PETER:
But you said you didn't want to marry me.

CATHY:
Because you said you didn't want to.

PETER:
No, I said I couldn't. I explained about the alimony and the child support. There's just not enough left for us to live on decently, until I get that promotion and the raise.

CATHY:
Then if you can't be committed, why should I be?

PETER:

I still say, there can be commitments other than marriage, just two people promising each other—

CATHY:

I've had that kind of promise in the past, in Chicago, and I wound up out in the cold. I commit myself, and then, when the man finds something he likes a little better, I get dropped. I guess I just want it all, or no commitment. I get too dependent. I don't really want anyone else, Peter. I didn't go to bed with Cliff. I didn't want to. But it made me feel good to go out with him. Free. Free of you.

PETER (hurt):

I didn't realize that you thought of me as just a ball and chain. I'm sorry.

DR. BACH:

You're mind-reading, Peter, without permission.

PETER:

Well, is that the way you see me?

CATHY:

No. And yes. I guess I mean it frightens me to be so very dependent on you. I'm afraid I'll lose you.

PETER (brightening):

Really? But I'm afraid of losing you. That's why it scares me so when you go out with other men. I'm afraid I don't have enough to offer you, to hold you.

CATHY:

Then why don't you want to marry me?

PETER:

I've told you and told you. The money. I *want* to.

CATHY (alert and delighted):

You mean that?

PETER:

Yes.

CATHY:

Then why don't you tell me?

PETER:

Because of all *your* talk about independence all these months. I thought I might frighten you off. Do you really want to marry me?

CATHY:

Oh, yes (She pauses.) I mean, on the one hand, I really want it very much. But then you—well, you do get so possessive, or something.

DR. BACH:

Cathy, it sounds as if you might have a gripe, and perhaps a demand for change of some kind. Do you think you should tell Peter about it? (She nods). Well, meditate first, and then perhaps this counterdemand will really clear some things up for us.

CATHY:

I'm not really completely clear about this, Dr. Bach. I know what I feel, but it's hard to express. I'm not as good with words as Peter is. If we argue about anything, he always seems to get his way. He talks me into it. I get exhausted and give in.

DR. BACH:

This is a fairly common situation, Cathy, when one person is more verbal or expressive than another. So what we try to do is balance the situation. We try to give the less verbal partner a chance to express what he or she feels without words, and without a distracting response from a partner who may be more clever with words. Would you like to try this, Cathy? There is no talking involved at all.

CATHY (looking doubtful, but somewhat relieved): I would, very much. I get terribly frustrated when I try to make my ideas stand up against Peter's.

DR. BACH:

Very good. One of our methods of nonverbal expression is what we call *molding.* One partner molds the other into an expression of what he or she wants the other to be in relation to themselves. Then the molder— we sometimes refer to him as the Pygmalion—places himself in a position which further clarifies the relationship that he wants in the pairing. But if you want to do it, Cathy, you must ask Peter's permission first. We never assume the right to manipulate or mold or invade another.

CATHY:

May I do this to you, Peter?

PETER:

Yes, dear. I want to know what you feel, and sometimes it's frustrating when I feel you can't tell me.

DR. BACH:

All right, Peter, then stand up and close your eyes. Please remain completely silent until this exercise is completed. Then you can open your eyes, and you will both have a chance to discuss the result.

Cathy, you may place Peter in any position you like. You can adjust his clothing, if he doesn't object, make him lie down, stand, kneel, whatever pleases you. You can also arrange his facial expression if you choose.

Cathy leads Peter by the hand to the center of the room. She looks up at him. He is seven or eight inches taller than she. Following Dr. Bach's instructions, she closes her own eyes and meditates for a moment, to let her feelings come through clearly. Then she smiles, as if she has the idea she wants.

She takes Peter's hands and puts them in his pockets. Then she studies him. She advances and lifts the corners of his mouth into a small, gentle smile. Stepping back, she looks up at him again, in a mildly dissatisfied way. Then she approaches and makes him kneel.

Now Cathy kneels in front of him. She straightens up as tall as she can. Kneeling, they are now close to being equal in height, she a foot or so away. Then she shakes her head and slowly backs up, until she is about three feet away from him. Now she smiles affectionately and extends both arms to Peter, but does not touch him.

CATHY:

You can open your eyes now, Peter.

PETER:

(He does, and looks a little puzzled.) I'm not sure I understand.

CATHY:

Well, think about it.

PETER:

You've brought us down lower and made us more the same height, more eye to eye. Does that mean you want us to be more nearly equal?

CATHY:

Yes, that's right. But there's more. There's a more important part.

PETER (studies the situation):

Why did you put my hands in my pockets? (He thinks about this.) Is it so that I can't touch you?

CATHY (a little uncomfortably):
Yes.

PETER:
But you're reaching out to me. Yet you're just far enough away so that you can't touch me. I don't think I get it. Do you mean you really don't like our physical relationship? (He asks it anxiously.)

CATHY:
Oh, no. You know I don't mean that. I love being physical. It's my best way to tell you how I feel. And you're a good lover. You're so affectionate.

PETER:
Then—what? I know I touch you a lot more than you like sometimes?

DR. BACH:
Has she said so?

PETER:
Sorry. Do I? Touch too much?

CATHY:
Not that. I like to be touched. It's different, what I mean.

DR. BACH:
If you're not sure what her molding means, Peter, perhaps you'd better ask.

PETER:
Yes. What does the rest mean, Cathy?

CATHY:
You get so close. It's funny, but I can say it now. Sometimes you make me feel surrounded. That's why I put your hands in your pockets. So you couldn't hold me, and I could reach out for you, when I was ready. That's why I backed up, too.

DR. BACH:
Why don't we all sit down, now, and Cathy, perhaps you have a demand for a change, too, that you can express.

CATHY:
It's still hard to pin it down. But it's as if Peter came too close, for too long.

DR. BACH:
Tell Peter, and try to be very specific.

CATHY:

I guess my gripe is that you seem to want to spend more time together than I.

PETER:

You think I want more time together than you want.

CATHY:

Yes. I'm afraid that if I say I'm bothered, that you'll think I don't love you. But I need time to myself.

PETER (he first feeds this back):
When do I do this?

CATHY:

Weekends, for example, we're never out of each other's sight. We sleep together Friday night, and then stay together all weekend. I need time to breathe. In a way, I'm relieved when you go out of town.

PETER:(he shows that he has listened first, by feedback):
I thought you liked the closeness. I know I've asked you.

CATHY:

You've asked if I liked the things we did together, if I liked sleeping with you and eating meals with you and going to museums and things. I really do. I like it all. But not all at once, not all of the time.

DR. BACH:

Well, what sort of demand do you make, since Peter seems to accept your complaint as valid?

CATHY:

It's hard to be specific. But I would like it sometimes if you would leave me a few hours on a Saturday and Sunday just to do my thing quietly, wash my hair or drip-dry my blouses, little chores I haven't time for during the week. My poor apartment has been a wreck for months. Or I might just like to read or watch television. You're a little too much for me. I'm exhausted by Monday morning, when it's time to go back to work.

PETER:

I know I do this. And the truth is, it tires me out, too. I see you getting restless, and when I do, it makes me feel anxious, as if you don't like being with me. So I cling all the harder. Maybe it would be good for both of us. I haven't been to a ball game for four months, for example.

CATHY:

Then you wouldn't mind giving me weekend afternoons or mornings to myself? I mean, you won't be hurt? I think maybe that's another reason why I keep wanting to escape to someone else. It makes me feel pressured to be so close.

PETER:

Let's try it out, and see if it doesn't help. Do you think it will, Dr. Bach?

DR. BACH:

I think so. One of the common differences between people is the problem of distancing: how much room each wants to allow the other or take for himself. You, Peter, seem to want much more closeness than Cathy can take. People in love often fear they will be engulfed, that they'll be overwhelmed by the partner, and exploited, if they give too much of themselves. Cathy has already expressed fears of exploitation, which seem to stem in part from past bad experiences, and in part from now knowing where she stands now. I think, by the way, that this may be what she means when she says she wants a commitment from you. Is that so, Cathy?

CATHY (she nods):

I can feel a great difference already, now that Peter has really told me more about how he feels.

DR. BACH:

You know, both of you, that you never really finished the fight for change that Peter began? I let it go unresolved, because I did not think it could be settled until Cathy could express more of her feeling. But what are you going to do about that? You had both taken nonnegotiable positions about whether or not she could date other men.

PETER:

I got the impression that you changed your mind, Cathy.

DR. BACH:

Mind-reading, Peter! And you don't need to read her mind. You only have to check out your assumption.

PETER:

Have you changed your mind?

CATHY:

Not really. Dr. Bach is right. I do feel more commitment from you when you level with me. But I still want to be free to keep my friends and see them. Maybe I will and maybe not.

PETER:

But Cathy—

CATHY:

You see, if I promise, it can only be that I won't go out with anyone, not that I won't want to.

PETER:

You mean I just have to trust you?

CATHY:

No more than I have to trust you in Cleveland.

DR. BACH:

Can you compromise your original demand, Peter, now that you have more information and understanding?

PETER:

Well, I do understand Cathy's point of view better.

CATHY:

But I want to know if you really accept it. Or will you just resent everything? Giving me more time to myself, leaving it open about whether I see male friends—

PETER:

We can try it out and see. (He thinks a moment.) One thing that would certainly help is if I can believe that you will keep me posted on what you do—especially if you want to be with someone else because they mean more to you.

DR. BACH:

Excuse me, Peter, but is it possible that you could phrase this question differently—that you are only asking Cathy to be open and level with you?

PETER (thinks it over):

I guess that really it what I mean. Will you, Cathy?

CATHY:

Of course, now that I start to feel that I can level, without your being angry or rejecting me. When you're open with me, it makes me trust you.

This fight is quite a discursive one. The reason is that so many problems existed in this pairing, unresolved, merely swept under the emotional rug. But the fight provides a number of suggestions about how self-assertion and leveling can handle many difficulties.

Among the basic principles demonstrated by this fight are these:

1. Be specific when you introduce a gripe.
2. Don't just complain, no matter how specifically; ask for a reasonable change that will relieve the gripe.
3. Ask for and give feedback of the major points, to make sure you are heard, to assure your partner that you understand what he wants.
4. Confine yourself to one issue at a time. Otherwise, without professional guidance, you may skip back and forth, evading the hard ones.
5. Do not be glib or intolerant. Be open to your own feelings, and equally open to your partner's.
6. Always consider compromise. Remember, your partner's view of reality may be just as real as yours, even though you may differ. There are not many totally objective realities.
7. Do not allow counter-demands to enter the picture until the original demands are clearly understood, and there has been clear-cut response to them.
8. Never assume that you know what your partner is thinking until you have checked out the assumption in plain language; nor assume or predict how he will react, what he will accept or reject. Crystal-gazing is not for pairing.
9. Don't mind-rape. Ask. Do not correct a partner's statement of his own feelings. Do not tell a partner what he should know or do or feel.
10. Never put labels on a partner. Call him neither a coward, nor a neurotic, nor a child. If you really believed that he was incompetent or suffered from some hopeless basic flaw, you probably would not be with him. Do not make sweeping, labelling judgments about his feelings, especially about whether or not they are real or important.
11. Sarcasm is dirty fighting.
12. Forget the past and stay with the here-and-now. What either of you did last year or last month or that morning is not as important as what you are doing and feeling now. And the changes you ask cannot possibly be retroactive. Hurts, grievances, and irritations should be brought up at the very earliest moment, or the partner has the right to suspect that they may have been saved carefully as weapons.
13. Do not overload your partner with grievances. To do so makes him feel hopeless and suggests that you have either been hoarding complaints or have not thought through what really troubles you.
14. Meditate. Take time to consult your real thoughts and feelings before speaking. Your surface reactions may make something deeper and more important. Don't be afraid to close your eyes and think.
15. Remember that there is never a single winner in an honest intimate fight. Both either win more intimacy, or lose it.

While some new partners suppress tension and conflict in order to cement the new relationship, others deliberately create fights. Typically, new lovers who are not yet sure of each other, argue a lot about what appear to be trivia. Deliberately or intuitively, they do this to gather "intelligence" about each other. They may even pose completely hypothetical conflicts to find out what the new partner would do if, for example, a rival suitor were to appear.

They may also criticize each others' tastes in clothes, choice of movies, etc. Once these imaginary or exaggerated conflicts have been handled in a bonding rather than tearing way, intrinsic tensions arise from the "I-and-You" relationships.

Typically they deal with such basic dimensions of intimacy as: "I'm not important enough in your life; I don't like being a side issue." Or who "wears the pants." Or setting the conditions under which others are to be included ("Strange that even at Christmas you didn't take me to meet your folks"). In realistic pairing both the initial apparently trivial and extrinsic conflicts as well as the later and more obviously significant intrinsic conflicts deepen intimacy because of the style of conflict management we teach.

We can even generalize that freedom from conflict is practically always limited to partners who act out well-defined roles under explicit contractual conditions. Examples are: tennis pals and smooth but highly specialized "Good Time Charlie" relationships between playboys and playgirls.

Sometimes one partner creates and/or reinforces self-deprecations. These are not tensions and confrontations focused on legitimate "I-and-You" conflicts, but alienating, ego-downers. Some examples are: "My God, the way you stumble when you walk!" or remarks about "The way you frown," or "The way you never read any books."

There are many other refinements to the system of intimate aggression. But this basic outline is enough to start any pair toward the constructive uses of aggression, toward the piercing of illusions and the reaching of reality.

————————————

*Most marriages today are firmly rooted in
the power principle—either the husband
or the wife wins or loses. But, asks a
wise and experienced woman, is this any
way to run a marriage?*

THE POLITICS OF MARRIAGE:
A DELICATE BALANCE

by Vivian Cadden

When you really stop to think about it, it seems almost incredible that two human beings can live for as long as, say, six months, let alone a lifetime, in the suffocatingly close proximity—emotional and physical— that marriage throws them into.

It seems reasonable to suppose that years and years ago, when marriage was a minuet choreographed to a fare-thee-well, a man and a woman might have mastered the routine. Husband moved three steps to his job, wife moved two steps to her kitchen; mother fed baby, father disciplined boy; husband initiated sex, wife demurred; husband insisted, wife acceded. As long as the partners followed the score that society had composed, remembered their steps and performed them with good grace, you had a marriage. Not necessarily a "happy marriage," whatever that may mean, but a workable relationship, a structure in which two people could function without stepping on each other's toes too much.

But today, for heaven's sake, a young man and woman must struggle to follow a faint, confused score, and there is no caller to direct their steps: "Husband steps to the right . . . wife will take a bow. . . ." I marvel that any marriage—and I mean *any* marriage—survives. As an avid amateur marriage-watcher I ponder, along with the professionals, the dynamics of this improbable institution. How do a husband and wife today create the dance themselves? By what ploys, what feints—to change the metaphor—by what maneuvering, what negotiation, what diplomacy, what politics, do they shape this happening called marriage?

Reprinted from *Redbook Magazine,* July, 1971. Copyright © 1971 The McCall Publishing Company.

Understandably, a lot of people have been concerned with this question since the marriage minuet broke down about 50 years ago. In fact,
that breakdown was responsible for the blossoming of an entirely new
breed of specialist, the "family-life expert." When family-life experts
aren't busy picking up the pieces of defective marriages and trying to
glue them back together again ("family therapy," that's called), they
are very likely poking into this very matter of the politics of the marriage
relationship and the way in which tasks and decision-making are distributed within the family (the "family power structure," that's called).

Riffling through the vast literature on the "family power structure,"
one can't help being struck by all the bristling terminology that abounds—
"husband-dominated," "wife-dominated," "controlling" the relationship,
and the like. The family-life experts and the Women's Liberation Movement share a vocabulary of power politics. But marriage is not, after
all, an adversary relationship—presumably no one wants to "win" or
"lose" the encounter. Why, then, this talk of *politics*, with its implications
of wheeling and dealing and throwing one's weight around? Why, when
two people have just vowed to "love, honor and cherish" each other, do
the experts assess their relationship in terms of *power?*

If one looks at the evolution of a marriage, particularly in its early
years, it seems evident that many aspects of the relationship fall into
place almost automatically—by preference, by default, by custom, by
the superior ability of one or the other at a particular task and, most
of all, by the shared expectations of the husband and the wife. (When
a National Institute of Mental Health research team asked newly married
couples how they happened to work out their particular arrangements
about cooking and serving food, many of them looked completely blank.
What was there to work out?) Neither power nor politics comes into
play if the husband likes to putter with the car and the wife doesn't
and if each of them always expected husbands to take care of cars and
the society in which they live expects so too.

But suppose he wants and expects to have children and she does not
or she wants to go to work and he doesn't want her to. How are such
questions settled? In times past there was no doubt that they were settled on the basis of power—the openly acknowledged legal, economic,
physical, God-granted power of the husband. It is not surprising, then,
that the family-life experts, trying to explain and illuminate modern
marriage, turned to a study of alternative sources of power within the
family. If the State to some extent and economic power to a lesser extent and brute force altogether and God more or less no longer regulated marriage, then who or what did, they asked?

They're a contentious lot, these family-life experts, with their surveys and their countersurveys; but if there is anything they agree about it is that the equilibrium—or the disequilibrium—of the family (what they call the "balance of power" in a marriage) is determined very soon, perhaps in the first year of marriage.

"Marriages groove pretty early," says John Gagnon, a State University of New York sociologist, and bales of research about the first years of marriage support this view. A marriage shapes up quickly.

John Haley, the director of the Philadelphia Marriage and Family Center, has a perceptive view of the mechanisms by which this happens. In an article written for the professional journal *Psychiatry,* Dr. Haley sets forth his belief that when one person sends a message to another— whether verbally or bodily, by gesture, by inflection, by the context in which he has transmitted the message—what he is doing is maneuvering to define the relationship between them. In the Haley model, a boy walks over to a girl and puts his arm over her shoulder. By doing so he has defined the degree of intimacy in their relationship. The girl has the choice of accepting or rejecting the relationship as it has been offered. She can let the arm—and the message—stand, thereby accepting the boy's definition. Or she can counter with a maneuver that defines their relationship differently. Or she can let the arm be but toss the boy a smile that says "I'm *letting* you do this." Each message acts out a jockeying to determine what kinds of behavior are to take place in the relationship, and who is to control what is to take place in it. Thus the relationship is defined.

Everyone, Haley believes, is constantly involved in delivering such messages and accepting or countering the other person's definitions.

A wife reaches out to her husband in bed, and by doing so says, "I too can be the initiator of love-making." The husband can either accept this definition of their relationship or reject it. He can respond to her gesture or he can kiss her affectionately on the cheek and roll over and go to sleep. Or by still other kinds of responses, bodily or verbally, he can qualify his acceptance or rejection of her message.

A husband tosses his dirty shirt on a bedroom chair. The message is clear enough: "You are in charge of dirty shirts." His wife can put the shirt in the hamper and later in the washing machine or she can let it lie on the bedroom chair. Or handing him a clean shirt the next day she can say, "I did your shirt," suggesting that she is aware that she has been maneuvered into doing it and that she has done it; still she is maintaining the option of *not* doing it.

And so in this view one may look at the beginning years of marriage as a series of definitions and redefinitions of the relationship: a million

messages accepted or rejected or accepted and rejected with qualifications, each determining what sort of behavior is to take place in the
relationship.

A key question to which family-life experts have been addressing themselves over the past decades is how these moves and countermoves finally come to rest. After all, two people can't bat around indefinitely the
matter of who is responsible for dirty shirts. If they do, they're in trouble.
As a matter of fact, Dr. Haley's definition of the unstable family is one
in which "neither the husband nor the wife is able to deal with the issue
of who has the right to determine the nature of their relationship and
under what kinds of circumstances." In this kind of family, Haley says,
"children, sex, relatives, recreation and other areas that call for collabo-
ration, or at least co-operation, immediately bring up the question of
'who will decide what,' which leads almost invariably to discord."

Not only does who-decides-what need to be settled, but also it's important to know how and on what basis the settlement was arrived at.
If it is true that the *unstable* family is one in which these crucial allo-
cations of responsibility have not been worked out, it may be supposed
that the *stable* family is one in which they have been firmly resolved.
But a moment's reflection is enough to dismiss this as a whopping *non
sequitur.* Who-decides-what can be settled, all right, but what if I hate
the settlement? Suppose I do accept a definition of the relationship that
puts me in charge of dirty shirts—but suppose I feel ready to scorch every
blasted one of them each time I set up the ironing board? Even an
amateur marriage-watcher can see that this sort of thing often happens,
and that it jolly well doesn't lead to stable marriages—and even if it does,
who needs *that* kind of stable marriage?

So we must know not only what the "balance of power" is but also
how it got that way. When push comes to shove, who prevails and why,
and on what basis?

The most important and influential stab at this problem was a book
called *Husbands and Wives,* written a little more than a decade ago
(and instantly noted by REDBOOK as a landmark) by Robert O. Blood
and Donald M. Wolfe. Blood and Wolfe had suspected, like many others,
that American marriages were no longer regulated completely by tradition and that decisions within the family were no longer made on the
basis of "rights" that accrued automatically to one sex or the other.
They set out to test this hunch, and if it was confirmed, to find out
where power did reside.

To this end they studied the decision-making process in 909 white,
middle-class Detroit families. They asked whether the "husband alone,"
the "wife alone," the "husband usually," the "wife usually" or "both" de-

cided: what job the husband should take; what kind of car to buy; whether to take out insurance; where to go on vacation; whether the wife should work or quit work; who the family doctor would be; how much money should be spent on food. On the basis of the answers, Blood and Wolfe characterized a marriage as "husband-dominated," "wife-dominated" or "equalitarian."

Looking more closely into the fabric of these marriages, they found that when husband and wife had more or less equal education and both worked, the relationship tended to be equalitarian. Parenthood, they observed, brought a sudden loss of power to the wife, since she gave up her job and had at the same time an increased need for her husband's support. The most clearly husband-dominated families were those in which the husband had a high-status job. In such families husbands were likely to decide unilaterally that their wives should not work—thereby further decreasing the power of the wife.

From these observations Blood and Wolfe concluded that power in the family "accrues spontaneously to the partner who has the greater resources at his disposal"—resources such as financial ability, education, competence.

Rereading Blood and Wolfe recently, I was struck again by its pioneering quality. *Husbands and Wives* really did open up a new way of looking at marriage. But I also was struck by a kind of fuddy-duddy quality the book had. My Women's Lib hackles kept rising. (I have a few anti-Women's Lib hackles too.) I kept wanting to say, "Oh, come on, now! That's not what marriage is like. You must be kidding!"

I wanted to say, "How can you suggest with a straight face that my deciding how much to spend at the supermarket (actually the supermarket decides how much I spend at the supermarket) is a sign of my power in the family? Who decided I was to decide about food? My husband, of course, disguised in something called 'tradition.' All right. Well, thanks a lot! I don't really mind doing the marketing, but don't let's pretend that I was the one who assigned me the job or that my momentous decisions about chicken once a week or chicken twice a week are an index to my power."

And if some interviewer came around and asked me who decides what about vacations, I'd say, "We both decide." (Pollsters in the family-relations trade almost always query only the wife—easier and cheaper to catch her in the home than her husband in the office—and if they do query both, they're likely to get different answers!) What I said about vacations was true—but it's also a lie. We talk about it a lot, but he decides. But then, he decides because I let him decide. So who, if anyone, is more powerful in that ploy? I let him decide because he likes to and because I'm too busy deciding what's for dinner—that particular "power" he has relinquished graciously to me.

And what about the one who influences the decisions? If decision-making is construed as "having the last word" on a given question, its meaning is clear enough: Someone finally has to take pen in hand and sign that lease or mortgage, and there's no doubt who does that. But how could I have a lifetime record of cajoling my husband into real estate he claims he had no intention of buying—or did he plan to buy it all along?

But if decision-making is considerably more complex than Blood and Wolfe made it out to be and if they chose some pretty inconsequential decisions to chart as well as some important ones, it still remains that who-decides-what in the family and who-decides-who-decides-what can be real clues to the power structure of a marriage. And Blood and Wolfe's theory about the resources that each partner brings to the marriage as determinants of power has basic validity even though over the past decade it has been refined and amended.

Many people have pointed out that their list of resources—financial know-how, education, status, competence—doesn't tell the whole story. Physical attractiveness, for example, can be a "resource" in quite the same sense that education can be. Just as the man with higher educational qualifications has "power" over his less well educated and perhaps less competent wife, so the physically attractive woman has some power to offset the resources that her successful but unattractive husband brings to the marriage. Dr. Gagnon has pointed out that under certain circumstances even weakness can operate as a resource. A sick or ailing partner can coerce his spouse. And everyone knows that the real tyrant in the family is the newborn baby, not to mention the mother who uses the baby to clobber her husband.

David M. Heer, a sociologist at the University of California at Berkeley, has carried Blood and Wolfe a step further. His focus is not so much on the relative resources the partners bring to the marriage but on their market value outside the marriage. He believes that husband and wife each conceive—consciously or unconsciously—the possibility of separation, divorce and remarriage, and that power rests with the one who can more afford to contemplate that possibility. This theory offers a good explanation of the phenomenon noted by all studies: the young mother with preschool children is low woman on the totem pole as far as power in the family is concerned. Coming on a hypothetical remarriage market with preschool children, she might have a pretty rough time of it.

All of which makes Heer think that ultimately the source of power in any marriage today is the greater willingness to dissolve it. The partner with the lesser resources, with the greater need for the marriage—whether financial or psychological or whatever—is, in the last analysis, the less powerful. Dr. Gerald Caplan, professor of psychiatry at Harvard Medical School, has added an important footnote—it is not actually this relative willingness to quit the relationship, but each partner's *perception* of that threat, that governs the marriage.

If the real source of power, then, is the greater power to go away, politics in marriage has to do with suggesting the use of that power. One plays politics in marriage by saying, in effect, "This is how it would be if I were not here." A wife suggests—not, of course, openly, unless the marriage is far, far gone—that there would be no sex, no food, no children, no warmth, no clean clothes, no smiles if she were not there. A husband suggests ever so subtly, that there would be no money, no protection, no sex, no status in the community, no one to put up the storm windows.

Husband and wife come to know where the particular power—and weakness—of the other resides. In particular situations they use this knowledge as a weapon, a threat. In the classic marital power play a wife who has to beg for money forces her husband to beg for sex.

In a recent issue of *Journal of Marriage and the Family*, Dr. Constantina Safilios-Rothschild, director of the Family Research Center at Wayne State University, has sketched a vivid picture of this kind of withdrawal of "resources" (and notice how she has broadened Blood and Wolfe's own list of resources) in a marriage.

"A wife," she says, "can prepare the husband's favorite dishes or torture him with badly prepared food; can take good care of his clothes or neglect them; keep a neat and attractive house or leave it sloppy and disorganized; be a great companion and host to his guests and colleagues or a miserable one; be a responsive sexual partner or a frigid one, or totally refuse to have sexual relations with him; be sweet, affectionate, understanding, supporting and loving or sour, cold, distant, critical, demanding and unfriendly. . . . Of course the husband also has at his disposal a similar range of 'resources.' A husband may share household tasks with his wife or refuse to do anything because of his 'heavy' schedule and spend that time drinking with friends; he may go out often with his wife or hardly at all, always disappearing in long meetings, conferences and business trips, even when he is by no means obliged to go to these meetings and trips.

"It must be clarified, however," Dr. Safilios-Rothschild continues (and here, alas, she lapses into the professional jargon that, far from clarifying anything, always manages to muck it up), "that the degree to which the above-mentioned 'resources' can be withdrawn without bringing about a serious marital disorganization, depends upon the duration of the withdrawal and most importantly, the degree of emotional-affective attachment of the 'other' spouse upon the withdrawing one."

In other words, the deliberately sulky, frigid, sloppy, critical, distant wife can go on playing this game for just so long, depending upon whether her husband has a greater need for her or she has a greater need for him. If the latter is true, Dr. Safilios-Rothschild says, "she will be forced to lose out in the power struggle in order not to have to face the possibility of total marital dissolution."

Pondering this, one realizes that Dr. Safilios-Rothschild has clarified something after all. For suddenly everything falls into place. It becomes crystal-clear that *every use of power,* whether open or veiled, whether perceptible or imperceptible, is a tiny step or a giant stride toward the dissolution of the marriage and/or the eventual vanquishing of one partner. Power politics turns marriage into a cold war.

To the extent that a marriage is governed by power and decisions are made on the basis of that power, it is characterized by conflict and rift or by the emotional pain of the powerless partner.

In modern marriages, if the balance of power is approximately equal, the continuous use of power tends to lead to conflict and sometimes to divorce. In the frankly authoritarian family, where power could not be challenged, the results were often despair and mental illness.

Where does that leave us? If we go back to Haley's framework—the defining and redefining of the marriage relationship to a point where who-decides-what is settled—and eliminate the destructive element of power as the determining factor, on what possible basis *can* the dance be composed?

In the introduction to a thoughtful, cogent book, *The Psychology of Power,* the British writer Ronald V. Sampson sets forth a view of human relations that is notable both for its simplicity and for the illumination it brings to many problems.

"Every human being," Sampson writes, "may seek to order his life and his relations with others on the basis of love or on the basis of power." To the extent that power is the prevailing force in a relationship—whether between husband and wife or parent and child, between friends or between colleagues—to that extent love is diminished. We can develop our capacity for power, Sampson believes, or we can develop our capacity for love. We cannot do both. Nor can we opt out of making the choice between the use of power and the use of love in our relationships. "For of necessity," Sampson holds, "everyone at all times and in all positions stands on a relationship with other men which will be predominantly of one character or the other."

Sampson develops his thesis with great skill in many areas, but nowhere is it more apropos than in the realm of marriage. When in those early months or years of marriage the dust of Haley's definitions and redefinitions has settled, husband and wife will stand on a relationship with each other that will be predominantly one of power or one of love. If the bountiful research on the power structure of American marriages suggests that more of them rest on power than on love, let no one despair of the institution, especially those who have newly entered into it.

For Sampson's options are clearly there, and the rewards of forsaking power are high. If those family-life experts have done anything in the past decade, it is to show us—inadvertently, sometimes—the futility of power politics in marriage. And if the Women's Liberation Movement has done anything, it is to make vivid the cost in human waste and human suffering involved in a power-ridden relationship.

It's important to note that Sampson's divergent poles of love and power cannot be reconciled by equal power as the governing force within the marriage. The equal distribution of power will guarantee, to be sure, that the same person does not always carry the entire psychic brunt of the relationship, as women were likely to do in the patriarchal family. But if power is still the guiding principle, you are back to Dr. Safilios-Rothschild's balky wife and balky husband, trading their withdrawals of resources but alternately giving in because of their equal, often neurotic, need for each other. What is needed, Sampson would say, is not equal power, but equal loving and honoring and cherishing.

It should be pointed out too that the existence of love between two people who marry is not a sufficient condition for a love-propelled relationship. There is no doubt that many an authoritarian husband dearly loved his wife and children. But love was not usually the driving force in such families. It was not the force that shaped decisions and allocated roles and responsibilities, and because "power corrupts," love was likely to atrophy. So too the successful young executive who ordains that it does not help his career to have his bride continue in her low-status job may be madly in love with her, but that marriage is as power-driven as one in which love is absent; and there exists the real danger that love may indeed become absent.

Sampson's framework makes it possible to understand how two marriages can have exactly the same profile as far as who-does-what and who-decides-what and still be vastly different in content. I can do those dirty shirts because I *must*, lest I face retaliation, whereas another woman may do them because she *wishes* to. One man can drop his shirts off at the laundry on his way to work because he doesn't want to face a sulking or snappish wife on Tuesdays; another husband may do the same thing because he feels his wife is overburdened and he wishes to spare her the chore. There is all the difference in the world, even in the trivia of married life, between subtle coercion and selfless giving.

If power politics in marriage consists of applying pressure by withholding something that is needed or desired, the politics of love are exactly the reverse. They consist of taking off pressure and giving as freely as possible of oneself. Possibly no marriage—no relationship of any kind—is entirely free of the politics of coercion. The reason Sampson's thesis holds so much promise is that every cultivation of our capacity to order our lives on the basis of love helps to dry up that crop of power and wither its bitter fruit.

Many husbands please their wives with gifts and many wives please their husbands with love. This exchange works well until either presents or love are given— or demanded—for the wrong reasons.

MONEY AND SEX: TWO MARITAL PROBLEMS OR ONE?

by Morton Hunt

What do most husbands and wives give each other to express their love? What do they withhold to express anger? What is offered as a reward for favors? What best expresses their masculinity or femininity, their feelings of worth, their value to each other? What is hardest for them to learn to use well in marriage? What aspect of married life are husbands and wives most secretive about?

Reprinted from *Redbook Magazine*, January, 1970. Copyright © 1970 The McCall Publishing Company.

The answer to all these questions could be sex—but it also could be money. Disconcerting though it may be, there seem to be sufficient similarities in the uses—and abuses—of sex and money in marriage to lead any reasonable observer to suspect a connection between them.

Many of us would want to reject the suggestion that money and sex are so closely related—at least as far as our own marriages are concerned—for it seems to degrade something we esteem. Conjugal sex is the embodiment of a loving relationship; how can it conceivably be akin to money? How can it possibly serve the same ends?

Yet in the course of 15 years of researching and writing about love and marriage I have been struck, time and again, by the unmistakable similarities in the roles both sex and money play in marriage.

I think, for instance, of a young woman who recently told me how the fluctuations in her husband's fortunes affect his behavior toward her:

"Every time Eric sells a major painting, he goes a little ape. He's giddy and carefree and generous—he'll buy me anything and take me anywhere—and he gets romantic and all charged up. But when he hasn't sold anything for a long while, he becomes moody and depressed. He starts talking about moving into some low-rent attic, gives me hell if I buy so much as a tea strainer and loses interest in sex for weeks at a time."

I have seen, too, a number of marriages in which both partners have similar feelings about each other but one expresses these feelings primarily through money and the other through sex. Many men, for example, find it difficult to put affection into words and caresses but easy to bring their wives gifts. Some women, on the other hand, may express affection in a score of ways but prefer to give the gift of themselves.

It is also common for one partner to choose sex and the other money to convey negative feelings toward each other. I know a junior executive and his wife, both of whom feel somewhat trapped by marriage; each strives to preserve a secret hideaway, a tiny domain of independence. The man is completely committed to his wife where money is concerned—he tells her everything about their finances and they own all possessions jointly. But when he feels hemmed in by marriage, he tells her he has an evening business meeting and makes the rounds of the downtown bars until he finds some agreeable girl with whom to spend a couple of energetic hours in a hotel room. Oddly enough, he does not feel guilty afterward, but cheerful and proud—and very fond of his wife.

She achieves the same goals in an opposite way. She is totally committed to him sexually—she has told him whatever there was to tell about her prior relationships, she is uninhibited with him in their love-making and she would not dream of being unfaithful to him. But from time to time, when they have quarreled, she shaves $10 or $20 off her household cash and deposits it in her secret "mad money" savings account. She thinks this is probably wrong of her but takes pleasure in seeing the total grow.

Most psychotherapists and marriage counselors to whom I have spoken say that their clinical files are filled with examples of couples whose conflicts take the form of sexual or financial problems. A recent survey made by a research team of the Family Service Association of America revealed that among troubled families who go to agencies for help, sexual problems are the commonest and financial problems are second.

The theory that money and sex are intrinsically related is really not new, except to modern men and women who do not wish to accept the thought openly. Historically, sex and money have long been traded unashamedly within marriage—from the customary "bride-price" paid by the grooms in primitive societies to the complicated dowry and property transactions of well-to-do Europeans in recent centuries. Even in America as late as the time of our grandparents, sex and money were the two major commodities exchanged within the marital relationship. It was the husband's responsibility, and his alone, to support his family; it was the wife's "conjugal duty" to provide sexual relief whenever her husband wanted it.

Today, despite half a century of female emancipation and equalitarian marriage, when a marriage is ending we acknowledge the equation between sex and money. In a divorce action, if a man can prove that his wife was unfaithful, he can hold out for smaller alimony payments; if a woman can prove that her husband was unfaithful, she can expect larger payments.

Damage suits too are an arena in which the dollar value of sex is recognized. If a man or woman is rendered incapable of intercourse by an accident or by medical bungling, the spouse can sue the responsible party for substantial cash damages for having caused "loss of consortium." This isn't a romantic view of conjugal love but it is historically based.

The idea that sex and money are connected within marriage may seem to imply a calloused bargaining that makes wedlock little better than prostitution. But in healthy marriages there is no such selling or bargaining; there is no overt trading. All one actually sees is that people deal with both their sexual drive and their financial affairs in remarkably similar ways. A regulated, cautious person, for instance, may stick to a budget, keep careful records of his expenses and weigh and judge every prospective outlay; comparably, he may schedule sex only for bedtime on the weekends.

The spontaneous individual, on the other hand, may perhaps spend his money and indulge in sex on impulse. The kind of person who can buy something he craves without first carefully examining the effect on his budget may also make love in midweek or midafternoon.

Only when some new influence upsets the handling of either sex or money does the unseen linkage become apparent. One prudent and rather rigid man, for instance, got into a business venture that forced him to spend his money freely and, to his mind, dangerously; while this situation lasted he not only economized in every other way, but he also lost much of his sex drive. He attributed the latter symptom to worry; in psychotherapy, however, he realized that it was an unconscious effort to conserve one of his forms of male power as compensation for the power he was squandering. In contrast, an impulsive and exuberant man lost his position and had to stick to a tight budget for a while; during this period he had a series of brief extramarital adventures that he himself recognized as an attempt to counterbalance the constraint he was under elsewhere.

Although each partner in a normal marriage may ordinarily be unaware of the ties between his sexual behavior and his attitude toward finances, he may be very much aware that he and his spouse deal with both things in different ways. For as Freud and many later psychologists have observed, a person with a strong personality style in an unwitting effort to complete himself often marries a person with a complementary style. The serious, self-controlled person often chooses a playful and impulsive mate who will make it easier for him to be freer. By the same token, the spontaneous and uncontrolled person generally chooses a mate who will be a steadying hand.

Passive people, similarly, most often fall in love with dominant people and vice versa, and the meshing of their styles is particularly evident in the areas of sex and money. Usually the woman plays the dependent role, letting her husband make the principal decisions about money and waiting for him to make the sexual overtures. Occasionally, however, the roles are reversed. A relatively passive or insecure man will sometimes put his wife completely in charge of the budget, turning over his salary to her and receiving a weekly cash allowance. I was told by several marriage counselors that such a man may be sexually passive also, waiting for his wife to make the first move.

Up to a point, such variations in the handling of sex and money are normal and can fit together in marriage; the complementation may be comforting and gratifying to both parties. But extreme variations are of neurotic origin in most cases and are likely to cause conflict.

An immature or neurotically impulsive person, for example, may see his mate as a parental ogre—restraining, disapproving and demanding— a person he feels impelled to disobey. His disobedience is annoying rather than destructive, except when it comes to money and sex: defiant behavior in these areas may shatter the trust and security essential to a happy marriage. A young woman, half weeping and half raging, told me what it was like to be married to a man who was at heart still a naughty boy:

"Things went pretty well until I got pregnant accidentally and against his wishes. Then his love seemed to turn to hate and everything about me represented burdens and responsibility he didn't want. He began to stay out until all hours and to take weekend trips without me; he said it was because of business, but he'd never discuss the business with me or give me a number where he could be reached. He kept his bank accounts hidden under fictitious names and he gave me cash each month, but always less than I needed, and the money was always accompanied by scolding about my extravagance and threats to cut me off altogether. And he refused to sleep with me for months at a time. He said he simply didn't feel like it when we weren't getting along well. The truth is, he was punishing me—and running around with other women. I think he really *wanted* me to know and to suffer."

Paradoxically, two relatively normal individuals also can run into sexual and financial conflict in marriage if their personality styles are not poles apart but too much alike; in this case the relationship becomes competitive rather than complementary. If, for example, husband and wife each have a strong need to dominate or a strong fear of being dominated, they may fall into a running battle for supremacy. Although there are many ways of exerting power over one's mate, almost no method can be more effective than the use of either sex or money or both together.

Some marriages that start out well enough because of a fitting together of complementary needs may fail if one partner's needs change. When a man is unsuccessful, for example, or still is completing his studies, he may be drawn to a strong and supportive woman who can take good care of him. According to campus psychiatrists I have spoken to, such a man may find it difficult to be sexually assertive with his wife. But when he completes his schooling and emerges into economic manhood, he may begin to feel dissatisfied with the basic male-female relationship in his marriage and strive to establish his manhood sexually. If the wife manages to adapt to the changing situation, the couple may rebuild their marriage; if she cannot, they may find that the relationship is an irreparable one.

So far we have been looking primarily at marriages in which the connection between sex and money was not obvious, but seen only after careful examination. In some marriages, however, the connection is very plain. Money and sex not only are seen as emotional equivalents, but also one is openly traded for the other. This sounds degrading, but it need not be.

Dr. Ernest van den Haag, a psychoanalyst and lecturer in psychology at the New School for Social Research, told me, "It is normal and healthy for married partners to feel, 'I give you this because I love you, just as you give me that because you love me.' Exchanging sex for money isn't pathological unless it becomes coercive or vindictive, taking the form, 'I won't do this unless you do that,' or, 'You haven't done this as much as I want, so I won't do that as much as you want.'"

But there is a world of difference between the spontaneous, loving exchange of sex and money and the deliberately manipulative or punitive bartering of one for the other that occurs in conflict-ridden or neurotic marriages. The commonest form of such bartering, long observed and reported by psychologists and sociologists, takes place when a husband, for example, becomes tight-fisted if his wife frequently refuses him sex, or when a wife refuses her husband sex if he is stingy or financially irresponsible. Such maneuvers, instead of solving the problem, conceal and eventually worsen it.

A 32-year-old accountant, basically a decent and well-meaning man, told me of the cynical and almost brutal arrangement he and his wife entered into, an arrangement that perverted their already-failing marriage.

"I suppose I'd been too damned bossy," he conceded. "I chose the house we bought; I gave her just so much cash each week; I told her what I wanted her to cook. Finally she evened the score by holding back in bed.

"When six months went by without sex, I told her I was going to see a lawyer and I stopped giving her household money. She asked me for money again and again, but I stalled her for more than three weeks. Then, almost in tears, she said that she couldn't buy food, she couldn't go to the launderette, she couldn't even put gas in the car—and what did I expect her to do? 'Come to bed,' I said.

"She didn't say a word, but after a minute or two she started unbuttoning her dress, and she headed for the bedroom with me right behind her. And you know what? It was as good as it ever had been, maybe even better. She was really *with* it; she seemed to get a special kick out of it. Things went on that way for eight months, until the divorce came through. All that time sex was good with my wife—and I was paying her for it."

Too late, he understood that he had been domineering and that his wife had fought back in the one way she could.

In general, forced exchanges satisfy neither party; the required giving angers the unwilling giver, and the need to extort makes the recipient resentful and contemptuous rather than loving. Besides, the unwilling giver is often able to cheat. As Dr. Nathan Ackerman, professional director of The Family Institute in New York, points out, "A man can force his wife to sell him sexual favors, but she can always outwit him at the game—she can seem to give in but lose her response, withhold her orgasm."

Sometimes she does so consciously, but more often unconsciously. In either case it is an effective revenge, for when the man senses that he has lost his ability to excite his wife, his own pleasure is diminished and his self-esteem damaged.

A man, too, can cheat on such a transaction in his own way. He can begin to do poorly in business, lose his job, make bad investments, all by the way of unconsciously contriving legitimately to shortchange his wife.

One well-to-do businessman, after grudgingly giving his wife the things she wanted in exchange for her renewed sexual response, began to grow increasingly worried about his business. He felt that he was about to be confronted by serious new competition; he thought his partner was planning to break away; he feared that a government audit might require huge additional tax sums. Finally he explained to his wife that he would have to cut down his drawing account to a bare minimum in order to stave off disaster. In actual fact, as he realized in psychotherapy, his business was in excellent condition and for the most part his worries were imaginary, he had unconsciously created them in order to have an irreproachable way of welshing on his bargain.

Another unhealthy exchange occurs when one partner—usually the husband—deprives the other of love and tries to make up for it by giving her more money or gifts. It is fairly common for a man to be generous to his wife in material terms when he is being inattentive or unfaithful. (The Italians say that you can always tell when a man is cheating on his wife—he's so good to her.) But this effort to compensate never really solves the problem. The wife almost always realizes—consciously or unconsciously—that she is being bribed to put up with neglect. Even if she accepts the bargain and believes that she finds some enjoyment in the extra compensation, her pleasure in the gift is likely to be bitter at best.

Here is how one young woman, in despair because of her husband's continuing affair with his secretary, speaks about the flawed satisfactions of such an arrangement:

"Crying, screaming, even begging him to stop, doesn't do any good. He knows I haven't got the inner strength to take legal action; he knows I'm terrified at the thought of being alone. So I've given up trying to make him break it off. Instead, I've been spending a fortune redecorating the house from top to bottom—Oriental rugs, hand-blocked wallpapers, dated antiques, crystal chandeliers. But he never complains about my spending; I guess he figures it's cheaper than a divorce. I may as well get *something* out of this marriage. I certainly don't get any love—he hasn't touched me in months."

At least this young woman is clearly aware of what a bad bargain she is making; she has recently begun to see a psychotherapist, seeking the strength either to repair her marriage or to break away from it. Many others, however, are less fortunate; they fail to realize that in trying to compensate for deficiencies in one area by an excess in another, they aggravate the defects of their marriages.

None of the illustrations I have given or the points I have made prove that the connection between sex and money in marriage is necessarily bad; they prove only that bad effects generally are produced when the connection is misused, when one is withheld to punish a husband or wife for being stingy or when one is used as a substantial for the other.

Here, as elsewhere in our lives, understanding is the prerequisite to happiness. Those who understand the connection between sex and money are at least able to realize what they are doing if they misuse that connection, to stop what they are doing and to look more closely for the underlying problem. Those whose marriages are sound and satisfying need not concern themselves about the connection, but can file their understanding away for future reference if ever a problem arises.

CONFLICT: MODELING
OR TAKING FLIGHT

by Carl E. Williams

Parents can model constructive conflict resolution or take flight and pretend conflict does not or should not exist. Many persons in our culture have a negative attitude toward conflict. Reasons for wanting to avoid conflict are frequently rooted in one's early childhood years. Socialization is a process involving the family, early experiences outside of the home in day care and nursery school centers, kindergarten, and the early elementary school years. In these years children may have received messages from parents and other adults which said, "don't be close, don't be intimate; don't express your feelings; you can't trust others; play it safe and don't get involved."

Research and clinical experience appears to suggest that conflict needs to be faced openly if one wants to develop intimate and trusting relationships with others. To avoid conflict is to create a barrier that militates against the very openness one wants to create.

Other barriers to facing conflict derive from some types of cultural conditioning. Some people have the idea about conflict that "this too will pass" or that "time is a great healer." Evidence is rather strong that it is only when persons act in time and face reality that change occurs. Waiting for time to pass does not change reality but may encourage one to submerge hostile feelings which appear at a later unexpected time. Our conditioning tends to suggest that love and conflict cannot coexist in a relationship where persons fight and are hostile to others in myriad ways. How for example, can one possibly love someone if they can tell them in the heat of an argument to "go to hell." For persons conditioned to feel this way about the reality of conflict, love is a cure all. Love conquers even the gut level feelings of intense anger, despair, and at times utter emptiness. This is quite an unrealistic burden for love to carry.

We may resist conflict in marriage and family relationships because we equate being "in control" of feelings with never letting these feelings be revealed. Instead a strong attempt is made to mask their overt expression at any cost. Males in our culture are strongly conditioned to maintain a facade of masculine control. To lose control is to indicate that one is not in charge of his life.

Rather than face conflict openly we are taught from a very early age to come to a mutual agreement. Don't rock the boat or ruffle the waters. Deep hurt is frequently the end result. Sometimes such hurt is revealed years later in a relationship between family members. For such persons their motto in regard to conflict could very well be, "come weal or come woe, my motto is status quo."

Change and growth rarely develop from status quo positions in life. Unless dialogue remains open and flows freely much of the time in human relationships, these relationships will stagnate and frequently become lifeless. To agree never to fight or argue is really to agree not to be close and intimate. To agree never to fight and argue in the presence of children is to agree never to model for them positive and negative ways of dealing with conflict including conflict resolution. Children can easily grow into adulthood with little knowledge about dealing with conflict and some of the options for resolution. Such positive models are usually not present in the world of education. In this important crucible of a child's developmental years he is shielded from the conflict between adults in that social system. His own conflicts with teachers and administrators are frequently resolved with the use of the paddle, service in detention periods after school, and other forms of withdrawal of privileges. These methods of conflict resolution deal with symptoms and rarely focus on causes. For teachers and administrators such means of handling conflict become the easy and convenient modus operandi.

Older children and adolescents are occasionally exposed to conflict through the news media. Here also the models for constructive conflict resolution leave much to be desired. Brute force through war, use of dogs, clubs, bitter accusations with words, charges and countercharges, and a variety of forms of other violence are the chief means of conflict resolution to which children and adolescents are exposed in the wider world.

As one reflects upon these societal forces of socialization in regard to facing conflict that begin in the earliest days of family interaction, it becomes quite clear why there are so few instructive models of conflict resolution anywhere in our society. If the model is not present in the family, one will find it quite difficult to develop constructive ways of handling conflict anywhere. Human personality, expectations of ourselves and others are much too complicated for conflict resolution to be a simple learning experience that occurs by accident.

Cindy, Tim, and Doug were from a family that pretended to hide conflict. A late evening fight and an early morning breakfast scene describes the results of the way the Parnell family handles conflict.

A decision had to be made that night about whether Alice would obtain a full time job or remain at home to continue fulfilling the role of housewife and mother as she had done since the early years of their marriage. John and Alice had been married for fourteen years and their oldest child, Doug, was twelve years old.

A long standing rule of the Parnell household was "never argue or fight in front of the children." The children will be certain that they are not loved, that their parents do not love each other, and that someone in the family is going to get hurt physically if fighting occurs. Alice and John felt that raised voices are the prelude to hitting someone or throwing things. Both wanted the children to feel that all was well between their parents at all times. "After all, we love each other too much to ever fight" was the attitude the children's parents tried to convey.

On this particular night John and Alice were certain the children were sound asleep before they started discussing whether or not Alice would obtain a full time job. The anticipated tense argument ensued for several hours. Voices were raised to a high pitch and the fight became quite bitter. The decision was unresolved at 12:30 a.m. when hostilities ended with both John and Alice physically and emotionally exhausted. Both wearily climbed the stairs and fell into bed. At this point the only positive feeling both parents possessed was that at least they had shielded the children from a bitter argument.

The next morning Cindy, Tim, and Doug slowly came downstairs at different times and sat down around the breakfast table. Tension and frustration were communicated nonverbally. There was no music or news from the radio. Mom and Dad were deathly silent other than a slight grunt now and then, and even these were directed to the children and not to each other.

This was not the norm for even an early morning breakfast atmosphere in the Parnell home. Almost always there was a feeling of reasonable warmth even if animated conversation did not frequently occur. Mom and Dad would frequently comment about something in the morning paper or a news item on the radio. Since John commuted to the office he left before the children were off to school. He never left without kissing his wife good-bye and giving his children an affectionate hug or caress. On this particular morning he expressed none of these feelings and confirmed fears already present in his children.

Each child slowly left the table, gathered his books and supplies, and went out the door for school. The only spoken words as they went to the bus stop were, "Wonder what is bugging Mom and Dad?" Unspoken thoughts were "Are they angry with me about something I have done?" Are they angry at each other?" "Wonder why they just don't talk about what is wrong if there is a misunderstanding?"

John and Alice Parnell were convinced in their own minds that shielding their children from conflict was doing them a favor. They would never have any doubts about whether their parents loved them or each other. Little did they realize two basic facts of life: conflict in any human relationship is inevitable, and children, consequently, need exposure to positive and constructive models of conflict resolution. Instead of shielding their children they had only confused them.

Disagreement about a wide range of issues in life is an inevitable result of the vast individual differences that exist among human beings. Repeated efforts to avoid conflict at all costs will only stifle human growth and impede the realization of greater human potential in a relationship with another.

In the Parnell family the model was to hide conflict and pretend that it just didn't exist. The fallacy is obvious! Cindy, Tim, and Doug Parnell are old enough to internalize the reality of conflict and the meaning of the search for conflict resolutions. Conflict situations are all around them in their relationships outside of the home. There is conflict in the classroom, on the playground, in the informal activities of scouting, community athletic programs, conflict with instructors of music, dance, and similar activities. They hear and read about and see conflict in the news media. Conflict in some form is a daily occurrence directly or indirectly for most everyone throughout life.

Whether Ms. Parnell works outside of the home or chooses not to directly affects the children and their attitudes toward themselves and others. Research is rather clear that the effects of a mother's employment outside of the home are determined by three basic factors: (1) her basic attitude about herself as a person and how this is related to her search for a job; (2) her feelings about her work and the degree of fulfillment she feels as a career woman and; (3) the feelings of the members of her family about her absence from the home.

Why not involve the whole family in discussing the alternatives along with both positive and negative consequences of each? How does husband and father really feel about his wife working? Can he openly and honestly state feelings of threat before his own children and wife concerning his wife's employment, if such feelings exist? What a positive model of being human for children to witness as part of resolving conflict! Too often parents are afraid to "ruin" what they conceive to be the "perfect" image of masculinity and femininity. The route to meaningful feelings about one's masculinity and femininity is to first of all be human. Being human is unrelated to being male or female per se.

The Parnell children could have witnessed bitter and even angry feelings on the part of both parents and each other as the discussion ensued. How do family members handle these feelings in themselves and each other? What happens as a result of how these feelings are expressed and handled? All of this is part of the model of destructive and constructive conflict resolution.

At some point in the encounter recognition that important data needed is not available may become evident. Some conflict situations cannot be resolved until all of the necessary data is at hand.

Children and adults need to be continually exposed to the reality that few conflict situations are resolved overnight. The idea that the sun should never set on a heated dispute or argument is a romantic myth. There are times when it is probably wise for an entire family to retire for the night intensely angry with each other rather than attempting to resolve conflict while emotionally and physically exhausted. Such conditions often encourage people to say things they really do not mean or feel; they tend to be somewhat more irrational, defensive and unable to cope with the here and now. A sense of humor which is frequently a crucial factor in resolving conflict is almost nonexistent in persons who are exhausted.

Other reasons for not attempting to resolve conflict immediately, in addition to insufficient data and physical and emotional exhaustion, are numerous. We live in a period where much of life is geared to the now. The inability to delay immediate gratification for a longer range goal is a stumbling block in the path to coping with conflict.

In some situations persons have difficulty in accepting a method of conflict resolution on both the intellectual and feeling or affective level. Sometimes one can work through and accept something intellectually but feelings are intensely involved. These feelings get in the way of acceptance. At other times the reverse is true. Until one can make progress in resolving conflict on both levels the conflict will frequently be present.

Much conflict occurs on the spur of the moment due to our being very human. An example is the father who returns home from work, at the close of an intensely difficult day. During the course of the day he lost two big business deals, learned he was being transferred to another department and that the transmission was going out of his comparatively new car. Upon returning home he turns into his driveway and suddenly confronts two bicycles, a tricycle, a go-cart, and a basketball, all of which are directly in his way. He can't park on the street and there isn't a child in sight. He angrily steps from the car, throws the objects quickly and roughly into the yard, gets back into his car, guns the motor, and screeches to a stop inches from the garage door.

Following this commotion his two youngest children innocently appear on the front door steps. Instead of his usual friendly tousle of the hair and greeting, father flies into a rage. He yells at the top of his voice about toys and other objects in the driveway, spanks both of them with anger, and tells them to go to their room. By this time he is in the house and begins screaming at his wife about the rough day he has had and her inability to discipline the children.

Little does he know about the day she has had. The washer broke down, the sewer clogged, Jon fell off the jungle gym and had to be rushed to the emergency room of the hospital to have his arm checked, and she learned that her mother has terminal cancer. One other problem to complicate her day is that she is to host the monthly bridge club that night.

This is the way one father and husband chose to handle conflict that was not anticipated but arose quickly. Whether conflict is the spur of the moment type or anticipated, positive or negative models are still conveyed. What do children learn about being more human from this type of interaction that analyzes the nature of conflict and options for resolution? What do children learn about themselves and others that may be unrelated to conflict in the process of internalizing feelings conveyed to them by parents in these situations?

Conflict is as natural and essential to human existence as breathing. We have no option about whether or not we will have conflict in the family or the wider world. Three chief options are available to everyone in regard to handling conflict. One can pretend conflict is unnecessary and suppress its reality. Another option is to recognize the reality of conflict in human relationships but to shield oneself and others from the realistic facts of conflict. The third alternative is to not only acknowledge its inevitability but to capitalize on the opportunities conflict potentially provides for unlimited growth and development. Conflict resolution is a basic goal in most human relationships. Parents, husbands and wives, decide whether they will ignore the existence of conflict, shield others from conflict, or provide constructive models for resolving conflict.

Conclusion

Each of the articles in the foregoing pages raises critical issues dealing with either the form and function of marriage or the quality, definition, and style of the marital relationship.

An extrapolation of the main points and critical issues leads us to postulate the following propositions as being absolutely central in a contemporary analysis of the institution of marriage.

1. The United States will need to adjust itself to pluralism in marital structure. While we see no lack of traditional or patriarchal monogamy, we also see no reversal of the present trends toward new styles and structures.

2. There is little evidence that monogamy is on its way out or that marriage and/or the nuclear family is on its last leg of life. Rather, the evidence points toward a need for the revitalization of the primary monogamous dyad. This requires an unlearning of the roles which have been handed down from generation to generation based on custom and tradition. The resulting role-binds constitute a series of double-binds sufficiently strong to create feelings of entrapment and enslavement, especially for the female.

3. The model of marriage as being a vehicle for the actualization of human potential requires far more than spartan resolutions about openness, sharing, and growth. Rather, it requires a far more rigorous premarital attitude toward mate selection, the courtship and/or engagement period, the rethinking of possible

benefits from a trial relationship, the question of changing human nature and changing vocational interests over the life span, the issue of ethics in human sexuality including the inordinate amount of emphasis on extramarital penile-vaginal relations as being the supreme threat to marital stability.

4. However private opinion may vary on the necessity for change, we hold that the styles and patterns a couple use in the facing and resolution of conflict is absolutely central to any dyadic relationship, be it traditional monogamy or open marriage, cluster marriage or group marriage. Conflict results from our individuality and our dignity as autonomous persons: It does not make sense to suppose that we can emphasize the development of human potential and self-actualization and then neglect the inevitable conflict that self-actualizing people will experience when their ideas, values, beliefs, and attitudes clash or interfere with one another's freedom. The need for "healthy fight models" is overwhelming as is the need for people to be helped to unlearn destructive practices in handling conflict. In the marriage of the future it may be axiomatic that "fight styles" or "conflict-resolution patterns" are the single most important factor in the prediction of marital stability and satisfaction.

5. The societal belief and custom of combining love and sex within a legalized institution called marriage needs to be carefully scrutinized. As a culture we have been, and most assuredly still are, socialized into a highly romanticized attitude toward sex, love, and marriage. We see no way for marriage to become a more fulfilling relationship until expectations are brought more in line with the human situation. Romantic notions celebrating the power of love to conquer all barriers and to enable two human beings to surmount the multitudinous challenges of life together *without proper attention to the tools, skills, and insight necessary* to accomplish these goals is a cruel and heartless hoax.

6. A recurrent theme in marital therapy revolves around the question: To what extent can the health (or quality) of the relationship exceed the health or growth level of the separate partners? Traditional marriage counseling has focused on the relationship without venturing into the behavioral patterns of the mates, leaving that area to the psychotherapists. Yet we would suggest that individual patterns and styles never be separated from the relationship. The relationship can hardly be understood without some knowledge of individual psychodynamics. Therefore it is of crucial importance that marriage styles and definitions be considered in the light of the individual personalities who are commited to the relationship. In essence, following Erikson's developmental

approach, identity must always precede intimacy, and, as we see it, individual identity necessarily precedes couple or dyadic identity. Another way of stating this concern is to say that a dyadic identity can be no stronger than the respective individual identities of the dyadic partners.

7. As a culture we share in a belief system which has built role expectations upon a double standard for males and females. While the emphasis today upon women's liberation is necessary, in the long run the male role-binds are no less important to the future of marriage than are the female role-binds. Whatever effect female-lib may have upon the society as a whole, as it pertains to marriage there seems to be little question that any growth-centered equalitarian model of marriage must take seriously the traditional customs and myths pertaining to both sexes. Only in this light can the crises in women's lives as well as men's lives be understood. Further, all talk about power and the balance of power within marriage would seem to be meaningless unless and until there is some consensual agreement regarding our inherent right as human beings to be what we are, without prejudice as to the behavioral role expectations laid upon us by our culture.

8. For countless generations the bearing and raising of children has been an "expected" and "assumed" part of our culture. There is increasing evidence that the presence of children, that is, their birth and early socialization, is in itself a crisis-producing phenomena within the marital relationship. Who today is justified in making the assumption, born in tradition and folklore, that no marriage is truly complete without children? Today there is a choice: Children or no children? If children, how many, how far apart, natural or adopted?

Dyadic marital relationships become vulnerable when children are present simply because the presence of a child or adolescent drastically increases the possible range of conflict, disagreement, and interruption of autonomous pursuits. Again, many of the "women's lib" issues correctly center on child care and socialization. Equalitarian relationships may one day serve as the ideal form of "modeling" for children and youth, yet such relationships must be able to handle conflict between the mates as a prerequisite for handling child-child and parent-child conflict. Few would argue the point that the socialization process is pivotal in the forming of beliefs, attitudes, and values in the young. The key issues are: 1) Into what kind of marital relationship is a child born? 2) What effect does the parent-child relationship have upon the child? 3) What effect does the parent-child relationship have upon the parents? 4) What effect does the parent-child relationship have upon the parent-parent relationship?

We conclude this series of writings about marriage by emphasizing once again that the issue is not: monogamy vs. polygamy, multilateral, communal, cluster, or group marriage. Just as there must be room for a pluralism beyond monogamy, there must also be room for a pluralism within monogamy. This means that the issue for countless people is "What kind of monogamy?".

glossary

Affect: emotion; feeling; *Affective level:* degree of emotional response to a stimulus.

Aggression: to move against someone or something. *Assertion:* to take a stand against someone or something moving against oneself. Aggression is often used to indicate violation of others' life space, while assertion is a protection of one's own life space.

Anxiety: a response to stimuli, sometimes identifiable and sometimes unidentifiable. Normal anxiety is in proportion to the stimulus severity. Abnormal anxiety or neurotic anxiety is out of proportion to the severity of the stimulus. Anxiety is usually indicative of some threat to the well-being of the inner self, in contrast to fear which is usually indicative of a threat to one's physical self.

Authoritarian: pertaining to one's attitude toward authority and authority figures. Persons who normally assert power over others or who submit themselves to the power and control of others are considered authoritarian personalities.

Autonomy: self-government; pertaining to an inner psychic state wherein an individual believes in and obeys his own inner code of ethics and life style. Usually, it refers to one who neither uses traditional authority in control of others or allows the authority and control of others over him.

Behavior modification: a method of psychotherapy with the stated purpose of changing portions or segments of a person's behavior. (It is often referred to as behavior therapy.)

Cluster family: an expanded family (not communal) whereby two or more family units share an intimate friendship characterized by deep mutual interaction.

Collective parenthood: a situation wherein a group of adults fulfill the parenting responsibilities usually assigned to the mother and father. It is usually found in communal and/or cluster families.

Commune: refers to a life style wherein two or more nuclear family units or individuals share the physical, economic, and emotional realities of daily life. Not all communes incorporate group marriage, but all group marriages are, by definition, communal.

Companionate: a marriage style wherein the two partners define the

228

core of their relationship as being one of companionship, partnership, and friendship as opposed to traditional male authority and female subservience.

Complementary needs: needs that are different, yet mesh well together. Traditionally, many marriages include a person with a greater need to dominate and one with a lesser need. Examples: slippiness and neatness; conservative with money and liberal with money; giving or nurturing, and receiving or being nurtured.

Crisis: any heightening of the severity of a problem to such an extent that the prior level of organization and adjustment no longer operates. Whether or not something is defined as a crisis depends on perception of the situation, prior experience in handling similar situations, and the resources one has to deal with the situation.

Defenses: a term applied to an individual's psychological-emotional method of protecting his or her ego from threat and danger. Defenses and defense mechanisms include projection, rationalization, transference, rigidity, close mindedness, prejudice, etc.

Demand feeding: in reference to infant care, the feeding of an infant via bottle or breast when the child appears to be asking to be fed. The term is used in contrast to schedule feeding, where the infant is fed according to the mother's schedule, whether or not the child is hungry.

Democratic child rearing: a term widely interpreted with varying degrees of conservative vs. liberal overtones. Basically, the democratic process involves the opinions, attitudes, and feelings of the children in the decision-making process. The term is used in contrast to authoritarian child rearing wherein the child's attitudes, etc. are not considered to be important.

Dependence: psychologically, a term referring to an emotional reliance upon a person or thing which is in excess of what is considered normal or rational. Dependency is generally viewed as undesirable due to the fact that it weakens the self-reliance ability of an individual, thus contributing to weak ego and identity, with precarious levels of self-esteem.

Double-standard: the condition under which judgment is rendered according to different standards for the same action or deed. There is a widely known male-female double-standard wherein what is sexually permissible for the male is taboo for the female. The double-standard, however, is applicable to politics, race, international affairs, etc.

Dyadic: a term used to pertain to a couple or a twosome. Wherever the essential components are in a one-to-one relationship it may be referred to as a dyadic relationship.

Egalitarian: pertaining to a state of equality. Thus, an equalitarian relationship wherein the participants are equals may be referred to as egalitarian.

Empathy: a feeling into; a capacity for identification with another. In contrast to sympathy which may imply a feeling sorry for, empathy feels into the dilemma of another without necessarily being sympathetic. In interpersonal relations, empathy is considered to be a very important trait since it facilitates understanding of other's situations, problems, etc.

Equalitarian: see egalitarian.

Extended family: a sociological term referring to the presence of a representative of three separate generations sharing a domestic household, e.g., grandparents, parents, children (grandchildren). Usually, but not always, they are related by blood.

Extramarital: literally, outside the marriage or beyond the marriage.

Family power structure: referring to coalitions and alliances within a family, whereby father and mother rule, father alone rules, mother alone rules, father-son dominate mother-daughter, or mother-son dominate. Many combinations are possible, including children in alliance against either or both parents.

Fidelity: traditionally, a sexual loyalty to one's mate, hence sexual exclusivity. Fidelity may refer to a more inclusive faithfulness or loyalty beyond the sexual.

Group marriage: a minimum of three persons wherein each person considers himself or herself married to at least two others within the group. Group marriages with large numbers are today being differentiated from small groups of between 3-8 people, termed multilateral marriage.

Human potential: a term gaining increasing public acceptance in the 1960s and early 1970s referring to the need for increased human fulfillment, i.e., self-fulfillment, self-actualization, and self-realization. The human potential movement encompasses many and varied kinds of emphasis, such as encounter groups, sensitivity training, and the increase of human awareness.

Homosexual: pertaining to relationships and associations between members of the same sex. Usually the term refers to preference in regard to sexual expression and/or desire. While homosexual is a correct term for both male-male and female-female relationships, the word lesbian refers exclusively to female homosexuals.

Heterosexual: pertaining to relationships and associations between the male sex and the female sex. Usually the term refers to preference in regard to sexual expression and/or desire.

Hedonism: the pursuit of pleasure; pleasure for pleasure's sake; a philosophy endorsing the experience of pleasure as either the chief meaning of life or one of the basic purposes of life.

Identity: the concept or image one has of himself/herself; how one interprets oneself and/or defines oneself; knowing who one is and what one is. A strong or healthy identity performs an integrative function within the personality, and a weak identity lacks a unified sense of self.

Infatuation: the idealization of a person based mostly on fantasy; the state of highly charged emotional attraction, often identified as love, toward a person who possesses traits of personality, body, and mind similar to a long-standing idealized object.

Infidelity: traditionally, the failure to be sexually loyal to one's mate. Infidelity may include disloyalty other than sexual, including a betrayal of growth, commitment to the other, and commonality of purpose and striving.

Inhibition: a nonvoluntary and nonconscious restrictiveness preventing self-expression in any number of areas, especially psycho-emotional-sexual expression. The psychoanalytic (Freudian) school holds that repression leads to inhibition.

Intentional community: generally, a term describing the goals, purposes, and commitment of at least three or more people toward establishing and maintaining a communal type life style, hence the *intention* to contract with each other. The term is often used in contrast with groups of people who drift into or fall into communal associations with each other.

Intimacy: the emotional and physical closeness between two people indicating the degree of unity and impact the pair feels in relation to each other.

Intimate fighting: game- and racket-free fighting where persons fully express feelings in a spirit of trust.

Life style: refers to marriage and family form and the values, attitudes, feelings and expressive behavior one manifests within a social system.

Marital health: the degree of positive well-being in the marital relationship and in the interaction patterns between the spouses.

Marital roles: roles performed by a husband or wife in relation to their marriage relationship.

Masculine: physical and psychological characteristics commonly stated to belong to males of the human species. Also refers to roles and behavior expected of the male.

Molding: sculpting of family members as we knew or know them.

Monogamy: marriage to only one legal mate at a time.

Multilateral: two or more families with or without children who are living together in a marital relationship.

Need: psychological or biological state which requires being met if a person is to function optimally psychologically or physically.

New marriage: a marriage that has moved from what it once was to the level of maximizing more of the potential of each of the spouses and their relationship together.

Nuclear family: a married couple and their children, if the couple have chosen to have children. A family is nuclear without children. This is the most basic irreducible unit in family composition, usually referring to parents and offspring. It is limited to two generations, in contrast to an extended family consisting of three or more generations and other relatives.

Orgasm: involuntary muscular contractions that occur at the peak of sexual excitement.

Pairing relationship: two people in the process of developing an intimate relationship, usually heterosexual but may include homosexual as well.

Passion: a powerful or compelling emotion or feeling usually related to affection, desire, or lust.

Patriarchal: general control of family members by the father in the family.

Personhood: the concept that persons in a marital and family relationship are individuals in their own right, whose individuality is to be respected by others forming the union.

Phobia: an excessive fear, such as fear of height, closed spaces, darkness, etc.

Pluralism in marital structure: more than one life style of married living, such as group marriage, homosexual marriage, childless marriage.

Polyandry: marriage of one woman to two or more men; a form of polygamy.

Polygamy: marriage of one man to two or more women (polygyny) or marriage of one woman to two or more men (polyandry).

Polygny: marriage of one man to two or more women; a form of polygamy.

Primary needs: needs relating to basic physical and emotional health, such as food, clothing, shelter, nurturance, and affection.

Primary relationship: relationship of husband and wife, parents and children as compared to relationships with friends; i.e., relationships with intimates as compared to others who fill utilitarian and instrumental needs.

Psychosomatic: a physical disorder that is produced by the emotional state of the person.

Residual: that which is left over upon which to build a marriage relationship.

Role: a social position or status characterized by personal qualities and activities, defined either by the prevailing social order, custom, tradition, or by oneself.

Role reversal: assuming the role of another, i.e., husband performs the roles his wife usually assumes and she performs the roles her husband usually assumes.

Romantic love: love characterized by the idealization and preoccupation with feelings about love and the one loved; an idealization and idolization of the beloved.

Romantic mystique: the idea that romantic love is the chief characteristic of a love relationship.

Sensuous: the degree of pleasure arising from the experiencing of one's body, especially the experiencing of physical warmth and closeness (as contrasted with sexuality, indicating attitudes, and responses to one's sexual identity, attitudes, and behavior).

Serial monogamy: a series of monogamous marriage relationships over time.

Socialization: the process by which the values, traditions, customs, manners, and mores of the society are transmitted to the ascending generation.

Solidarity: a relationship growing from common interests and responsibilities.

Spontaneity: acting upon impulse without giving extensive thought to what, why, and how; a state of being inwardly free to be self-expressive without undue consideration to others' reactions.

Status: position of persons in relationship to society.

Stereotype: a generalized feeling or thought that is often inaccurate when applied broadly.

Swinging: mate swapping; the custom of husband and wife interacting sexually with another couple.

Sympathy: outward expression of concern for persons who are experiencing physical or emotional hardship.

Temperament: refers to an individual's emotional nature, how he responds, and prevailing moods over time.

Token system: money won or accumulated that may later be cashed in for an object or event.

Transactional analysis: a system of therapy wherein the structure of personality is based on the concept that every person has a child, a parent, and an adult within herself/himself. T. A. or Transactional Analysis studies the communications between one's own parent, adult, and child in addition to the communications and transactions between the parent-adult-child of other people.

index